Recovering the U.S. Hispanic Linguistic Heritage:

Sociohistorical Approaches to Spanish in the United States

Recovering the U.S. Hispanic Literary Heritage

Board of Editorial Advisors

Recovering the U.S. Hispanic Linguistic Heritage:

Sociohistorical Approaches to Spanish in the United States

**Edited by Alejandra Balestra,
Glenn Martínez and
María Irene Moyna**

Recovering the U.S. Hispanic Literary Heritage

Arte Público Press
Houston, Texas

Recovering the U.S. Hispanic Linguistic Heritage: Sociohistorical Approaches to Spanish in the United States is made possible through grants from the City of Houston through the Houston Arts Alliance and by the Exemplar Program, a program of Americans for the Arts in collaboration with the LarsonAllen Public Services Group, funded by the Ford Foundation.

Recovering the past, creating the future

Arte Público Press
University of Houston
452 Cullen Performance Hall
Houston, Texas 77204-2004

Cover design by Pilar Espino

Recovering the U.S. Hispanic Linguistic Heritage: Sociohistorical Approaches to Spanish in the United States / Alejandra Balestra, Glenn Martínez, María Irene Moyna, editors.
    p.   cm. — (Recovering the U.S. Hispanic Literary Heritage series)
Includes bibliographical references.
ISBN: 978-1-55885-528-1 (alk. paper)
    1. Spanish language—United States— History. 2. Spanish language—Study and teaching—United States—History. 3. Spanish language—Social aspects—United States. 4. Hispanic Americans—Languages. I. Balestra, Alejandra. II. Martínez, Glenn A., 1971- III. Moyna, María Irene.
PC4826.R38 2008
467'.973—dc22

2008016605
CIP

8 9 0 1 2 3 4 56 7   10 9 8 7 6 5 4 3 2 1

Contents

Part I
Recovering the U.S. Hispanic Linguistic Heritage

Part II
Analyzing the U.S. Hispanic Linguistic Heritage

Acknowledgments

Alejandra Balestra thanks Nicolás Kanellos who has been very supportive since 1997 when she started working at the Recovering the U.S. Hispanic Literary Project. A few years later, Nicolás once again supported her academic endeavors by accepting this book project for publication. She thanks Manuel Gutiérrez and Marta Fairclough for their encouragement to pursue historic sociolinguistics studies and for always being supportive. She is most thankful to her husband, Nelson Andara, who is always by her side, and to her daughter Carla Romina Haramboure, who reviewed her contribution to the Introduction and always shared her dreams; this work would never have been done without their constant love and support. She thanks Marcela Walter Salas, Marina Tristán, Eleuterio Santiago Diaz, Kelly Bilinsky, and Catherine Travis who supported this project from the beginning. She thanks Rena Torres Cacoullos for proofreading her contributions to the Introduction. Special thanks to the anonimous reviewers and staff at the Recovery Project, Arte Público Press, who make this volume possible, and to the staff at the Bancroft Library and the New Mexico State University Library who helped locate documents. Finally, a very special thanks to Antonia Castañeda, who shared several valuable documents.

Glenn Martínez acknowledges the intellectual leadership and support of Manuel Gutiérrez, Juan C. Zamora, and Roger Higgins. Special thanks to numerous colleagues who read previous versions of the manuscript including Ana Carvalho, Javier Duran, Daniel Villa, Jennifer Leeman, and the graduate students in his courses on historical sociolinguistics at the University of Texas at Brownsville, the University of Arizona, and the University of Texas Pan American. He also thanks the historians and archivists who helped him locate critical documents: George Gause, David Mycue, Mark Glazer, David Montejano, and Cecilia Hunter.

viii ❖ ❖ ❖ ❖ ❖ ❖ ❖ ❖ ❖ ❖ *Acknowledgments*

María Irene Moyna would like to thank several colleagues who have shared with her their interest for and expertise in the use of letters in linguistic and historical research, most especially Walter Kamphoefner, Wolfgang Helbich, Joe Salmons, and Stephan Elspaß. Special thanks go to those who attended her presentations and read her work on this topic, including Domnita Dumitrescu, Brian Imhoff, Daniel Villa, and Susana Rivera-Mills. Her students in history of the Spanish language at San Diego State University were a constant source of inspiration. Some of them even became treasured assistants and co-authors, in particular Wendy L. Decker, María Eugenia Martín, and Israel Sanz. Finally, a word of thanks is due to the knowledgeable staff of the archives she visited for data collection, in particular John Panter at the San Diego Historical Society Archives, and Bill Frank at the Huntington Library. This work is dedicated to all the peoples who have lived in the American Southwest, including the hundreds who left their written legacy, and the thousands who were silenced by time and circumstance. May we honor you by creating a more just society for all.

Part I

Recovering the U.S. Hispanic Linguistic Heritage

1. Introduction

Over the last thirty years or so, the main focus of the study of Spanish in the United States has been synchronic, and has yielded abundant research on the formal, social, and pragmatic features of the language in its present day form. The historical dimension of Spanish in the territory of the current United States has had to wait considerably longer for recognition as a field of linguistic exploration, although recently some authors have devoted themselves to historical recovery, paying attention to colonial manuscripts (Perissinotto 1992, 1998; Craddock 1998, Craddock & De Marco 1999-2000, Imhoff 2002), or indirectly, using data from dialectal atlases as evidence (Bills & Vigil 1999). This has made available to the historian and linguist a growing collection of competent transcriptions and exegesis and has made possible further exploration in the field (Acevedo 2000, Bernal-Enríquez 2000, Bills & Vigil 2000, Trujillo 2000). To date, however, little has been done in terms of applying sociolinguistic methods to historical documents from the area (with some notable exceptions, cf. Balestra 2002, 2006, Martínez 2000a, 2000b, Wolford 2005).

The purpose of the present project is to look at the Spanish language in the United States from a sociohistorical perspective, taking a stab at a field that is ripe for development. Sociolinguistic analysis can give insights into the direction of language change and hint at the social forces that motivate it. It opens a window onto society and offers a way to gauge conflicts between its various groups and sheds light on how these conflicts have been resolved or perpetuated. Language thus becomes a barometer of the power shifts among groups. This work also sets the stage for the booming field of synchronic and dialectal studies of Spanish in the United States, closing the gap in scholarship between synchrony and diachrony, and helping to highlight the long tradition of multilingualism in the present-day territory of the United States. Ultimately, it is hoped that this increased awareness will help dispel the myth of an English-only Arcadia that is at the base of much of the xenophobic sentiment that prevails today. This work will have succeeded if it motivates others to apply sociohistorical research methods to Spanish in the United States.

Recovering the U.S. Hispanic Linguistic Heritage: Sociohistorical Approaches to Spanish in the United States is structured as an extensive introduction and a collection of seven articles that touch upon numerous related fields and may be of interest to a number of scholars, such as historians, sociologists, and linguists. In that sense, it is truly multidisciplinary, even if the main focus is language and linguistic change. The purpose of the introduction is to provide a historical background, including a discussion of the linguistic policies that emerged in the Southwest during the periods of Spanish, Mexican, and U.S. rule. We also discuss the location and characteristics of the archival sources that may be used to study these periods, in an attempt to entice other scholars to carry out their own fruitful explorations. Finally, we include a brief discussion of the quantitative and qualitative methodologies, borrowed from sociolinguistics, as well as the main challenges encountered when applying them to historical data.

2. Historical background

The modest purpose of this historical introduction is to provide a general overview of the various periods of Spanish, Mexican, and American domination in the area now known as the American Southwest. Because the emphasis of this work is on language, particular attention will be paid to the demographic characteristics and the power dynamics between the various groups, since those are known to shape linguistic behavior. In most instances, however, it will be little more than an exposition of the main historical facts, with no attempt at in-depth analysis. The first reason for this is the need to compress into a few pages a history that spans several thousand years, when we include the pre-Columbian period. The second reason is that there are already many excellent works that cover the history and social evolution of the area in much greater detail than this introduction can. The interested reader may consult works on the history of the Southwest from a number of perspectives (cf. for example, Richardson 1934, Hollon 1967, Faulk 1968, Perrigo 1970, Cutter & Engstrand 1996 for general accounts; Bolton 1921, McWilliams 1990 [1948], Bannon 1970, Weber 2003 [1973] for pioneer works on the Spanish-Mexican borderlands; Wellman 1954 & Kessell 2002 for narrative histories; Barrera 1979, Griswold del Castillo 1979, 1984, Griswold del Castillo & De León 1996, for sociological and political reappraisals from a Chicano perspective; and Duingan & Gann 1998,

González 2000, for works that consider the history of all Latino groups in the United States).

The tradition of American history begins with the arrival of the English on the eastern seaboard in 1607 and the establishment of their colonies. This is, of course, not based on historical precedence but it is rather the result of an Anglo-centric assumption that American civilization as we know it is the child of English parents exclusively. Thus, we are told, the powerful Anglo-American thrust for exploration, and conquest swept the country from east to west, gradually taming nature and natives, and gaining ground over alien European powers who got in the way of the unstoppable force of "Manifest Destiny", as the nineteenth century U.S. expansionist policy came to be known. Although for many years Spanish borderlands historians have been striving to present a more accurate picture (cf. Bannon 1970:8), the myth has been hard to dispel in popular culture. This erroneous view provides a false argument for many of today's ethnically and linguistically exclusionary political and social movements. At a time when the future appears increasingly dependent on multicultural integration on a global scale, it would be well to look back on the past of the United States and recognize that diversity is part of the very warp and weave of the nation. The multiple contributions of its early inhabitants, both native and European, have shaped the physical, economic, social, cultural, and linguistic landscape of vast territories of the country. The main purpose of this work is to shed light on one specific strand of this variegated tapestry, namely, the Spanish-Mexican heritage. We do so on the basis of an in-depth analysis of textual sources that highlight the linguistic, social, and ethnic diversity present even then.

Let us begin, then, by stating the oft-overlooked fact: the Anglo settlers to the territory of the present-day United States had been preceded by other Europeans, envoys of the Spanish crown, who set foot on the Florida shores in 1513. These first explorers would be followed by conquerors, and then by missionaries and settlers. The first European language known for a fact to have been spoken on American soil was therefore not English but Spanish, and some speakers of U.S. Spanish today are the direct descendants of those early arrivals. By the time the first English colonies were founded, the Spaniards had already made considerable inroads on the northern frontier of New Spain, and were well on their way to establishing stable settlements in the area. They would continue to do so for a period exceeding three hundred years altogether, until they collided with other European settlers moving south and west.

In the course of the three centuries of Spanish rule over New Spain, the northern borderlands came to constitute a vast swathe of lands to the north of the furthermost expanses of the Aztec empire. They included vast territories in the north of present-day Mexico, comprising from east to west, Nuevo Santander (now divided between south Texas and the Mexican state of Tamaulipas), Nuevo León, Coahuila, Nueva Vizcaya (present-day Chihuahua), Sinaloa, Sonora, and Baja California. Additionally, they included territories which are now within the United States, namely, Florida, Louisiana, Texas, New Mexico, Arizona, and California. Further forays were made into present-day Kansas, Nebraska, Utah, Colorado, Nevada, and as far north on the Pacific Coast as Oregon, Washington, and Alaska (for details, cf. Cutter & Engstrand 1996:2).

The movement was not a neat progression from south to north, however. It is better to understand the conquest as a three-pronged advance, which has been aptly described as "the extended fingers of an upraised hand" (Kessell 2002:xiv). There was a central thrust from Mexico City to the north, covering northern Mexico and New Mexico. A western wing climbed up the western slope of the Sierra Madre into Sinaloa and La Pimería (present day Sonora and Arizona) and was joined by a northward expansion from Baja California that was later pushed even further into Alta California. Finally, fanning from the central plateau northward, expeditions were sent to the western Texas plains to defend against the advances of the French established in the Mississipi valley. In fact, these French territories of the lower Mississippi would also come into Spanish possession briefly and will therefore occupy us when discussing the eastern borderlands. Finally, Florida, which had been the site of the earliest explorations and which was reached more frequently from the Antilles than from New Spain, remained in general marginal to the borderlands and retained its military outpost status, failing to develop into a regular colonial settlement. In what follows, we provide a brief outline of the geographic characteristics of these areas, a description of the main groups of their early inhabitants, and the stages of Spanish northern conquest and settlements.

2.1. Early Settlers and Inhabitants

From the geographical point of view, the Spanish borderlands were a vast territory with two mountain ranges running from north to south in Mexican territory, i.e., the Sierra Madre Occidental and Oriental, continued within the boundaries of the United States by the Sierra Nevada and the Pacific Cordillera, on the west, and the Rocky Mountains, further east. Between these slopes lie fertile valleys in California, while Baja California is a narrow, arid corridor, split down the middle by a mountain range and a desert. The central areas in the south of Arizona and New Mexico are rugged and dry, with vast expanses of desert interrupted by forbidding mountain ranges and almost impassable canyons. To the east of the Rockies lies the dry Llano Estacado (Staked Plain) in Texas, and further east still, the swampy Gulf coast of Louisiana and Florida (Cutter & Engstrand 1996:Ch.1).

The main waterways are constituted by the Colorado, flowing into the Gulf of Cortés, the Rio Grande, which crosses New Mexico from north to south before bending eastward to flow into the Gulf of Mexico, and the Mississippi, which also flows into the Gulf from the north. Aside from these, there are few reliable rivers with sufficient flow year-round to provide irrigation or transportation of people or goods. On the other hand, those same trickles can overflow with seasonal rains, which in colonial times slowed down the progress of overland packtrains. Reaching Alta California was particularly difficult: the land passage through the Yuma desert was made dangerous by the presence of natives; the sea voyage, too, was perilous and uncertain. At the mercy of currents and winds, ships could be destroyed at sea or take so long to get there from the ports of Acapulco or La Paz that crews were often ravaged by scurvy.

These vast areas were not uninhabited upon the Spaniards' arrival. Estimates of the indigenous population in 1492 vary, but some think that there were approximately 700,000 people living in the current territory of the United States, while another 200,000 lived in the northern Mexican frontier (Griswold del Castillo & De León 1996:2). The first settlers, small bands of hunters, must have arrived in the proto-Asiatic migrations across the Bering Straight, sometime between 50,000 and 20,000 B.C. They continued southward, with some groups branching off to the east of the Rockies, while others travelled south along the Pacific coast between 12,000 and 9,000 (Cutter & Engstrand 1996:8). They arrived in Baja California around 8,000 B.C., and populated the peninsula in waves of migrants who left their most puzzling modern traces in cave paintings in the central desert (León Portilla 2000:59 *et passim*).

At first these peoples were hunters of large game, but by 3,000 they had a more diversified diet, practiced agriculture, and had started living in villages. For example, the Mogollón-Mimbres culture, went as far east as the Rio Grande Valley and as far west as south central Arizona. They planted corn and supplemented agriculture with hunting and gathering. To their west was the culture of the Hohokam, who developed a canal system allowing them to irrigate the Sonoran desert and plant corn, squash, beans, and cotton (Cutter & Engstrand 1996:10). To the north, in the territory of the Four Corners (where Arizona, Utah, New Mexico, and Colorado meet) were the Anasazi. They were a basket weaving culture, who later learned to weave cotton and make pottery. They obtained their sustenance from agriculture and some hunting. Originally they lived in caves, but eventually they built pithouses which they turned into complex apartment structures, by adding rooms to existing dwellings. In the 13th century Arizona cultures declined, maybe due to drought, epidemics, or the migration of hunters from the north and east. For whatever reason, the people of Arizona abandoned their cities and moved to the Rio Grande Valley or became entrenched in isolated areas (Perrigo 1970:8; Cutter & Engstrand 1996:14).

The invading newcomers were Athapascan hunters, such as the Apaches and the Navajo. The latter, although originally an Apache tribe, eventually acquired sedentary traits. The Apaches, on the other hand, continued to be nomadic, increasingly so with the appearance of horses in the territory. Another nomadic people, further east into west Texas, were the Comanches, buffalo hunters like their Apache enemies. In the south and east of Texas, the Caddo, a buffalo-hunting people who also knew corn and vegetables, formed a confederacy with several divisions and subtribes (Perrigo 1970:12).

According to Milanich (1998), Florida was inhabited by Paleoindians around 8,000 B.C., when the weather in the area was cooler and drier than today, and the peninsula itself is estimated to have covered more land, due to lower sea levels. The weather would gradually become wetter, giving rise to wetlands in some locations and leading the early inhabitants to an increased reliance on the sea for subsistence. With time, the early inhabitants would construct stone and bone artifacts, and by the year 2,000 they were making pottery and trapping animals. In east and central Florida, the Mayaca and the Timucuan peoples collected animal and plant life, and by 750 A.D., the Timucua were growing corn, and they also consumed beans, peas, pumpkins, citrons, gourds, and tobacco. In the north of the peninsula there is also evidence of intense farming around the same time by the Apalachee, which in turn led to more complex social organization.

In the west, the fertile soil of California provided sustenance to a high population of diverse indigenous peoples. According to Cutter and Engstrand (1996:9), they added up to somewhere between 135,000 and 350,000 and spoke 135 distinct language varieties. Even small areas could allow for very dense occupation by semi-sedentary groups, due to the abundance in animal and vegetable life in the valleys. From south to north, those groups included the Pericues, the Guaycuras, the Huchities in the south and center of Baja California (López Portilla 2000:61 *et passim*), the Yumans around the border area, the Mission Indians (as the coastal tribes came to be known after the arrival of the mission fathers), and a number of other groups including the Penutians and the Miwok in central California (Cutter & Engstrand 1996:15).

2.2. Early Explorers and Conquerors

To summarize the historical periods corresponding to the Spanish conquest and settlement of the borderlands, it makes sense to have recourse to one of the most succinct and classical works in that tradition, adding, where appropriate, from other sources that help to nuance and flesh out the account. In what follows we discuss the early explorations of the borderlands, followed by a geographical presentation that focuses in turn on each one of the three fronts of the Spanish conquest (central, eastern, and western).

The first European to set foot on the mainland United States was Juan Ponce de León, who landed on the shores of Florida in 1513, eight years before Hernán Cortés reached Mexico Tenochtitlan. In 1521 he repeated his feat, as did Pánfilo de Narváez in 1528 in an ill-fated expedition of 600 men which would have lasting consequences. One of the members of the expedition, Alvar Núñez Cabeza de Vaca, managed to make his way on foot across the territories of modern-day Louisiana, Texas, and New Mexico, and after a nine-year journey, made it back to Spanish-occupied territory in New Spain. He and his men had managed to move from one Indian group to another with ingenuity, collecting information about the resources of each area. However, the hardships took a heavy toll: by the time they were met by other Spaniards, their party had dwindled to four survivors (Kessell 2002:Ch.1).

The Spaniards who met them in northern New Spain were the men of Nuño de Guzmán, a rival of Hernán Cortés in New Spain, who had founded San Miguel de Culiacán while moving beyond the Aztec borderlands to the west, and after exploring Nayarit, Jalisco, and southern Sinaloa. The Spaniards had started hearing fantastic stories about the Seven Cities of Cíbola, purportedly located in the north and reputed to be rich beyond compare. Their imagination was further stirred by Cabeza de Vaca, whose men had seen stone arrowheads they thought were made of emerald. This was all the Spaniards needed to hear to believe that north of New Spain there might be another Mexico, as rich as the one that had yielded so fast to their conquest in the south, and as willing to convert to Christianity. This set the wheels of exploration and conquest of the northern borderlands in motion and placed the Spaniards face to face with challenges they had not encountered before.

The first expedition sent to the north was a small exploratory group headed by Fray Marcos de Niza, who, after a fateful trip that cost the life of most of his companions, returned with claims that he had seen the smallest of the seven cities of Cíbola (Bannon 1970:16; Kessell 2002:23-27). Viceroy Mendoza saw his chance to best his rival Cortés and planned for an *entrada de conquista*, financed with his own resources and sanctioned by the king. The expedition, headed by Francisco Vázquez de Coronado, moved north and explored in every direction. It encountered the Pueblo Indians and the nomadic buffalo hunters of the east, and reached Arkansas in search of the purportedly rich kingdom of Quivira, encouraged by an Indian guide who later confessed he had made up the story to divert the Europeans from Indian lands, a bit of misinformation that cost him his life (Kessell 2002:41-44). Coronado's report upon his return to New Spain was disappointing: the north did not hold gold, silver, or a rich empire.

Meanwhile, in the east, Hernán de Soto was testing the possibility that Cíbola might be to the northeast in Florida, rather than due north from New Spain. Following the trail of other explorers, he set out to the area again in 1539. After pushing northeast possibly all the way to the Carolina Piedmont, he headed south again, bordered the Florida peninsula, and reached the mighty Mississippi. There, de Soto's death led his companions to return to New Spain. Upon their arrival in Pánuco, these explorers also told a disappointing tale of hardship and had little to show for their efforts (Bannon 1970:25).

In the west, developments were also taking place that would lead to the first European contact with the Californias. As part of the campaign to conquer and secure the Philippines for Spain, Viceroy Mendoza sent two ships north from the west coast of Mexico. Commanded by Juan Rodríguez Cabrillo, the expedition skirted the Pacific coastline all the way to Oregon (Cutter & Engstrand 1996:47-48). Upon Cabrillo's death, the expedition turned around, but on the way back located San Diego Bay, having missed Monterey and San Francisco further to the north. This expedition, which was also a disappointment from the monetary point of view, concluded the age of the *conquistadores*, placing the northern borderlands firmly on Spain's map of the New World. On some of these fronts, like New Mexico, Spanish settlement would soon follow. On others, such as California, more than two centuries would elapse before any concrete steps towards colonization were taken.

2.3. The Central Route North: Northern Mexico and New Mexico

Once it was clear that no rich kingdoms lay ahead that could be easily raided, the Spaniards turned to prospecting and mining. They were successful in several points of Nueva Galicia and as a result started opening up the territories of present-day northern Mexico. In their progress northward, the Spaniards would gradually become acquainted with indigenous groups unlike any they had encountered before. Accustomed to dealing with peoples who had been previously subdued by the Aztecs, and for whom the transfer of power from one group to the other was simply a matter of adjusting to a new dominant group, the Europeans were unprepared for the belligerent reception they were given by these peoples (collectively known as the Chichimeca), who had never had masters and had no urge to acquire them. They so hampered the travel of overland packtrains necessary to supply the mining camps, that a war of extermination was seriously considered as the only possible "solution." Instead, the Spaniards turned to a uniquely Spanish borderlands institution, the mission (Bannon 1970:29). If the natives could be "reduced" in missions under the supervision of priests, then their labor could be harnessed to provide badly needed supplies for the mining camps. The justification for this form of economic exploitation was found in religion. By bringing Indians into the fold of Catholicism, the Crown would be doing good by increasing the capital of Christian souls and by granting the Indians the gift of eternal salvation.

Thus started a series of missionary and exploratory expeditions, which brought back information about the northern expanses of the empire. The largest and most important of those expeditions into New Mexico was led by Juan de Oñate, a wealthy Spaniard who used his own resources in the endeavor. The expedition was plagued by difficulties, both with the Acoma Indians and with Oñate's own enlistees and settlers, who revolted and attempted to return (Kessell 2002:71-96). By 1607 Juan de Oñate was ready to resign, but a promising increase in the numbers of neophytes in the northern missions led the king to a change of heart: New Mexico was to be held and turned into a province, with the crown to foot the bill. The capital of the province was established in Santa Fe, which by 1630 had a population to 250 Spaniards, 750 mestizos and as many as 50,000 Indians in 25 missions (Bannon 1970:41). Over the centuries, it would prove its worth as a defense bastion, first against Indians, and later, against Europeans.

Between the new outpost of New Mexico and New Spain in the south lay vast territories that needed to be effectively controlled for the new settlement to survive. The seventeenth century would test the effectiveness of the mission as a form of control over the natives in the area. As the friars moved northward on the eastern slope of the Sierra Madre, they opened missions through northern Durango and southwestern Chihuahua, coming in contact with groups such as the Tepehuans and the Tarahumaras. However, this contact was not always peaceful: in the first half of the century the natives rebelled several times against Spanish ill-treatment and forced labor practices (Bannon 1970:77). However, by the last quarter of the 1600s, the south of Chihuahua was under control and civilian occupation ensued, while the Jesuits moved into the Tarahumara Alta and the Franciscans founded San Francisco de Cuéllar (Ciudad Chihuahua), an important point to reach the outpost of New Mexico (Bannon 1970:54 *et passim*).

In New Mexico, the first half of the seventeenth century was not one of exciting developments. Having discovered that there would not be any quick rewards, the population set about to carve out an existence through farming and sheep herding. Adding to their discomfort was the fact that, for anything they did not produce, they were dependent on the caravan trade. Their supply line was the 1,500-mile-long *Camino Real*, which made transportation of goods precarious and slow, and led to high prices. To complicate matters further, a Church-State dispute raged for much of the period (Kessell 2002:97 *et passim*). In light of these hardships, why did the settlers not simply return to the safety and comfort of New Spain? Many of them no doubt would have preferred to do so. The reason was that Spanish frontier settlers had no freedom of movement: they were bound by royal orders and could only leave with royal permission (Bannon 1970:6).

The Pueblo Indians of New Mexico had their own set of problems, as shown in Bannon (1970:80 *et passim*). Since the only resource the Europeans could benefit from was the labor of the indigenous population, the newcomers often resorted to abusive measures such as requisition of goods and forced labor. Although the Pueblos had converted, they resented the immobility forced upon them by the mission system and the persecution of their old ways. The medicine men in particular resented the unfair competition from Catholic religious practices and the repression to which they were subjected. In 1680, Indian discontent boiled over into a revolt which led to a total abandonment of the New Mexico settlements by the Spaniards, who were forced to retreat to El Paso, Texas. It would take several years and several governors to successfully reconquer the area. In 1692, Diego de Vargas finally moved north and recaptured the towns, obtaining pledges of allegiance from the Indians in exchange for royal forgiveness. By 1694 Santa Fe had been recovered, resistant Indians were being suppressed, and the missions were being repopulated. It became obvious that the colony's priority should be self-sufficiency, so that it could become stabilized and act as a bulwark against the nomadic Plains Indians during the centuries to come.

2.4. The Eastern Borderlands: Florida, Texas, and Louisiana

The eastern borderlands of Florida were never fully integrated into their western counterpart, being more directly linked to the Caribbean islands than with the mainland. They were also different in that from beginning to end, they had a defensive purpose, with missionary work and settlement subordinated to the *presidios* set up against the encroachment of French corsairs first, and English settlers later. It was this purpose that led Pedro Martínez de Avilés, Florida's *adelantado*, governor, and captain-general, to repel the French in bloody encounters, to found St. Augustine in 1565, and to build a string of forts around the peninsula. He also tried to convert the Indians with the help of Jesuits and Franciscan friars, but in this endeavor he met with less success.

Starting in 1570, the Jesuits worked hard in Florida under very dangerous conditions. They expanded towards South Carolina and also on the Gulf Coast, so that by 1655 there were missions in the Apalachee territory (around modern-day Talahassee), and a port on the Gulf. These missions grew in size and importance, in spite of the fact that epidemics reduced the Indian populations. To protect the missions and the Atlantic coast, garrisons were established along the shore. However, the crown could not spare sufficient manpower to make them really effective in stopping intruders. It was clear that Indian allegiance would be crucial to secure this border. With the establishment of an English colony in South Carolina in 1670, competition for the trade and friendship of the Indians in the interior started. English prices were too tempting for the natives to refuse, so that the balance was tipped against Spain. The missions on the coast thus shrank gradually, until the governor of South Carolina, James Moore, came all the way from Charleston and attacked St. Agustine (Bannon 1970:107). Although he did not succeed in taking it, Spain was now cornered in Florida, forced to recoil in order to keep control over the remaining settlements. The fate of the Indians was even more dire: the destruction of the Apalachee and Timucuan missions in the eighteenth century would lead to the decimation of the Indian groups themselves (Milanich 1998:173).

Nearer Texas, it was French explorers who threatened the Spanish borderlands by moving into the Mississippi, on their way from New France (Quebec) in 1673. Apprised that it flowed into the Gulf Coast, they made plans to start a settlement at its mouth. However, the party that was sent in 1684 to accomplish this task, led by Robert Cavelier, sieur de La Salle, landed on the Texas shore instead, and built a fort at Garcitas Creek (Bannon 1970:96). The expedition, beset by privations, disease, and internal strife, was totally decimated by the time the Spaniards reached it. It did, however, bring to the fore of the Spanish consciousness the need to defend and fortify the territory that lay between the French territories around the Mississippi and their own colonies on the west and south. This would bring Texas into the fold of the borderlands.

Although West Texas had already been the object of some exploration from New Mexico in the sixteenth century, the eastern corridor would be opened in the seventeenth century, starting with the settlement of what is now Nuevo León and Coahuila. Juan Domingo de Mendoza and Fray Nicolás López pushed further east, returning with information about eastern Texas and requests for missionaries made by the Jumano Indians. In the 1680s other expeditions by sea and land would gather more information and by 1690 two missions had been established among the Texas Indians on the Neches river (Bannon 1970:102). The next year Texas became a province, but the absence of any signs of French invaders led to a retreat from the area back into Coahuila and Nuevo León, in spite of the friars' urgent requests to attempt mission efforts among the Hasinai Indians.

Bannon (1970:109 *et passim*) shows that the Spaniards who thought the French incursions were over in the area would soon find out their mistake. By

1712, Louisiana had been given over to a private proprietor, Antoine Crozat, who was interested in trading with the Indians and with the Spaniards, too, even if it meant having to act illegally and resort to smuggling. It was clear to both sides that the tug-of-war between Spain and France would be won by whoever managed to win over the Indians, because neither had enough troops to secure the area permanently. Each side thus resorted to the method they knew best, which in the case of Spain was missionizing, and in that of France, trade. Thus, in 1716 a reoccupation of Texas by Spanish forces was attempted, but there were never sufficient funds to properly protect the area. To make matters worse, in spite of the founding of several missions, the nomadic Indians would not congregate.

The Indians of the Plains were not amenable to the mission system because of their nomadic lifestyle and the fact that they had no difficulty finding food in their surroundings. However, Europeans themselves may have magnified the power of the native peoples with two imports which increased their raiding potential and their range. These were the horse, which they obtained by stealing the Spanish *caballadas*, and the gun, which the French traded with them. These innovations not only caused Indian groups to prey on the Spanish *pueblos* but also on each other, upsetting the balance between groups that in turn created more instability for the Spanish settlements. Thus, for example, the attempts at creating a mission for the Apaches in San Sabá failed because of Comanche raids in the area (Bannon 1970:137).

In 1762, a new international development would have an impact on the eastern borderlands. In that year, Spain acquired Louisiana from France as compensation for the loss of Florida to the English at the end of the French and Indian War (Cutter & Engstrand 1996:176). The Louisiana territory was not seen as an asset, though, since it meant stretching the protection of the borderlands to the east beyond breaking point. Additionally, without the convenient buffer zone provided by the French, now the Spaniards came face to face with the English in the southern colonies, and, after the 1780s, with the Americans. The boundary against the new Anglo-American land-hungry settlers was destined to become a thorn on the Spanish side. The recovery of Florida in 1783 did little to avert the problem, because by then it already had Protestant settlers. In fact, in the last years of the American revolution, Spain may have worsened the situation by allowing Americans to establish themselves in New Orleans and western Florida, where, it was thought, they would act as a line of defense against the expansionism of their former countrymen. This solution did not work: by 1810, the Americans had occupied western Florida, while in eastern Florida the Creeks, who were allied with Spain, suffered a defeat in Horseshoe Bend which ultimately led to the loss of Florida by Spain, ratified in the Adams-Onís Treaty of 1821 (Bannon 1970:206-208).

The retrocession of Louisiana to France in 1800 might have provided some respite to Spain had it lasted. However, after the Americans purchased the territory from Napoleon in 1803, they had a closer base from which to penetrate Texas. Filibusters and settlers kept coming into the territory, as well as traders eager to reach the Santa Fe trail from the Mississippi valley. The American government also exerted pressure on the Spanish borderlands, both from the east and from the north, encouraged by a new expansionist dream that led it to question the boundaries of Texas.

2.5. The Western Borderlands: Sinaloa, Sonora, and the Californias

As we have seen, Spanish interest in California was directly linked to the Manila trade of the sixteenth century. Once Spain had secured the Philippines as an entrepot for trans-Pacific trade by the 1570s, there was growing interest to find bays in the Pacific coast that would act as way stations to effect needed repairs on ships and to obtain fresh food and water after the long trip so as to help crews recover from the ravages of scurvy. Additionally, trespassers working for the English crown (such as Francis Drake, Cavendish, and others) were a nagging problem for the valuable Manila galleons. A port on the California coast, it was thought, could act as the seat of a coast guard.

The first step taken by the crown was to entrust the viceroys to draw up maps of the area. This led to the Vizcaíno explorations, which reached San Diego Bay in 1602, and Monterey a year later. A Carmelite friar that accompanied the expedition chronicled the voyage and urged the conversion of the many Indians they encountered. However, for the next century the Californias would lay untouched; the first European settlement in the long peninsula of Baja California would be Nuestra Señora de Loreto Concho in 1697, while San Diego would have to wait until 1769 for permanent settlement. The California enterprise would be preceded by movement along the western slope of the Sierra Madre, which made it possible.

The western flank of advance into the northern borderlands was orderly and continuous (Bannon 1970:53-72). As we saw above, Spanish interest lay in mineral wealth, but prospecting in the western slope of the Sierra Madre in Nueva Vizcaya uncovered no riches. Additionally, the local Yaqui people proved troublesome and unwilling to settle in missions. In 1591, the Jesuits moved into Sinaloa, and started their missionary efforts on the valleys. These paid off: by 1620 there were 80,000 baptized Indians in the Pimería Baja. By 1638 the fathers had moved into the valley of the Río Sonora, to the northwest into the Opatería and the Pimería Alta. The Opata were already farmers, but the priests diversified their crops with the introduction of wheat, brought new irrigation techniques and livestock, and taught them manual skills. The fathers were accompanied by defensive military garrisons, whose function was to defend and police the mission Indians and to bring back runaways. In spite of their supposed unity of purpose, however, there was frequent friction between missions and *presidios* over the soldiers' un-Christian behavior.

In a pattern that was to be repeated throughout the borderlands, the missions made civilian settlement possible by acculturating the indigenous population to the type of labor and consumption patterns of colonial New Spain. Thus, civilian settlers started arriving in the area during the second quarter of the seventeenth century. Bannon (1970:61) states that by 1678, Sinaloa had 600 families of Europeans and *mestizos*. By the end of the seventeenth century there were also civilians in Sonora.

An important development in the second half of the seventeenth century was the appearance of non-Spanish Jesuits in the area, after the crown lifted its ban on foreigners. Among them the Tyrolese Jesuit Eusebio Kino stands out. Having been assigned to the Pimería Alta, he travelled indefatigably—an average of 30 miles a day—exploring and mapping the Pimería and the Papaguería (Cutter & Engstrand 1996:122-124; Bannon 1970:65-70). Among other things, he pointed out that California was not an island, but a peninsula—a fact proven by Francisco de Ulloa's travels in 1539, but that has been ignored by mapmakers since. The area could therefore be reached by traveling a mere 100 miles from Sonora-Arizona. For Kino, this was an important discovery because it meant it would be relatively easy to send provisions to the friars working in arid Baja California. Kino thus proposed the founding of a town in the Colorado River valley, which would act as a stopping point on the overland supply route from the Pimería to his brothers in the mission of Loreto. The Baja California missions needed supplies from the mainland because they were still not self-sufficient, and although northward progress was steady, it was also slow. The Jesuits had been successful in preventing any civilian settlement in their territories, and they only grudgingly accepted the presence of military garrisons. Then, in the 1760s José de Gálvez was appointed *visitador general*, and among other duties, was in charge of implementing the expulsion of the Jesuits (Bannon 1970:153). However, the fathers' plans of extending the line of California missions were not abandoned. In fact, appraised of the news of Russian settlement plans in North America, Gálvez moved to occupy Alta California. San Diego would act as the anchor in the south, while Monterey in the north would be the main center, base for defense, and a port of call for the Manila galleons. These two points would be linked by a line of missions and *presidios*. The expedition was organized in two ships and two land companies, one of the latter headed by a Franciscan, Fray Junípero Serra, and manned by Catalan soldiers as well as local *soldados de cuera*. After a rough start, the Alta California missions progressed steadily under the supervision of Father Serra, followed by Palou, and Lasuén. Together they lay the foundations for two important California industries: agriculture and stockraising. Alta California, the last of the Spanish borderlands, prospered to such a degree that by 1777, the governor would move his seat from Loreto to Monterey (Bannon 1970:164).

Until the second half of the eighteenth century, the Spanish borderland provinces were administered directly by the viceroy of New Spain (cf. Bannon 1970: Ch. 10). This proved less than ideal, since the problems of the border were too distant and too complex to be understood, let alone handled, from Mexico City. The solution would come in the form of a reorganization of the frontier into a new administrative jursidiction, the *Provincias Internas*, independent from the Viceroyalty of New Spain. In 1772, acting by recommendations made by the Marqués de Rubí after an extensive inspection of the borderlands, a royal order from Charles III of Bourbon created a new office, the inspector-commander of the *Provincias Internas*. Additionally, in 1776 the Northern provinces were erected into a separate administrative unit, the *Comandancia General*. With some setbacks and changes in their exact composition, the *Provincias Internas* would be maintained until the end of the Spanish period in America.

2.6. The Borderlands After Mexican Independence

When Mexico gained independence from Spain in 1821, the embattled new nation accepted the settlement of boundaries that had resulted from the Adams-Onís treaty. The fledgeling country was internally destabilized by the ensuing struggles between federalists and centralists. Independence also resulted in the lifting of trade restrictions between the United States and Mexico, which led to increased numbers of American settlers, traders, and fur trappers throughout the borderlands.

In Texas, the American presence increased due to colonization plans carried out by agents known as *empresarios*, of whom the best known is Stephen Austin. In exchange for cheap land, the Anglo settlers had to convert to Catholicism and pledge allegiance to Mexico (Perrigo 1970:103). Many of them were cotton farmers from the South, who came into Texas with their slaves. The local Mexican population was soon flooded by newcomers; according to some estimates, by 1834 there were 16,000 Anglos; 4,000 Black slaves; and only 5,000 Hispanics in Texas (Perrigo 1960:109).

In New Mexico the American infiltration took the shape of transient trappers around Taos and traders in Santa Fe. The latter were encouraged by the success of the Santa Fe trail caravans, which left Saint Louis loaded with manufactured cloth and hardware, and exchanged them in New Mexico for skins, horses and mules on the hoof, and silver at a good profit. The New Mexicans could then extend the trade south to north Mexico (Griswold del Castillo & De León 1996:20).

In California, the first Americans came by sea, on a global trade route that connected Boston with China. The merchants would bring cotton and cutlery to California, exchanging them for local otter and beaver skins, which were in high demand as a warm clothing material in China (Cutter & Engstrand 1996:284). They would then complete their business by buying tea and silk for the Boston markets. Occasionally, they would take California hides and tallow to Peru, or leather for the New England industry (Perrigo 1970:111). Some of the merchants, both American and British, settled in California and New Mexico and became members of the local gentry. In order to acquire lands, however, they had to become Catholics and Mexican citizens, something they often achieved through marriage. This family alliance with locals gave them an opportunity for profit but also gave some advantages to the local elites, who could strengthen their claims to "whiteness" as well as their financial base, by connecting with capitalism (Griswold del Castillo & De León 1996:21). By 1840, the overland route to California had been opened, and pioneers also started to pour in from the east. As a result, by 1848 the non-indigenous population had grown to a total of 15,000 inhabitants (Marschner 2000), of whom the non-Hispanics accounted for 6,500, over a third of the total (Francis 1976).

The presence of ever-increasing numbers of Anglo-Americans less and less willing to assimilate with the locals upset the Mexican institutions, especially in Texas, where foreigners greatly outnumbered the original Spanish-speaking settlers. For example, there was friction when the Mexican central government abolished slavery, a measure the Anglo slaveholders resented and which was later suspended for Texas (Perrigo 1970:116). Moreover, the overtures of the American government for buying territories in Texas insulted Mexico, and resulted in the prohibition of further Anglo settlement in the area. Amidst this atmosphere of increasing animosity, the incident that precipitated the war between the Texas territory and the central government was related to refusal on the part of the latter to grant the Texan request for statehood and its state constitution draft of 1833, as guaranteed in the Mexican liberal constitution of 1824. In 1835 the Texans gained independence from Mexico, but neither of its neighbors was too quick to recognize the Lone Star Republic. Soon, it was being militarily threatened by Mexico and facing increasing public debt (Perrigo 1970:124). In spite of this, a steady flow of immigrants, among them 40,000 Black slaves, led to an increase in the population (Perrigo 1970:132).

Texas made several attempts at annexation with the United States, but the northern abolitionists did not support this move, which would increase the number of slavery states in the Union. However, by 1845, annexation was approved by U.S. Congress and by Texas, the first concrete move by the United States to conquer the borderlands (21970:133). The ensuing war between the United States and Mexico and its consequences for the Southwest are discussed in Section 2.11.

In California and New Mexico, meanwhile, Mexican independence had hailed a new era which, it was hoped, would end the severe neglect the area had seen in Spanish times. Among the tangible changes was an increase in self-rule, with local *criollos* acting as Political Chiefs and representing their provinces before Mexican Congress. However, these positive changes could not forestall the internal strife that resulted both from national and local conflicts. For example, in California there were conflicts between liberals, who were in favor of the secularization of the missions, and the Church authorities, who argued that their native wards, who were the owners of the property, could not manage them successfully without the friars (Perrigo 1970:137-139). Plans for a gradual process of secularization, were unsuccessful: a hasty process of privatization of mission lands resulted in the Indians often losing everything. *Californios* also reacted bitterly against the arrival of ex-convicts as part of colonization plans encouraged by the central government (the Híjar-Padrés expedition). They felt that any new lands made available by the secularization of the missions should be theirs to distribute, rather than for outsiders to dispose of. The end of the Mexican period saw struggles between the authorities of the central government and the *Californios* as well as internal conflict between northerners and southerners.

In New Mexico, Indian raids were particularly problematic after Mexican independence, so that many peasants stopped planting and took refuge in the cities, adding to the civil unrest. The centralism of Santa Anna's government led to a revolt against his local representative, governor Albino Pérez, and to his replacement by Armijo, who in the last years of Mexican rule would be in charge of the lavish distribution of land as a result of mission secularization (Perrigo 1970:154). Both in California and in New Mexico, the arrival of increasing numbers of immigrants from the United States was seen with alarm by the central government, and led to unsucceful attempts to stop them.

2.7. The Economy of the Borderlands

The lure of precious metals had been the original economic incentive of much exploration into the northern borderlands. The dream of striking it rich quick by discovering gold and silver mines was a strong motivation for most early explorers, and one that was fed by the improbable but all too real experiences of the conquistadors in Tenochtitlan and Peru. Gold and silver were also an incentive for the crown to grant permission and supplies to embark on the expensive exploratory journeys. However, with the exception of the northern regions of Nueva Galicia and Nueva Vizcaya, the borderland territories would prove to be a disappointment. The seven cities of gold never materialized and the northern frontier acquired strategic value, acting as a buffer zone against the incursions of hostile Indians and other European powers.

According to Perrigo (1970), in the absence of precious metals or stones, the economic life of the outermost Spanish borderlands revolved around agriculture and especially, extensive stock raising. The Spanish patterns of land exploitation were adapted to the new milieu, which was not ideally suited for many crops, due to scanty rainfall in many areas. It was mainly a subsistence economy, which frequently had to be supplemented with royal supplies or annuities, especially during the early years. Eventually, however, most ranches and missions achieved a measure of self-sufficiency. Their main activity was livestock and sheep raising, so that there was an abundance of meat for consumption and tallow for candles and fuel. Leather and wool were also used as raw materials in the manufacture of boots, harnesses, and blankets. The dietary staples were corn and beans, supplemented with produce from small orchards and gardens. In some areas, such as Baja and Alta California, the missions introduced crops, such as vines, which were destined to become cornerstones of the local economy for centuries to come.

To assure economic exploitation, the crown had traditionally encouraged settlement by offering grants of *encomienda*, which made the grantee responsible for the conversion and wellbeing of the indigenous population in an area, in exchange for an annual tribute to be paid by that population to the *encomendero*. However, with the exception of the Pueblo Indians of New Mexico (Kessell 2002:111 *et passim*), borderlands indigenous populations were not subjected to this modality of exploitation, because they were not amenable to a system of personal service and tribute (Bannon 1970:29). The *encomienda* itself would be outlawed in 1712, and thus could not be applied to territories settled after this date, such as Texas and California. Most land was therefore apportioned through a royal proprietary grant, which was given to an individual who guaranteed that he would found a colony with families. A community of ten or more families could also obtain a charter to found a village, following exacting royal instructions regarding urban layout and the building of communal edifices. In some areas, such as New Mexico, European settlers founded *villas*, while the local indigenous population could acquire the rights to their *pueblo* lands. Individuals could also obtain grazing land, in the form of a *sitio*. In general, these *sitios* were vast, aridity requiring large expanses of terrain to make cattlebreeding profitable. Vast lands were also given in usufruct to various religious orders, who were in charge of converting Indians to the Catholic faith at their missions.

The labor required to make the land productive came from two main sources. On the one hand, there were converted mission Indians, called neophytes. Their lives were strictly regimented, with labor divided so that while some were devoted to working in the fields, others were apprenticed to master carpenters, blacksmiths, and so on. The women were often in charge of food preparation, spinning, weaving, and candle-making. The Europeans and *mestizos* who did not live at the mission had to do their own tilling and harvesting, although owners of large *ranchos* often had tenant farmers to work for them; debt servitude was not uncommon as a means to guarantee the stability of the workforce in the large estates. Labor for construction and public works was provided by soldiers and Indians, whom the missions often "leased" for that purpose.

Bannon (1970:80) notes that travelling and transportation in the borderlands were slow and dangerous. The roads were virtually non-existent, flooding over in winter when the rains would swell rivers which were barely a trickle the rest of the year. The main force of traction came from beasts of burden such as donkeys and oxen to pull from two-wheeled wooden carts, and horses to transport soldiers. The poor often did not travel far on their own, adding to the isolation and boredom of their borderland existence. On the other hand, government and church officials would embark on year-long exploration or missionary journeys across this terrain, made dangerous by topography and enemy Indians.

These difficulties in transportation meant that royal supplies reached the far corners of the borderlands infrequently and that the merchandise thus transported was outrageously expensive. We have already mentioned the reliance of New Mexico on the long *Camino Real*, which took eighteen months to complete. California was equally dependent on a tenuous sea route from the ports of the west of Mexico (Acapulco and San Blas). The possibility of licit trade with other countries was precluded by Spanish mercantilism, and even later provisions of free trade under the Bourbons did not allow commerce with foreigners. However, these stringent rules were often hard to apply, as the population was scattered and there were few resources for enforcement. Illicit trade was therefore practiced with abandon, because, while local authorities turned a blind eye, smugglers stood to make huge profits with little risk and local populations obtained necessary goods that were otherwise unavailable (Cutter & Engstrand 1996:283-285).

These smuggling activities were the first step in the gradual weakening of the economic links between the northern borderlands and Central Mexico. Over time, the area's market and strategic positioning would awaken the interest of traders from the United States and other powers. With Mexican independence, trade was legalized and gained momentum, with the opening up of the Santa Fe trail connecting St. Louis to New Mexico in 1822, the connection of Texas with Louisiana's cotton trade, and the increasing presence of Yankee traders in California.

2.8. Society During the Spanish-Mexican Period *which area?*

Owing to their lack of economic promise, the northern borderlands were never too heavily populated. After the original settlements were established, few newcomers arrived to renew the stock, so that the population grew mostly through births, and the area turned into "a colony of cousins" (Kessell 2002:110). The settlers came from two main sources, which in time became intermingled and created a *mestizo* culture. On the one hand, there was the indigenous population, and on the other, European and *mestizo* settlers, mostly from New Spain. The population of Christianized Indians always exceeded them in number, in spite of horrific mortality rates. For example, although by 1680 the Pueblos of New Mexico had been reduced in number to 20 thousand from 50 or 60 thousand, they still outnumbered the Hispanic population eight to one (Kessell 2002:111).

Spanish borderlands society was very different from its English counterpart in its internal ethnic makeup. Although in general it followed Spanish cultural patterns as far as language and religion are concerned, miscegenation had been a feature of Spanish colonization from the earliest periods, and continued to be so in the northern borderlands (Bannon 1970:6, Cutter & Engstrand 1996:187). This resulted in a society stratified along ethnic and racial lines, though more loosely so than in New Spain (Ríos-Bustamante 1993:89). At the top of the pyramid were the full-blooded Spanish officials, born in Spain (*peninsulares*) and acting as representatives of the crown, and the Spaniards born in New Spain (*criollos*). There were also *castas*, i.e., people of mixed blood such as *mestizos* and mulattos. Finally, there were Indians brought over from New Spain and local Natives who had been integrated to colonial society through the adoption of orphans or illicit slave trade of prisoners.

The origin of the settlers was not uniform throughout the borderlands. In general, however, the frontier was settled from the adjacent provinces, with little influx from central Mexico and even fewer colonists from Spain (Griswold del Castillo & De León 1996:6). Among the Spanish authorities, there were also shifts in origin which reflected the changes in demographics and policies of mainland Spain over the centuries. Thus, although the earliest settlements of New Mexico had links to central Spain, California colonization reflected a shift of power to the peripheral provinces of the north, northwest, and east (Killea

1977). On the other hand, the rank and file and the *pueblo* settlers were generally enlisted from the colonial population, from locations such as Sonora, Sinaloa, and Baja California (Perissinotto 1992, Mason 1998:65). From the initial settlements, the population in general increased mostly due to the high birth rate, not further migration.

In most of the Spanish borderlands, society was divided among religious, military, and civilian classes which loosely followed ethnic lines. The religious class was represented by priests, whose power and prestige derived from their association with the Catholic Church and from the large holdings they administered in the name of their Indian wards. The military class was constituted by the soldiers and officers at the *presidios*, whose function was to police the border against attacks from hostile Indians and foreign forces, and often to prevent or stop the flight of mission Indians. The civilians could be rich, if they had been granted lands or *encomiendas*, or poor landless tenant farmers and servants.

The government of the borderlands was exercised by the Spanish crown through local authorities appointed to that effect. The viceroy, who represented the king himself, appointed the provincial governors, in charge of supervising the *presidio* captains, the rural *alcaldes*, and the *cabildos* of the larger towns. The *presidio* captains had control over their soldiers. The rural *alcaldes* were justices of the peace in charge of enforcing the law and supervising the non-mission Indians. In a bigger town, administration was done through two *alcaldes ordinarios* and elected *regidores*, who formed a *cabildo*. The *cabildo* gave the locals a taste of self-rule, since it had the power of administering justice, executing royal ordinances, and could even write their own, but these had to be approved by the governor (Perrigo 1970:86-87).

In the borderlands, the Church had two distinct functions. On the one hand, its secular branch was in charge of ministering to Christians in the *presidios* and *pueblos*. On the other hand, its regular branch was in charge of reducing the Indians in the missions. Several religious orders carried out this work in the Spanish northern borderlands, including the Jesuits, the Franciscans, and the Dominicans. If the Indians already lived in towns, the fathers would build chapels among them and consider the entire town their "reduction." If they were not gathered in *pueblos*, then a mission was built to house them. It was imperative for the mission fathers to be able to keep a close watch on their wards for religious instruction and supervision. For example, unmarried women were secluded in their own halls, in an effort to control their sexuality. The lives of all mission Indians were strictly regimented, with periods devoted to religious duties followed by others of labor. The lands around the mission were said to belong to the Indians, but the friars considered themselves entitled to their usufruct in exchange for their trusteeship. The products of Indian labor were used to support the mission population, but surpluses were also sold to the outside world.

Although the accounts of the mission period from the point of view of the Indians are not numerous, and we may wonder how they felt about their new lifestyle, one thing is certain: the Indian population was ravaged by astoundingly high mortality rates (for a detailed account, cf. Jackson 1994). The causes for this must be found in a combination of factors that may have affected different groups to different degrees. The integration of the missions into New Spain tied them into a single disease pool, so that epidemics spread along the trade routes and hit indigenous populations in major outbreaks at least once every generation. The fact that not only small children but also adults were affected meant that populations had a reduced ability to rebound from losses. In some areas, such as Alta California, non-epidemic causes seem to have been more important. Among these were the fact that women of childbearing age were often cut off from their ancient sources of knowledge of prenatal care and forced to work in the fields, both of which may have increased rates of miscarriage. Abortion and infanticide were practiced, especially if the mother suspected the child of being the result of rape by white soldiers or settlers. Small children were particularly vulnerable to diseases due to poor sanitation and overcrowding. For all age groups, the congregation of hitherto dispersed populations into spatially compact communities was detrimental because it led to water pollution and faster spread of germs. This problem was particularly acute among young women of childbearing age, due to the custom of locking up unmarried women at night in closed quarters.

Additionally, Jackson (1994) notes that other lifestyle changes brought about by the missions may have directly contributed to the weakening of the Natives' health. For example, although it is a matter of debate how substantial the food rations at the missions were, there is little doubt that the priests were under pressure to provide surpluses to support the garrisons at stable prices. Thus, bad crops reduced what was available for consumption by the Indians. That the missions were not a free meal ticket is evidenced by the Indians' frequent attempts at fleeing (Jackson 1994:136). Corporal punishment was commonplace, another piece of evidence that the mission Indians were not always willing participants in the process of Christianization. It is little wonder, considering the severe disruption the mission wrought on indigenous patterns of culture. Native people were forced to follow systems of government, social structure, and division of labor they did not participate in creating and which did not take into consideration their customs, traditions, and values. They were forced to adopt the Spanish dress code, language, and even family structure. This forced acculturation created a psychological dislocation, of which the melancholy and listless attitude which many visitors noted was probably symptomatic (Jackson 1994:139).

Jackson and Castillo (1995) note that the decimation of the indigenous population was acutely felt by the priests. In fact, it forced the closure of several missions and the relocation of survivors in order to consolidate the work of tending to these ever shrinking flocks. Additionally, the priests, who were under obligation to supply the garrisons, had to go farther and farther to get recruits to work for them. However, they were not equally proactive in their response to epidemic outbreaks. On the one hand, they refrained from interfering with the divine punishment they assumed the plagues to be. Thus, for example, they failed to inoculate the population against smallpox when a vaccine was already available and in use in New Spain (Jackson & Castillo 1995:42). On the other hand, they justified the deaths with the argument that suffering was necessary for salvation. Neither the missionaries nor the colonial officials were ready to connect the dots between mission life and the decimation of the Indians living it, and never made adjustments to lessen the impact of the one over the others. It is estimated that by 1848, the California indigenous population had dwindled from 200,000 to 80,000, while in New Mexico and Arizona their losses had been even deeper, from 454,000 at the time of the arrival of the Spaniards, to 215,000 in 1800 and 176,000 by 1848 (Griswold del Castillo & De León 1996:6).

2.9. Daily Life

Daily life in the borderlands, as elsewhere in New Spain, was strictly regulated by the Crown and by Catholic religion. Unlike Anglo-American frontiersmen, those of the Spanish borderlands had little freedom and were closely supervised by the authorities. Their movements were dictated by official instructions, and they could be liable to penalties if they deviated. Withdrawal from an assignment was tantamount to desertion, and punishable as such.

The Church also closely monitored the lives of borderlands inhabitants. In fact, church and state were two sides of the same coin in the Spanish colonies, each one supporting the other in the advancement of its purposes. It theory, they were to act as two close allies, though often they were pitted against each other over the right to the Indian labor supply. The Catholic Church was guaranteed a spiritual monopoly by the Crown, which made it a formidable power if inimical to the lay authorities. Misbehavior could lead to the withholding of the sacraments and to the ultimate punishment for a Catholic, i.e., excommunication. More importantly, perhaps, was the fact that after 1626, the Catholic Church authorities acted as agents of the Holy Office of the Inquisition (Kessell 2002:99), with the power to charge, incarcerate, and transport any person accused of a number of crimes such as bigamy, sodomy, and heresy, to await trial in Mexico City.

Amid the hard life of the borderland frontier, the family was a strong institution, and provided a bulwark against adversity. Griswold del Castillo (1984:42) notes that it provided the rich with a secure means of preserving, increasing, and transferring wealth from one generation to the next, while for the landless, it was a "social insurance against hard times." The family went beyond the nuclear unit to incorporate a large network of relatives. Some of these relations were not based on blood, but on the religious institution of *compadrazgo* (god-parenthood) sanctioned by the Catholic Church. The *padrino* or *madrina* acted as sponsors for religious occasions, and committed to give the *ahijado* or *ahijada* moral and economic support. In turn, *padrinos* became closely connected with the child's parents, who became their *compadres*.

Within the family, the authority was patriarchical, with the *pater familias* completely controling his wife's legal acts, property, and person and imposing his will over other members of the family (Arrom, apud Griswold del Castillo 1984:26). This pattern was rooted in the need to maintain female honor so as to guarantee the purity of the family lineage. The authority of parents, especially fathers, extended to areas as personal as the selection of marriage partners for their children and their profession of religious faith. This paternal authority did not end when the children reached adulthood, but continued as long as the father lived. The women's influence was most strongly felt within the house, where the husband would defer to her for matters of childrearing and home management. However, it must be taken into account that Spanish law gave women the right to inherit property and titles, testify in court, and sign contracts, as well as a high degree of economic independence, which some of them exercised.

The family and the Church were also mostly responsible for educating the young. Formal school attendance during the colonial period was not mandatory or enforced, in spite of the efforts of some authorities. The development of public education was limited by the area's low population density, by political instability, and by the difficulty in securing funds for schools and trained teachers. Few children, mostly boys, attended school, and they did so briefly. There, they were taught reading, writing, arithmetic, and religious doctrine. Very occasionally, children of wealthy families were sent to study in Mexico City (Griswold del Castillo 1979:84-85).

The mixing of cultures on the Spanish borderlands did not result in as thorough an amalgamation as it had in New Spain. Spanish settlers imposed certain features of their motherland on their colonies and on the Indians they lived with, most notably, Catholicism. But the indigenous peoples did not accept all aspects of the new religion wholeheartedly and often rebelled against them. They were faster to adopt the utilitarian innovations, such as metal tools, livestock, and crops (Kessell 2002:107). Likewise, the Hispanics accepted the Indians' ancestral knowledge of their environment, in particular their methods for harnessing water for irrigation. The architecture of the Southwest was a blend of Spanish styles with autochtonous construction patterns and materials. Most buildings were made of a mixture of mud and hay known as *adobe* and covered by mortar (Perrigo 1970:76).

2.10. The U.S.-Mexico War and the Treaty of Guadalupe Hidalgo

As we saw in Section 2.6, the annexation of Texas to the United States in 1845 led to war with Mexico. To counter the Mexican grievances over the loss of the Texan territory and the blockade of Mexican ports, the Americans had their own claims for monetary losses incurred by American citizens which Mexico had failed to pay in their entirety. The United States attempted to use this debt as leverage to further its plans to purchase California, an attempt which did not go over well with the Mexican government (Perrigo 1970:157). Additionally, the Americans contested the Texas southern boundary, where had traditionally been the Nueces River, but which the Americans were attempting to stretch south to the Rio Grande. It was in this disputed land where war would break out, in an incident that both sides claimed had been a foreign aggression on their territory.

The United States attacked on four fronts, with one army crossing the Rio Grande into northern Mexico, another travelling overland through New Mexico and Arizona into California, a sea expedition to the California ports, and finally, one from the port of Veracruz on the Gulf Coast onto Mexico City itself (for details, cf. Perrigo 1970: Ch. 9). This overall plan was followed and encountered little direct and immediate armed resistance on the part of the borderlands population. In New Mexico, it was the Taos and the Pueblo Indians who offered the most resistance, while in California, after the battle of San Pascual the *californios* capitulated at Cahuenga. This is not to say that there was no resistance, however. The arrival of the American troops was valiantly, sometimes heroically, resisted by the local populations of Monterrey, Nuevo León, Sonora, Chihuahua, Coahuila, and Tamaulipas. But valor alone could not make up for the enormously unequal battle, and the war ended when the American army took Mexico City in 1848. The ensuing peace treaty of Guadalupe Hidalgo resulted in the cession of the borderlands to the United States, in exchange for a payment of 15 million dollars. Mexican citizens in the ceded territories were given the option of moving south to Mexico or remaining in their ancestral lands and becoming U.S. citizens.

There are many reasons that can be cited for the fast and decisive American victory. According to Piñera Ramírez (1994:183), an important one was the very low population density in the Mexican borderlands, a feature inherited from the colonial period. It has been estimated that the area, which constituted 51% of the Mexican territory, was home to only 1.6% of its population (Piñera Ramírez 1994:183). The states immediately to the south of the borderlands were not very populated either, with half a million inhabitants out of the country's seven million, this led to the mobilization of armies from the south in their defense. Mexico's internal political situation also militated against the country's ability to defend itself from attack. The new republic was torn by struggles between federalists and centralists, which led to instability in the central and local governments. For example, Mexico had eight presidents during the 20 months the conflict lasted. The army that had to face the invasion was inadequate, with a rank and file made mostly of conscripts and lacking basic training, food, and equipment. Their arms were no match for American artillery and led to disproportionately high numbers of casualties on the Mexican side.

In order to understand the consequences of the Mexican-American War, it is necessary to consider the interests that stoked it in the first place. Some have argued that the doctrine of Manifest Destiny was the ideological engine behind the war (Perrigo 1970:115), but others have claimed that in fact the doctrine was used as a *post facto* excuse: "Manifest Destiny was essentially a manipulated appeal and an attempt to secure broad public support for an expansionist policy of particular benefit to certain political and economic interests" (Barrera 1979:13). According to this author, all productive sectors in the United States stood to win from the war against Mexico: the south would benefit from the addition of Texas territory to cotton growing, while the industrial Northeast would gain from the opening up of California ports on the Pacific for trade with the Orient. Thus, the political parties representing these sectors voted for financial support to the war, in spite of voicing opposition to it. Industrial and technological development, which was partly one of the causes for the war, also made it possible to envision a country extending from the Atlantic to the Pacific, unified by fast new means of transportation, in particular the steam engine.

2.11. The Southwest After American Annexation

After 1848, the Southwest began a series of rapid transformations which would bring the area into the fold of the capitalist economic order and would have a number of social consequences. In California, Texas and Colorado, the Spanish-speaking were outnumbered by Anglo newcomers; in California and Texas, moreover, population figures grew so much that they were soon granted statehood. In New Mexico and Arizona, on the other hand, the Spanish-speaking continued to be a majority, and these two territories had lower population figures which delayed statehood until the early twentieth century.

In California, transformations were accelerated by the discovery of gold in the north of the state before the ink was dry on the peace treaty. Thus, the following years brought large numbers of immigrants from the east coast, so that the population of the state stood at 200,000 in 1852 (Marschner 2000:7). This led to economic prosperity for some, as they became rich either through mining or in the businesses that provided miners with necessary goods and services. Even southern California ranchers stood to benefit from the sale of their cattle at inflated prices. However, the rapid arrival of Anglos also led to considerable social unrest, as the authorities scrambled to maintain law and order over a variegated and often unruly population (Pitt 1966:52). In this sea of newcomers, the outnumbered *californio* population stood to lose the most. The fact that they were more experienced at mining only exacerbated ethnic envy, making them liable to prejudice and summary justice and lynchings in the mining towns (Pitt 1966:51, for details cf. Gonzales-Day 2006).

Another serious obstacle to the prosperity of the local Hispanic population was the application of the provisions of the Treaty of Guadalupe Hidalgo that had to do with land ownership. For example, in California the Land Law of 1851 placed the burden of proving ownership on the ranchers, who often lacked any documentation to back their claims to land that had been in their families for several generations. Because they normally had few liquid assets, ranchers could not face the new taxation or the cost of litigation, so that they often lost their land to the state, squatters, or greedy lawyers (Pitt 1966:86 *et passim*). In this respect, the situation was even worse in New Mexico, where delays over decisions about land grants lasted over 50 years in many cases. In Texas, on the other hand, the legal issue was less problematic because more land had been distributed to *empresarios* by the Mexican government, using procedures that were easier to reconcile with American legislation. However, there is evidence that even here the local Hispanic population lost land steadily (Barrera 1979:30).

Although it was purported that the land of the large *ranchos* would be subdivided among small individual farmers, in fact it became concentrated in the hands of large agriculture capitalists (Barrera 1979:22). In northern New Mexico, where land ownership was often communal, the loss of land was particularly hard for the small subsistence farmers and shepherds. This led to their downward social mobility, as they were reduced to the role of laborers.

According to Griswold del Castillo and De León (1996), the strengthening of communications with the east, achieved through several railroad projects started after the Civil War, had direct and indirect consequences for Mexican

Americans. On the one hand, the track gangs were a source of employment for displaced rural labor. On the other, the train brought increasingly large numbers of Anglo migrants from the east and changed the demographic make-up of the area. The railroad also affected other industries in the Southwest, by making it possible to bring the heavy equipment needed for mining as well as to haul out the product. It also had an impact on cattle breeding, whose profitability until then had been limited by the cost of transporting animals on foot to distant markets. Agriculture also benefitted from the expanded markets for Texas cotton and corn, and California fruit and vegetable crops.

Griswold del Castillo and De León (1996) observe that the new American economic order proletarized a large number of Mexicans, sometimes through labor arrangements not too different from the older forms of *peonaje*. Those who did not have the necessary skills to fit into the new economy were unemployed or had to migrate leaving behind their families. In some cases they were displaced forcefully from profitable ventures, such as freighting in Texas. Increasingly they worked as day laborers, cooks, servants, miners, or seasonal *vaqueros*. The women too started joining the work force.

At first, it seemed like the members of the elite would withstand the onslaught by establishing alliances with the Anglo majority (Griswold del Castillo & De León 1996: 43 *et passim*). Eventually, however, most of them too would suffer dispossession of one kind or another, as they had no capital to compete with companies funded by east coast ventures. In the process, however, the Mexican-American population became increasingly heterogeneous, as people acculturated to the mainstream to different degrees and with different rates of success.

The Mexican-American population also started to feel Anglo contempt, which manifested itself in outright violence or, more subtly, through negative stereotyping and inimical legislation which banned some of their customs (i.e., the so-called "greaser laws"). As they became increasingly urban, they were relegated to certain sections of the city, often the historic Spanish or Mexican town, which suffered neglect and deteriorated. In spite of their numerical disadvantage, Hispanics did make attempts to resist, in the form of rebellion and banditry. Among many examples, one can mention Juan Nepomuceno Cortina, who confronted Anglo authorities in Texas to show his opposition to fraudulent land disposession, starting a rebellion that bedeviled the Texas Rangers and the Mexican authorities on both sides of the border around 1860 (Thompson 1994). In California, the actions of real bandits such as Tiburcio Vásquez and others were aggrandized into the feats of the mythical figure of Joaquín Murrieta (Pitt 1966:284).

Rosenbaum (1981) also notes collective rebellions, such as the El Paso Salt War, which pitted locals against a company which impinged on their rights to exploit communal salt deposits. Although largely ineffectual or neutralized by the authorities, these movements flared up in the Southwest practically throughout the rest of the century (e.g., Gregorio Cortez in Texas, the Maxwell Land Grant, and the Gorras Blancas of San Miguel county in New Mexico) (Rosenbaum 1981). The fact that the rebels often had the support of the local Mexican American population shows that they were manifestations of a more generalized discontent. Finally, as the century progressed and the Mexican-American population started its own newspapers, the intellectual class used them to decry the discrimination to which they were subjected. Working-class Mexican Americans in the fields and mines also fought back against their exploitation by staging strikes in several instances throughout the Southwest.

2.12. Social Changes After Annexation

Griswold del Castillo and De León (1996) note that after annexation, Mexican families continued to maintain many of their old customs, especially their tolerance of multirracial marriages, their close ties, the institution of *compadrazgo*, and the subservient status of women. However, patriarchy underwent changes as young men were forced to leave their wives to fend for themselves while they looked for work in distant locations, women also started to look for their own employment, which increasingly required relocation and uprooted them from their communities.

The Catholic Church, which had been a strong bulwark of traditions in the Spanish-Mexican frontier, also underwent many changes. For one thing, it started to respond to the American ecclesiastic authorities in Baltimore, so that priests and other church appointees were no longer connected to Mexico. Generally, the new local authorities were Europeans who could speak Spanish but were against traditional local manifestations of religiosity, such as *curanderismo* (faith healing) and the New Mexican tradition of the *penitentes*. This was a reflection of a broader mandate of the American Catholic Church to assimilate large numbers of Catholic immigrants to their new country. In the Southwest, however, this move hurt the relationship between the Church and its parishioners, who often rejected these changes and retaliated by refusing to pay their tithe (Griswold del Castillo & De León 1996:36). Another change in the patterns of religion was the fact that now Catholicism faced competition from several Protestant denominations, which started evangelizing in the new territories. This process was more intense and successful in New Mexico and Texas, and less so in the rest of the Southwest.

As noted by Griswold del Castillo and DeLeón, in general, the geographic and social isolation of Mexican Americans in rural areas and certain specific parts of the urban centers, on the one hand, and in the lowest paid occupations that were rejected by Anglos, on the other, meant that they succeeded in maintaining their language and customs. In the latter part of the century, this sense of community flourished into the founding of mutual aid societies, such as the Alianza Hispano Americana of Arizona (1894), which had the mission of offering assistance to the poor and maintaining cultural pride and a sense of identity. At the same time, the fact that Mexicans and Mexican Americans kept moving into new areas looking for work, coupled with the continued arrival of Anglos, resulted in increasing social intercourse and blending of sociocultural traits. The Spanish-speaking came in contact with new consumer products and with new ideas in school, which changed their outlook, their aspirations, and their language.

2.13. Summary

In this historical introduction we have seen how the vast territories of the borderlands were conquered and settled by the Spanish Crown starting in 1513. The conquerors and settlers moved in three directions: straight to the north of New Spain, to New Mexico; to the east, into Texas and Louisiana; and later, to the west, into Arizona and California. In so doing, they encountered numerous indigenous groups that had lived in the area for several millenia and had succeeded in making a living from the often harsh environment.

The Spanish settler population was small and tended to stay that way for the entire period, with the exception of New Mexico, where it reached a total of 50,000 to 60,000 inhabitants. The first settlers were more often than not from the nearby frontier areas, rather than from the Peninsula. This was due in part to the fact that the rugged terrain was not economically attractive, as it provided little more than the bare necessities, a fact exacerbated by poor communications with the rest of the colonies. As in other parts of the Empire, mixing with and acculturation of the local indigenous population was common. The main institutions of social control were the Church and the Crown, supposedly working in unison but often clashing on important matters, such as the management and treatment of Indians. Because the survival of the settlements often depended on this labor pool, the steady dwindling of their numbers posed serious problems.

After two centuries of continuous settlement, the Spanish colonies underwent an internal upheaval due to the independence of Mexico from the Spanish Crown. Additionally, they were being increasingly threatened by other European powers with a stake in North America. These two facts conspired to bring the newly independent Mexico face to face with the United States in an unequal battle that eventually led to the cession and purchase of the northern borderlands by the latter. After that, rapid economic transformations fueled by capitalism ensued. The Spanish-speaking minority underwent a process of proletarization and displacement, as they lost their land and saw competition from Anglo settlers for jobs in the new economy. The Mexican Americans were also the object of racial prejudice, punitive legislation, and outright violence, and responded sometimes by rebellion and banditry, but most often by retreating into their families and networks for protection and solidarity. Although it has often been blamed for not blending into the American majority more readily, the Spanish-speaking did show a knack for adjusting to their unfavorable new realities. Through it all, however, they fought hard to preserve their identity, including in many cases their ancestral language.

3. Language Policies

3.1. Language Policies During the Colonial and Mexican Periods

According to some estimates approximately 147 languages were spoken in New Spain in 1521 (Swadesh 1959). The Spanish explorers and settlers thus faced daunting linguistic challenges the likes of which they had never encountered before. Throughout the colonial period, the empire's response was a mixture of idealism and pragmatism which led to different linguistic policies at different times and achieved mixed results. As in other areas of colonial administration, there was often a disconnect between the letter of the law and the measures actually implemented by those in charge of their application. Additionally, the linguistic policies favored by the Crown and the Church were often at odds. In what follows, we present a brief summary of the language policies applied during the process of exploration, conquest, and colonization.

During the period of exploration, sheer survival and the success of entire expeditions depended on finding people capable of interpreting between the locals and the explorers (Brooks 2001, Luca 2004). The urgency of the situation led to different measures, such as employing local interpreters or Spaniards who had been stranded in America on previous trips. Explorers also routinely captured indigenous youths and took them back from their trips, with the purpose of teaching them Spanish and indoctrinating them so that they would act as go-betweens in later voyages (Luca 2004). The success of these measures varied, because, among other things, it was hard to guarantee the survival of these children and to prevent them from betraying the Europeans once they were back among their people. Moreover, the extreme linguistic fragmentation of the Americas greatly limited their usefulness. The challenges of communicating with indigenous populations were apparent from the very first incursions into New Mexico. For example, Kessell describes Oñate's reliance on a "polyglot corps of interpreters who knew Nahuatl, Towa, and Pecos" (2002:78). More dramatically, the dangers of poor communication are exemplified by the earlier case of Estebanico, one of the four survivors of Cabeza de Vaca's expedition. When he returned to the area of New Mexico he had traveled through before, as a guide for a new expedition led by Marcos de Niza, his offensive behavior, coupled no doubt with his inability to communicate with the local chief, led to his death and to the failure of the entire expedition (Kessell 2002:27).

Linguistic diversity also hindered the Church and the Crown in their settlement efforts. One of their main stated objectives of colonization, the conversion of heathens, could only be achieved if the indigenous population understood the sermons and followed Catholic rites. For the missionaries it was clear right away that it would be impractical to postpone conversion until the Indians had mastered Spanish and Latin. Sheer numbers made an abrupt shift to Spanish unthinkable. Additionally, the priests considered it undesirable to allow much communication between the indigenous population and lay Spaniards, since that could lead to economic exploitation and moral depravity. According to Moreno de Alba (1993:53), linguistic unintelligibility between both groups was not deemed entirely bad, since it acted as a form of protection when coupled with physical isolation in towns and missions. One exception to this rule were the children of the nobility. For them, the priests opened boarding schools such as the Colegio de Santa Cruz de Tlatelolco, where these young noblemen were taught Spanish as the language of daily life and Latin as the language of religious indoctrination.

If the majority of the indigenous population would not learn Spanish, then the missionaries would have to learn the languages of the communities in which they intended to catechize. They did so with mixed success. A few expended considerable effort in documenting and recording indigenous languages in treatises and glossaries (Amate Blanco 1992). On the other hand, many missionaries had only rudimentary notions of native languages, which impeded their work. Since interpreters were banned from confession, some had to skip this rite altogether, and could do little more than read ready-made sermons. The situation was especially dire in missions that congregated indigenous peoples who spoke several different languages or where the missionaries had to move frequently from one post to another (Hausberger 1999).

One practical solution to deal with linguistic diversity was to extend the use of indigenous lingua francas beyond their pre-colonial boundaries. Thus, the Church changed the linguistic ecology by favoring some indigenous languages at the expense of others. In New Spain the chosen languages were Nahuatl, Mayan, and the main languages of Oaxaca, already widely used for trade (Cifuentes 1992:10). Other languages such as Tarahumara, Pima, and Guaycuru were also adopted as regional languages in the north. The priests also altered the linguistic map of New Spain by resettling and mixing indigenous groups in the missions, probably accelerating processes of language shift and loss (Hausberger 1999:66). Finally, Spanish came to join the mix as the language of administration and as a lingua franca.

The language policy of the Crown was not just motivated by religious fervor, as shown by Moreno de Alba (1993:51-56). Achieving the Hispanization of the New World was a matter of empire building, aptly summarized in Antonio de Nebrija's characterization of Spanish as *compañera del imperio* "partner of the empire." This led to shifting priorities over the years. For example, under Charles V, efforts were made to promote the learning of Spanish among the Indians. In 1570 Philip II, advised by the Franciscans, decreed that Nahuatl should be the official language of the indigenous population of New Spain, a move meant to simplify the friars' work, but opposed by other groups. In 1596, the king's *Real Cédula* urged for voluntary Spanish instruction instead. To encourage this, it was decreed in 1690 that when choosing officers in Indian villages, priority should be given to those who could speak Spanish (Hausberger 1999:62). By the eighteenth century, Charles III went as far as to order the abandonment of all languages other than Spanish, a measure which reflected the new priorities of the Crown.

These shifting policies had limited possibilities of implementation in the face of the complex realities of America. As a result, the linguistic make-up of the colonies was still very diverse at the time of their independence. For example, in Mexico over 60% of the population did not speak Spanish as their mother tongue in 1810 (Cifuentes 1992:12). This was also true of the vast area of the Mexican borderlands at the time of their annexation to the United States. There, large contingents of Indians continued to use their own languages, sometimes alongside Spanish, sometimes exclusively. For example, in records of criminal court cases from California, Indian defendants are routinely recorded as speaking through interpreters (Beebe & Senkewicz 2001:242 *et passim*). Unlike what happened in New Spain, Spanish in the Southwest acquired very few borrowings from the local indigenous languages, possibly a reflection of the low status of these languages (Trujillo 2000). On the other hand, speakers of indigenous languages often resorted to Spanish for borrowings and as a lingua franca. The effects of this tendency are still observable today (Brown 1994, 1996).

3.2. Language Policies in the U.S. Southwest

Bilingualism and the policies of English Only are a preoccupation shared by all Spanish-speaking communities in the United States and, as will be mentioned later, also by all communities using languages other than English. The restoration and revalidation of the Spanish language is an objective shared by

Puerto Ricans, Mexican Americans, Cuban Americans, and other Spanish-speaking groups that have grown considerably in recent years, including Colombians, Venezuelans, Argineans, and Dominicans.

These struggles for the legitimacy of minority languages date back to the eighteenth century, when the U.S. Congress rejected a bill allowing for the publication of some copies of the law in German, as requested by some citizens of Augusta County, Virginia (Kloss 1977:28). Still, regardless of the concerns of citizens and the numerous attempts to recognize the languages of minorities in general, the history of linguistic policies in the United States has consistently been that of imposing English in possible social domains and the devaluation of all minority languages. It has not only been Spanish that in most possible situations has been placed in the status of dominated language; so have indigenous languages slowly eliminated from the linguistic map of the United States.

However, Spanish has faced a better fate than other minority languages in the United States. Despite suffering continuous attacks, it is the most widespread and best maintained minority language in the Union; as pointed out by Rosales (2000):

> Mexicans keeping their language in the United States territory longer than most other non-English-speaking ethnic groups is partially due to continuous Mexican immigration and because of the resistance to Anglo domination. After the Anglo conquest, Southwest Mexicans continued to speak their language, regardless of political and cultural domination. (26)

Although the presence of the Spanish language has persisted over time due to the factors mentioned by Rosales, the Union's linguistic policy has followed a process of Anglicization as observed by Hernández-Chávez, who points out that "Following the Mexican-American War (1846-1848) and the annexations of Texas, California, and New Mexico, policies in the West followed the pattern of Anglicization policies in the East and Midwest" (1994:145). This pattern attempts to achieve the cultural and linguistic assimilation of immigrants and people who use languages other than English. The linguistic pattern of English Only summarizes U.S. policies from the beginnings of its history to the present day.

Still, as mentioned earlier, often this linguistic policy is countered by reality. Various factors have intervened, resulting in the continuous use of Spanish in the United States. A major factor is that Spanish-speaking immigrants continue to arrive in the United States, thus keeping the Spanish language alive in the country.

We will present a brief history of the linguistic policies related to the superimposition of a dominant to a dominated language in the U.S. Southwest. We will also mention the means of resistance, if any, to the policy of English Only.

3.3. New Mexico

The process of change from the Spanish to the English language in New Mexico was slow, but eventually a switch was made to the dominant language, in spite of the opposition posed by different sectors of society.

The Anglo-American invasion was resisted by the Spanish-speaking inhabitants of New Mexico, leading to the 1848 revolt in Taos where the Anglo-American governor was assassinated along with other settlers (Espinosa 99). In addition to the opposition posed by those denominated *mexicanos*, New Mexico was not a territory of interest for the Union. Poor and lacking gold, it was composed in great part by desert and inhabited by a mostly Mexican and indigenous population by the time it was abdicated by Mexico (Hernández-Chávez 1994:147). These factors made it unattractive in the eyes of the Anglo-Americans, who moved to the different regions with intentions of developing a capitalist economy. It is for these reasons that the territory was not integrated into the United States as a state of the Union until 1912, after awaiting sixty-four years, and following fifty petitions to Congress (Hernández-Chávez 1994:147). The reasons why statehood was finally granted are varied. It must be noted that by 1912, the arrival of the railroad promoted the immigration of Anglo-Americans. As the Anglo population outnumbered the Mexicans they obtained positions of power and began to seize New Mexicans' lands, gradually imposing patterns of colonial domination over the rest of the population of Hispanic origin (Gonzales-Berry & Maciel 2002:15).

During the period in which the territory was not a state no laws were passed with regards to the Spanish language, mostly for practical reasons. People spoke Spanish, so all official documents continued to be written in Spanish and then translated into English. As Hernández-Chávez points out: "in 1853, a petition to authorize translators was granted by the Congress, and in 1884 funds were appropriated for translation and publication of proceedings" (1994:147). Toward the end of the nineteenth century, Amado Chávez defended the teaching of Spanish in public schools. He used original arguments to defend the native language of the New Mexican population, including "two additional attributes to sustain his argument: the inherent beauty of the Spanish language and its utilitarian value" (Gonzales-Berry 2002:171). Chávez also emphasized that being bilingual did not prevent New Mexicans from possessing the characteristics of good citizens (Gonzales-Berry 2002:171). In the early twentieth century though, there was an increased pressure towards teaching in English and for teachers to learn English. "The New Mexico Enabling Act of 1910 stipulated that schools were to be conducted in English . . . " (Hernández-Chávez 1994:148).

Along with the growth of the Anglo-American population came a resurgence of resistance movements. One of the first forms of resistance, as in the case of California, were newspapers and other periodicals. From their pages many editors and readers put up a defense of the Spanish language (Maciel & Gonzales-Berry 2002:18) or promoted the use of the periodical as a means to acquire or improve the Spanish language:

> To neglect the original language is an indolence. Even though English is the national language, Castilian is the language of the Hispanic home. They will say that there is a lack of teaching of the Castilian tongue. That is true, but lacking teachers, look for a good periodical that is written in this language; look for a publication that has the purest Castilian, and if you cannot learn the Spanish language through this medium, with due correction you will learn much, enough to understand what the cinema artists say, where they express themselves in correct Spanish. (Juan Montano, 25 de julio de 1930, *La Bandera Nacional*, New Mexico)

The fight for the preservation of the Spanish language in New Mexico was arduous and New Mexican legislators sought ways to negotiate its maintenance while simultaneously fighting to have New Mexico granted statehood. From the earliest attempts, however, there was a push for a policy of English Only, as it had been applied to other states of the Union. Education played a paramount role in the imposition and spread of the English language. From the beginning, New Mexicans opposed public education, not due to lack of support for public education, nor due to the distance separating the different pueblos from each other, as pointed out by Gould quoted by Gonzales-Berry and Maciel, but because the acculturation meant by adopting the English language: "the Nuevomexicano population feared public education would spell cultural and native-language erosion" (Gonzales-Berry 2002:171).

Gonzales-Berry points out in an article published in *La Opinión* that the Spanish language in New Mexico had a legal and symbolic status until 1987, when there was a new attempt to pass a bill granting official status to English. This bill was eventually voted down even by the representatives who presented it in the first place: Marta Lambert and Don Silva (Gonzales-Berry & Maciel 1987).

Even the most rabid defenders of English as an official language recognize New Mexico's special status. For example, Gerda Bikales, executive editor of U.S. English, the national organization promoting English as the official language of the United States, stated that "one picks and chooses one's battles in this business, and New Mexico isn't a very promising situation. We would not expect to pass a bill there now" (Groves 1987: D1).

Although they have succeeded in maintaining the language of their ancestors, the state's Spanish-speaking inhabitants have seen it affected. For example, during the 1930s English had already taken the place of Spanish in the public domain and restricted it to the position of a language spoken only at home. Gonzales-Berry explains:

> Spanish had given way to English as the main language for communication and by the thirties the repression of Spanish in the schools had become the unyielding rule. As the vision of the foreseeing writers of the New Mexican Constitution blurred, Spanish became a subordinate language. Seeing themselves being denied their right to teaching in their native language, New Mexicans acquired an informal body of Spanish at home. Spanish remained an everyday source of the group's internal cultural identity. As a public social note their language was stigmatized and qualified as strange, rare, and of the streets. (Gonzales-Berry 1987)

Toward the end of this section we will mention some of the efforts to revitalize Spanish in New Mexico and the rest of the states of the U.S. Southwest.

3.4. California

The Spanish language arrived in California with the first missionaries. In the beginning, and with the help of soldiers, they taught the language to the indigenous people as a component of the "civilization" they would eventually impose on them. As the eighteenth century progressed and the nineteenth century began, the Spanish-speaking population became quite powerful in the region, imposing their language, political, and economic ways on the local inhabitants.

During this period of Spanish and Mexican domination a formal means of education that would contribute to the consolidation of the Spanish language was not developed. Nonetheless, some means of education existed to alphabetize the inhabitants of California, including the indigenous population, and oftentimes it was women who took the primary responsibility as educators (Castañeda 1993:77).

The arrival of the Mexican Governor José María Echeandía was a push towards the creation of public schools. This liberal governor was a passionate believer in free, public, and compulsory education for all, rich and poor, Indians and *gente de razón* "people of reason," as the Spanish-speakers called themselves. Echeandía believed that education was a fundamental aspect of wealth. However, he not only faced opposition from the Church, but also had to deal with the disinterest of the people. In spite of many attempts to promote the creation of public schools in the *presidios*, his success was scant. On the one hand, he lacked enough funds to build the schools; and on the other, he faced complete indifference toward education among the population; both reasons led Echeandía to abandon his desires to end ignorance (Guinn 1903:60).

Another passionate fighter for public and mass education during the Mexican era was Governor Manuel Micheltorena, who made a great effort to implement a system of public education in California. Schools were created in all *pueblos* and they were assigned funds extracted from the territorial treasury (Guinn 1903:60).

In 1844, Micheltorena enacted what is considered to be the first education law in California (Guinn 1903:60). It consisted of a decree of ten articles indicating what should be taught in schools, hours of operation, ages of schooling, and other regulations. However, his good intentions did not last long, and due to a lack of funds all schools were eventually closed (Guinn 1903:61).

Although during this period there were some attempts to foment formal education, it was limited and restricted to males. In fact, all teachers were males. During the California War of Conquest, as well as during the Gold Rush, schools remained marginal. The lack of teachers was in part related to the lack of men, who preferred to earn more money in the goldmines or were obligated to go to war.

The lack of educational facilities under the Spanish and Mexican governments had implications for the Spanish language. In the absence of any institutional educational policies, Anglo-Americans in California developed their own formal educational system in English. Hispanic parents opposed it at first, but began to accept it with the passing of time, due to their wish to integrate their children into the developing capitalist economic system.

As mentioned earlier, those Anglo settlers that had arrived before the war integrated and assimilated themselves to the Hispanic population of California. On the other hand, those who arrived after the war and the signing of the Treaty of Guadalupe Hidalgo (1848) had no intentions to assimilate. On the contrary, they arrived to impose their own customs and language. Due to the development of this Anglo majority and to their representation in positions of power, the laws related to language were changed as the nineteenth century reached its end. In 1849 laws could be published in Spanish and English; however, the 1852 "statutes required their promulgation in Spanish in the counties most heavily populated by Mexicans . . . but the Constitution of 1855 specified that English was to be the language of instruction . . . " (Hernández-Chávez 1994:146-147). This process of imposition of the English language in California culminated in 1879 with the Constitution's elimination of the use of Spanish from all official spheres.

California was one of the first states to initiate a linguistic debate related to the preservation or loss of the Spanish language. The change in government following the signing of the Treaty of Guadalupe Hidalgo represented for the Hispanic inhabitants of California a process of cultural and linguistic schizophrenia. This manifested itself in the fight for the preservation of the Spanish language while at the same time recognizing the need to learn the language of the colonizer, as expressed in periodicals of the time (Kanellos 2002:xx).

Hispanic newspapers in California, as well as those of other states of the Southwest, expressed this debate on their pages. On the one hand, due to territorial interests of the inhabitants of California and the need to defend the lands they had owned during the Spanish and Mexican-rule in the courts, the publications encouraged the learning of the English language. For example, Francisco Ramírez, in his editorials published in *El Clamor Público*, was a supporter of learning English. Kanellos points out that Ramírez "considered that it was important not only for business purposes, but to protect the rights of Californians" (Kanellos 2002a:xx). Conversely, bilingual education was defended by Antonio Coronel from the pages of his newspaper, *La Crónica*, of Los Angeles. This preoccupation with preserving the Spanish language can be observed in a majority of periodicals published during the period immediately following the Anglo-American invasion. Arturo Rosales mentions in *Testimonio* that "After the Anglo conquest, Southwest Mexicans continued to speak their language, regardless of political and cultural domination" (Rosales 2000:26). He adds that the Mexicans of the Southwest "published hundreds of Spanish language newspapers to cover not only news and advertising but also to support their own ideas, language, and culture" (Rosales 2000:26).

In California the preoccupation with the preservation of identity and the maintenance of language as a symbol of that identity was evident. As explained by Griswold del Castillo,

> In the Spanish and Mexican periods, Los Angeles had no newspapers. There had been little need for them, since the pueblo was small. Few could read, and few had interests outside of their immediate localities. During the American era all of this changed. Suddenly Los Angeles' population grew, almost tripling in ten years. Literacy became more widespread, and the Spanish-speaking took more interest in outside affairs. There followed a journalistic revolution, as at least 16 Spanish-language newspapers made their appearances not just a local phenomenon but part of a movement among Mexican-Americans throughout the Southwest. (1979:125).

However, and in spite of these efforts, the English language was imposed with time. An era of intense Americanization started with the beginning of World War I. Americans began to feel threatened by the growth in the number of immigrants whom they feared had no intentions to assimilate as other immigrant groups had done earlier (Nichols 1989:15). The Americanization movements promoted the teaching of U.S. history and the pledge of allegiance, and also imposed restrictions on the teaching of foreign languages. The most affected language during WWI was German; however, other European, Asian, and Native American languages were also targeted. Schools imposed English as the sole language of instruction, a move that facilitated the process of shift towards the English language.

3.5. Arizona

Although its linguistic history was similar to that of the language in New Mexico, California, Texas, and other states, Arizona Spanish-speakers did not enjoy the same degree of tolerance as their New Mexico counterparts..

Attempts to impose the English language in Arizona predate statehood. During the time when the territories of New Mexico and Arizona were fighting for their integration as states of the United States, Arizona saw the preeminence of Mexicans and the Spanish language in New Mexico as a negative factor for statehood. From the moment it became a part of the United States with the signing of the Treaty of Guadalupe Hidalgo, Arizona did not mention anywhere in its Constitution that it would follow the indications of the treaty. When language is mentioned in Arizona's Constitution, English is indicated as the adopted language for the state. For example: "Article XX, Section 7: Provisions shall be made by law for the establishment and maintenance of a system of public schools which shall be open to all the children of the State and be free from sectarian control, and said schools shall always be conducted in English." In Article XX, Section 8, English is declared the language of all state officers and members of the State Legislature. Finally, in 1988, Arizona voters approved an English language amendment, making English the official language of the state (Nichols 1989:50). This amendment was ruled unconstitutional by the U.S. Ninth Circuit Court case *Yniquez vs. Arizonans for Official English.* Nonetheless, the voters of the State of Arizona passed Proposition 301 in 2006 which once again insists that English is the official language of the State and that any communications carried out in a language other than English must be deemed legally unofficial.

3.6. Texas

Texas has also been touched by the English Only movement that has swept through other regions of the U.S. Southwest. After the Mexican-American War (1846-1848) and the annexation of the state, Texas continued the policy of Anglicization that had been implemented in other regions of the country (especially in the East and Midwest). Following the battle of the Alamo (1836), growing Anglo-American resentment was reflected in the policies implemented against the Spanish language. Martínez (2000) interprets this development as an imposition of bilingualism with English, in a state where the dominant language had been Spanish.

In 1841 Texas ceased to publish its laws in Spanish, although in 1846 the governor of the new state of the union "was authorized to disseminate the laws of the State in either Spanish or German" (Hernández-Chávez 1994:146). The elimination of Spanish from the schools was the strongest step towards the imposition of the policy of English Only. In Texas, during 1858, English became the language of instruction in schools. The Spanish language, was thus constituted into a foreign language beginning in 1870, when the teaching of a foreign language is allowed during a transitional period, until the students finally acquired English (Hernández-Chávez 1994:146). Around 1905 English was imposed as the sole language of instruction, leaving Spanish completely relegated to the status of a foreign language, creating a precedent that would facilitate the process of declaring English as the language of the state (Luebke 1980:2).

In all the states mentioned, the measures taken at the state level were accompanied by federal moves promoting the policy of English Only; for example when "Congress amended the naturalization laws to refuse citizenship to aliens who could not speak the English language. This requirement also appeared in the Nationality Act of 1940. The requirement of an ability to read and write English was added later in the Internal Security Act of 1950" (Nichols 1989:19-20). Nichols points out that the United States allowed the use of other languages when it was convenient.

Between the late 1950s and 1970s a growing tolerance towards minority languages emerged. The fight for civil rights can be tied to aspects concerning minority languages. In the majority of cases, the defense of a language other than English was based on the protection of individuals regardless of national origin, and not so much on the right to maintain the language in question. In other words, the laws did not protect languages, but rather foreign citizens' rights to live free of discrimination. Thus, laws were approved related to minority languages, such as "the Bilingual Education Act, the Court Interpreters Act, and the Voting Rights Act, which tolerates non-English languages." (Nichols 1989:21). Still, some were of great importance for the revitalization of the Spanish language, such as the Bilingual Services Act of 1973 passed in California, which "required State and local agencies that render significant public services to linguistic minorities to hire bilingual employees or interpreters" (Hernández-Chávez 1994:150). In other states, a "transitional bilingual education and protections for voters" was imposed gradually (Hernández-Chávez 1994:151).

At the federal level, laws were passed that would be of great importance for the recognition of minority languages: "the Voting Rights Act of 1965, Title VII of the Elementary and Secondary Education Act of 1968, and the Court Interpreters Act of 1978" (Hernández-Chávez 1994:151). Although these laws were a step toward the acceptance of other languages, in reality they displayed certain weaknesses and were not able to protect the linguistic rights of the Spanish-speaking population. As an example, the Title VII Act provides for transitional bilingual programs, in which children are ultimately led toward Anglicization. During the early 1980s this situation prompted a reaction by those who perceived a threat in the advances, albeit limited, of minority groups. These groups pushed for the establishment of English as the official language, not simply de facto but also by law. At the state level, various states had already established English as their official language. In 1986, California passed a constitutional amendment declaring English the official language of the state and various states followed this example afterwards.

In conclusion, the English Only movement has progressively gained ground and minority languages have been increasingly displaced from public life in the United States. This process of English advancement over other languages, and in particular over the Spanish language, has resulted in language loss or in linguistic contact situations, leading to phenomena particular to bilingual zones, as will be demonstrated in some of the essays in this book.

4. Methodology

One of the concerns of historical sociolinguistics is the methodology used for the collection and analysis of linguistic data. In this volume we present a varied sample of data collection methods, different sources, and diverse analyses. On the one hand, surviving informants are interviewed in studies with a sociolinguistic focus such the essay by Pratt, who interviews "Adaeseño" speakers, descendants of the Spanish colonists in Northwest Louisiana. On the other hand, aspects of the language from the past can be analyzed through written texts (Balestra, Gubitosi, Martínez, Moyna, and Decker) or the comparison of manuscripts (Cunningham). Whichever approach is utilized to study the language of the past, limitations will be encountered.

To start we will present fundamental aspects of sociolinguistics, a relatively new field of linguistics. Although dialectological studies had been the initial step in the development of sociolinguistics, this discipline emerged as a separate subject during the early 1960s. The basic principle of sociolinguistics is the empirical study of variations in language and the correlation between these variations and linguistic and non-linguistic factors. The studies by Labov in

Martha's Vineyard and in New York (Labov 1963, 1966) pioneered this new discipline. Although other linguists have taken into account the varied nature of language, it is Labov who began to study it systematically.

Among the most important principles in sociolinguistics is the recognition that human languages are inherently variable. This variability is a structured phenomenon which can be analyzed empirically. Linguistic variation is linked to internal as well as external aspects of language. Frequently, sociolinguistics employs quantitative methods, including a systematic compilation of data, use of linguistic variables, and statistical methods to analyze such data.

The sociolinguistic study of linguistic variation employs the methodology of apparent time as well as real time (Labov 1994:43-112) and these studies have demonstrated that variation could be indicative of a progressive change in the language. Sociolinguistic studies have identified several social factors that can be correlated to linguistic variation, the most frequently cited being age, gender, education, and social class. Controversy arises when attempting to define the latter, due to the complex nature of the variable. Defining it requires the identification of a series of subfactors which would be difficult to quantify, such us profession, education, income, etc. Additionally, this is a variable that cannot be applied to pre-industrialized or non-industrialized societies. The majority of the studies in this book, including those about the second half of the nineteenth century, correspond to the pre-industrial stages of the U.S. Southwest. Confronted with these difficulties, linguists have resorted to alternatives such as equating class with professional categories, among others. Among these studies are Milroy's investigations (1987) of the maintenance of non-standard English in Belfast, Northern Ireland. A predominant factor in this study is the integration of individuals in the social network of the local community. According to this model, the social network is described in terms of proximity and density of the links among its members. The degree to which the members of the community know each other determines the density of the network; the degree to which the members interact is what Milroy and Milroy call "multiplexity" (Milroy & Milroy 1987, 1992). If the social networks are solid and there is much density and "multiplexity" then the language persists with little variation. Variation is incorporated in the community when the social networks are weakened (Milroy and Milroy 1987, 1992, L. Milroy 1980, J. Milroy 1992, 1999).

Sociolinguistic models of this type are properly applied to contemporary societies as well as past ones, as noted in Romaine (1982), a pioneering study of historical sociolinguistics. The author demonstrated that it is possible to resort to sociolinguistic methods that had been used to study phonological variation in industrialized urban areas to study grammatical variables of the past. Current investigation trends in historical sociolinguistics (Richter 1985, Milroy

1992, Machan & Scott 1992, Nevalainen & Ramoulin-Brumberg 1996) also use sociolinguistic methods to study the language of the past.

Historical sociolinguistics has a number of limitations and some advantages when compared to current sociolinguistic studies. Table 3.1 (from Nevalainen & Ramoulin-Brunberg 1996) presents a comparison between sociolinguistic research used for the present and for the past.

	Current research	**Past**
Object of research	Phonological variation and/or change.	Grammatical variation and/or change.
Research materials	Spoken language.	Written language and/or speakers using a linguistic form in danger of disappearing.
	All people.	Only the literate (upper ranks, men), and/or people with little or no education.
	Authentic speech; observation, elicitation, evaluation.	Randomly preserved texts
Social Context	Known society, much data available.	Social structure has to be reconstructed on the basis of historical research.
Standardization	Significant element.	Significance varies.
Associated discipline	Sociology, Statistics.	Social history.
Time and results of change	Unknown	Known

Table 3.1. Comparison between current and historical sociolinguistic studies. Adapted from Terttu Nevalainen and Helena Ramoulin-Brunberg (1996:18).

Diachronic and synchronic sociolinguistic studies use different sources. In very limited cases, oral data can be obtained through interviews with the last survivors of a vestigial language. Written data can be obtained from newspapers, periodicals, testimonials, legal documents, and personal correspondence. Another problem frequently encountered by language historians as they use written sources is the inevitable delay between the introduction of new forms in speech and their appearance in text. To limit this gap, written texts can be considered as real representatives of what occurs in speech. The data obtained for historical research are those that have been accidentally preserved for future generations. As pointed out by Labov, "historical linguistics can . . . be thought of as the art of making the best use out of bad data" (Labov 1994:11).

If working with written texts (correspondence, diaries, and testimonials), it must be taken into account that the language of those at the lowest tiers of society cannot be studied because the vast majority of them could not read or write. Only the privileged class kept in written communication with people from other places. Nevertheless, and fortunately for us, there are exceptions. Such is the case of Josefa and Laureana Cuevas, two sisters that worked at the house of a Mexican family of means in mid-nineteenth century California and wrote to their brother. Therefore, the historical sociolinguist must recognize the limitations of the work in terms of the population or the data that can be recovered, and in no way can she or he attempt to represent society as a whole. It must also be taken into account that the concept of a literate society is not absolute, but rather a continuum. Some individuals reached more advanced levels of literacy than others.

Current language researchers have at their disposal the social structure that they wish to study as well as a great number of facts and social analysis provided by sociologists and statisticians. In historical studies, social historians are consulted to reconstruct societies of the past. This is necessary to create classifications that are relevant and to analyze the linguistic data.

Another difference, which is an advantage for the historical study of languages, is that both the initial stage of the process of change and the end result are known. This advantage provides historical sociolinguists with an excellent opportunity to test the veracity and relevance of the analysis in apparent time in contrast with changes in real time (Ramoulin-Brunberg 1996:19).

Finally, for those studying the languages of societies which have suffered colonization by speakers of a different language finding written documents in the dominated language can prove challenging. Archives tend to preserve documents from socially prominent individuals and this judgement is left to the criteria of archivists or the families that supply them with documents for preservation.

Another approach to the study of a dead or dying language is through surviving informants. These informants may be "tainted" through contact with the dominating language (as in the case of Spanish speakers in the Anglo-American society). The difficulty for the linguist is to find and interview those individuals, especially considering their age. Interviewing the elderly has drawbacks, such as problems with diction and lapses in memory.

Results from pilot studies about historical sociolinguistics show that relatively general levels of analysis must be utilized. For example, it may be possible to classify all speakers according to their social status, but only a few of them offer adequate material for stylistic analysis. The lack of detailed social profiles of the subjects causes problems. For instance, it is impossible to analyze the social attitudes in the manner Labov did in Martha's Vineyard (Labov 1966), or to evaluate ambitions by interviewing the informant and their friends

(Chambers 1995:95-100). Alternatively, there is real time information about those people's social advancement. Social networks cannot be established to the degree Milroy (1980) and Milroy (1992) did in Belfast, but their characteristics can be discussed at the societal level.

In synthesis, historical sociolinguists face several difficulties when attempting to rebuild the linguistic forms of the past. However, by adapting the procedures used in current sociolinguistic research and bringing together a variety of historical and social ancillary data, it is still possible to provide a rich and nuanced description of language variation in the past. The fact that the end result of the change is generally known gives historical sociolinguistics added importance to assess the predictive value of contemporary studies.

5. Language Maintenance and Language Shift

The study of language maintenance and shift is a central aspect of the historical sociolinguistic investigation of bilingual and multilingual communities. Uncovering patterns of maintenance and shift allows the researcher to understand more fully the social background of the linguistic changes that emerge in textual analysis. Patterns of maintenance and shift can also be useful in periodization efforts if the evidence points to sustained historical moments of either strong retention or rapid decline of a minority language. Synchronic studies of maintenance and shift have been carried out using three basic methodologies. Some researchers have used sociolinguistic questionnaires in order to uncover the relative vitality of the minority language in an individual's routine linguistic interactions (Gal 1979, Mejías, Anderson-Mejía & Carlson 2003, Silva-Corvalán 1994, Bernal-Enríquez 2000). Other researchers have focused on structural factors in a community that may or may not support continued use of the minority tongue (Giles, Bourhis & Taylor 1977, Jaramillo 1995). Finally, some researchers have used census data in order to gain a broad perspective on the ways that minority language speakers shift toward the dominant tongue (Hudson, Hernández-Chávez & Bills 1995, Bills, Hudson & Hernández-Chávez 2000, Portes & Rumbaut 1996). In this section, we will survey these three methodologies and point out how the historical sociolinguist can use them in order to uncover patterns of language maintenance and shift from a diachronic perspective. Furthermore, we will illustrate each methodology using data from nineteenth century Texas.

5.1. Sociolinguistic Questionnaires

Sociolinguistic questionnaires have been a useful tool in uncovering patterns of maintenance and shift in minority language communities. Researchers familiar with the area under investigation elaborate questionnaires and submit them to a random sample of speakers from the area. The questionnaire normally asks respondents to indicate the language most frequently spoken in a given place—school, work, home—or with a given interlocutor—grandparents, parents, teachers. The results of the questionnaire oftentimes shed light on well defined patterns of intergenerational differentiation where the older generations prefer the minority language in more contexts than the younger generations. For example, Susan Gal (1979) used this methodology to uncover patterns of language shift in Oberwart, Austria. She demonstrated how a long standing situation of bilingualism between German and Hungarian systematically underwent language shift. Her findings indicated that German progressively encroached on all domains for the youngest speakers and that Hungarian was maintained in all domains for the oldest speakers. From these data it was patently obvious that within a matter of generations Hungarian was to become an obsolete language.

The historical sociolinguist will likely have no direct access to the type of information garnered from sociolinguistic questionnaires from the archival records available. However, the insights gleaned from these studies can prove to be a valuable resource for the study of language maintenance and shift patterns in the past. For example, documentary evidence from letters and other correspondence can give us a general picture of the language of interactions between different members within a family unit. Memoirs are another source for determining the relative degree with which a minority language was spoken. To illustrate with the case of Texas, Jovita González's recollections about her educational formation in Starr County, Texas, during the early twentieth century suggest important patterns of language use. She reminisces:

> Previous to our moving to San Antonio, I had attended, for one year, a one-teacher school in English, taught by Miss Elida García at the San Román Ranch. Even though the English I learned was elemental, it helped me a great deal. This, together with my knowledge of Spanish, enabled me to enter the fourth grade at the age of ten. With the aid of a dictionary and my father's constant help, I was able to be promoted at the end of the school year. Another thing that helped us was the fact that all our neighbors were English-speaking. (González 1997:xi-xii)

While González's recollections do not explicitly refer to her patterns of language use, they do suggest that she generally spoke Spanish at home with her parents and siblings and English at school and with her neighborhood friends. Archival records also provide additional types of evidence for the investigation of language maintenance and shift. Newspaper editorials, in particular, are a rich source for obtaining attitudes and sentiments about language that can, over the course of several generations, result in language loss. For example, an editorial column from the 1855 San Antonio newspaper *El Bejareño* clearly suggests a favorable attitude toward bilingualism among Texas Mexicans. The editor wrote:

> . . . nos empeñaremos siempre en promover la fundación y el formato de las Escuelas Públicas en las cuales, sin perder el idioma de Cervantes, los niños Méjico-Tejanos, adquirirán el idioma nacional, serán instruidos en los deberes de ciudadanos, su creencia religiosa será respetada, y se harán ciudadanos útiles y dignos de pertenecer a un país libre. (*El Bejareño* February 7, 1855)
>
> ". . . we will work diligently in promoting the foundation and format of the Public Schools in which Mexico Texan children, in an atmosphere of respect for their language and religion, will acquire the national tongue and be instructed as to the duties of citizenship. They will thus become useful citizens and worthy subjects of a free nation. (*El Bejareño* February 7, 1855)"

The same sentiment was expressed by Jovita Idar, editor of the Laredo-based *La Crónica* in 1910, while decrying the overt Americanization efforts in Texas Public Education.

> In our previous article we stated that "most regrettably, we have seen Mexican teachers teaching students of their race in English without taking into consideration, at all, their mother tongue." With that we did not intend to imply—not in the least—that the language of the land they inhabit should not be taught, as it is the medium available for direct contact with their neighbors, and that which will allow them to ensure that their rights are respected. What we wanted to suggest, simply, is that the national language should not be ignored, because it is the stamp that characterizes races and nations. Nations disappear and races sink when they forget their national language . . . We are not saying that English should not be taught to Mexican Texan children, but, whether appropriate or not, we are saying you should not forget to teach them Spanish. In the same way that arithmetic and grammar are useful to them, English is useful to those people who live among English speakers. (Kanellos 2002a:142-143)

Such editorials attest to the conflictive nature of language loyalties in nineteenth and early twentieth century Texas in particular and in the U.S. Southwest in general.

In summary, while the use of sociolinguistic questionnaires is not a possibility for the historical sociolinguist seeking a clearer picture of the past language situation of Spanish speakers in the United States, synchronic studies equip the historical researcher with important insights and heuristics that can aid in the qualitative analysis of letters, memoirs, and newspaper editorials.

5.2. Structural Factors

Patterns of maintenance and shift can also be studied by looking at the structural factors in a given society that contribute to the continued vitality or demise of a minority language. Sociolinguistic researchers have begun to think about these basic sustaining relations in a contact situation under the rubric of "ethnolinguistic vitality." Giles, Bourhis, and Taylor define ethnolinguistic vitality as "that which makes a group likely to behave as a distinctive and active collective entity in intergroup relations" (1977:307). Ethnolinguistic vitality, therefore, is indicative both of how different languages pattern in a contact situation and of the relative likelihood of survival or demise of each of the languages in contact. Giles et al. propose that the measurement of ethnolinguistic vitality can be empirically gauged by considering the relative weight of three socio-structural factors: demography, status, and institutional support.

The framework proposed by Giles et al. stresses the importance of demography in language maintenance or shift. A community that supports two or more languages will display a set of demographic patterns that structure the relations between the languages in contact. The distribution of distinct language group members over a given geographic region is crucially important to this structure. When the territory occupied by the minority group is perceived as an ethnolinguistic homeland rather than as a foreign land, there is a greater likelihood that the group will maintain its vitality as a collective entity. In other words, conquered groups are more likely than migrant groups to sustain ethnolinguistic vitality over many generations. Group concentration also plays an important role in the structuring of languages within the multilingual ecosystem. "Minority group speakers who concentrate in the same geographic area may stand a better chance of surviving as a dynamic linguistic group" (Giles et al. 1977:313). Distribution and concentration, however, oftentimes become confounded by group proportion. When the minority group becomes extremely outnumbered by the majority group, it has little chance of maintaining its distinct ethnolinguistic identity regardless of its perception of the territory as an ethnolinguistic homeland and of its dense concentration in isolated pockets throughout the region. The absolute number of the minority language population thus takes on added significance within the multilingual ecosystem. Mixed marriages can contribute to the sustenance of multilingualism as well. When the rate of endogamy exceeds the rate of exogamy, subordinate languages are afforded greater odds of survival. If the converse holds true, however, i.e., the rate of exogamy exceeds the rate of endogamy, then the dominant language is more likely to engulf the subordinate language community. "Subordinate groups then are likely to have more vitality . . . when the incidence of ethnolinguistically mixed marriages is low" (Giles et al. 1977:314). Immigration patterns also affect the demographic structuring of the multilingual ecosystem. "Migrants who move into an area where linguistic groups are in overt or covert competition appear to be willing to adopt the language and culture of the dominant group rather than that of the subordinate group" (Giles et al. 1977:314). In sum then, massive immigrations, mixed marriages, and asymmetric demographic distributions upset the ecological balance by threatening the vitality of the ethnolinguistic minority.

Inasmuch as language maintenance depends on the sustained occurrence of social acts of verbal interchange and negotiation between speakers, the demographics of the subordinate language community must be seen as a key material condition contributing to its success or failure. Demography has traditionally been evaluated as a deterrent to language shift when subordinate language speakers demonstrate relatively high absolute numbers, a relatively low incidence of mixed marriages, and a relatively low proportion of immigrant groups who identify with the dominant language and culture.

In the nineteenth century Southwest, demographic patterns were not uniform. There were clear differences in terms of absolute numbers, mixed marriages, and immigration between the towns closer to the border along the Rio Grande and the cities further away from the border. In San Antonio, Texas, for example, the presence of Anglos was pervasive as early as 1850 and continued to rise steadily throughout the course of the century. In the Rio Grande Valley along the border, on the other hand, Anglos averaged a mere 10% of the entire population throughout the nineteenth century, reaching a high of only 16% (De León & Stewart 1989:12). This ethnic distribution suggests that there were sharp differences in the relative demographic dominance of Spanish speakers in each of the two regions. Similarly uneven geographical patterns were evident throughout the Southwest thus favoring maintenance of Spanish in some regions and more rapid shift to English in others.

Political factors in some regions of the Southwest were also more conducive to Spanish language maintenance. In the border towns of Texas, for example, the fact that the region was not formally incorporated into the State until the end of the Mexican-American War in 1848 contributed to continued maintenance of Spanish. As stated in Section 2.8, the territory between the Nueces and the Rio Grande had been in dispute from the time of General Santa Anna's defeat at San Jacinto up until General Zachary Taylor's march on Brownsville in 1846. Therefore, the Tejano perception of the region as an ethnolinguistic homeland was probably more intense than it had been in other more northern regions such as San Antonio. In her historical novel *Caballero,* Jovita González dramatizes this sentiment. Doña Dolores responds to the news that

Texas had been incorporated into the United States saying: "What nonsense . . . We do not choose to be [dirty] *Americanos*. We are Mexicans, our mother land was Spain. Not all of their laws can change us, for we are not them. *Americanos*, indeed!" (1996 [1938-39]: 9).

Intermarriages between Anglos and Mexicans have existed since the beginnings of social contact in the Spanish borderlands. The cultural and linguistic results of these mixed unions have varied significantly over the years, however. During the initial years of contact, intermarriages often resulted in the Anglo male adopting the culture of the Mexican bride (Carver 1982). After the Texas Revolution, however, mixed marriages most often resulted in the Mexican bride's adoption of the Anglo groom's culture. Dystart claimed that between 1830 and 1860 "the vast majority of . . . children of mixed marriages established identity with their father's ethnic group rather than with their mother" (cited in Matovina 1995b:57). The trend follows Giles et al.'s assumption that when one of the parents is from the dominant group, the children tend to adopt and identify with that language and culture. The varying ethnic identification among the children of Anglo-Mexican marriages responds to the social and cultural milieu of the time: in the pre-revolutionary years children tended to adopt the mother's ethnic identity because it was the dominant one but in the post-revolutionary years they often opted for the father's.

Language maintenance or shift also depends on the status assigned to each of the language groups. Economic, social, and linguistic factors affect the status of an ethnolinguistic minority group within a given multilingual ecosystem. The economic factor relates to the group's relative control over the economic life of the community. A minority community that is composed largely of merchants and landowners will often carry higher status than a group composed of peasants and laborers. The social factor, on the other hand, refers to the degree of esteem that the group has of itself as a distinctive collective entity. It derives primarily from the remembered historical moments that inspire individuals to bind together as a viable social group. Linguistic factors refer to how the community perceives the minority language. Linguistic status was initially conceived within Giles, et al.'s framework as the relative international prestige of the minority language. Haarmann (1986), however, has criticized this formulation as much too broad to yield any significant explanatory value. That a language carries international prestige in an area that is far removed from the ethnolinguistic minority has little bearing on the status of the minority's language in a unique social setting. Indeed, it seems possible that the very fact that an internationally prestigious variety is spoken in some part of the world may contribute to an even lower linguistic status of the minority variety. If the minority variety diverges from the standard variety, this will often serve as an opportunity for the dominant group to downgrade the subordinate group in opposition to the "true speakers" of the language.

The structured diversity of languages in a multilingual society often derives from societal hierarchies separating the speakers of different languages. These hierarchies, in turn, can be viewed as ideological outcomes of a set of patterns emerging from the status assigned to different groups. Status within a community may be measured in many different ways. On the one hand, we might consider a group's relative economic status by determining the amount of wealth it controls in relation to other groups and the degree of prestige assigned to the type of work that its members do. On the other hand, we can also evaluate a group's relative social status by delineating the degree of esteem that it is afforded both on the part of society at large and on the part of the group itself. To the extent that individual speakers will want to associate themselves with groups of greater social prestige, we may assume that higher economic and social status are conducive to language maintenance.

In nineteenth century Texas, for example, the economic status of Tejanos can be related directly to their status as landholders. In 1833, 436 Tejano-owned ranches existed between the Nueces and Rio Grande rivers. After the Texas Revolution, however, Tejano land tenure decreased significantly. Along the Rio Grande, land tenure loss began during the middle of the nineteenth century and proceeded systematically into the twentieth century. In Hidalgo County, for instance, Mexicans accounted for 83.5% of landholders in 1852. By 1865, this figure had decreased to 48.7%, and finally bottomed out at 29% in 1900 (Alonzo 1998:163). A sharper and more rapid decline in land tenure affected Tejanos in the regions around the Nueces and San Antonio rivers. As early as 1850, Tejanos represented only 38 (32%) of the wealth holders in Bexar County with an average dollar value of personal wealth at $1,371. In the same year, Anglos represented 80 (68%) of the wealth holders with an average dollar value of $4,010 (De León 1997:115). The decline in economic status based on land tenure was conducive to language shift inasmuch as the minority language came to be associated with a relatively poor and landless class.

Social status is more difficult to ascertain in the nineteenth century Tejano community because there is little direct historical evidence to indicate the degree of self-esteem the group had of itself. De León, however, offers the following assessment of Tejano ethnic identity in the nineteenth century.

> To have been Mexican American in Texas in the nineteenth century was to have been bicultural. Thus, political campaigning and court trials in South Texas were often conducted in Spanish. Rancheros worked the range according to the Mexican method, then traded their stock to out-of-state buyers. Children attended Anglo schools while retaining their customs.

Entire communities celebrated patriotic holidays of both countries. Such dexterity explains why at times Tejanos divided along ideological or economic lines. It clarifies why in some instances they demonstrated against oppression and at others they joined in support of the same system that oppressed them. Even if only a few could function in a bicultural setting, the community in general looked at itself as Mexican American. The titles of mutualistas (names like *Sociedad México-Texana*), the names of newspapers (*El mexicano de Texas* and *Las dos Américas*), the designations of political clubs (*Club Republicano México Texano*) reveal the sentiments. (1997:205-206)

De León's observations seem to indicate a rather high level of cultural and ethnic awareness among nineteenth century Tejanos. Matovina agrees that Tejano cultural heritage was firmly retained throughout the century. "The presence of other nationalities, Protestant denominations, and a new political order in San Antonio after U.S. annexation served to sharpen rather than diminish Tejano identification with their cultural and religious heritage" (1995:79). The conflict and contrast brought about by Anglo newcomers heightened Tejano ethnolinguistic awareness and concomitantly raised their self-esteem as a group. However, even though social status in terms of in-group self perceptions may have been quite high; we would be hard pressed to ignore the effects of out-group perceptions on Tejano social status. De León states that "segregation, blatant discrimination, disparaging names, and public abuse all reflected a[n Anglo] state of mind redolent in the nineteenth century" (1983:103). In San Antonio these negative attitudes surfaced shortly after the victory of the Texas Revolution. Before his flight from San Antonio, Juan Seguín wrote: "at every hour of the day and night, my countrymen [fellow Tejanos] ran to me for protection against the assaults or exactions of those [Anglo] adventurers" (Matovina 1995b:32). The racialization and continued discrimination against Tejanos continued and intensified after Texas was admitted to the United States as a state. By 1850, negative attitudes about Tejanos seem to have been common in both regions of South Texas. Thus, Oscar Addison described the Brownsville Mexicans in 1850 as "a class inferior to the common niggers" (De León 1983:17). The sharp contrasts between in-group and out-group perceptions, however, may in fact be two sides of the same coin. I would argue that the resilience Tejanos found in the integrity of their group was molded and incited by the constant attacks they suffered from the outside. Their ethnic identity was defined and strengthened by their alterity within the new social order. Paredes argues that "the Mexican saw himself and all that he stood for as continually challenging a foreign people who treated him, for the most part, with disdain" (1993:9). The Tejano identity bred of conflict and contrast incited a distinctive folk tradition in the region, and this tradition helped sustain and elevate the sociohistorical status of the community. The historical acts of resistance and defiance of Anglo hegemony served as a major impetus of heightened ethnolinguistic awareness and pride. Grassroots rebellion movements, such as those of Antonio Canales (1839-1840), Juan N. Cortina (1857-1861), and Catarino Garza (1891), figure prominently in the lore of South Texas. These heroes had been kept alive in the memory of the community through the well-known *corrido* or folk ballad. The singing of these *corridos* represented at once a challenge to Anglo hegemony and a call to in-group solidarity against the injustices perpetrated against them. The social status of the Tejano community appears to have been rising and developing a more ethnolinguistically centered foundation and thus contributing to language maintenance.

Status variables supported the maintenance of the Spanish language among Tejanos inasmuch as they served as a catalyst for greater degrees of in-group solidarity. Even while the Spanish language was coming to be associated with a landless, laboring class within the dominant society, it was also emerging as a symbol of membership in a marginalized group that, through its folklore and its grassroots activism, sternly resisted cultural and political absorption.

The last of Giles et al.'s variables, institutional support, refers to the extent to which social institutions legitimize both the use of the minority language and the existence of its speakers. Giles et al. draw an important distinction between formal and informal institutional support of minority languages. The latter refers to the extent to which the minority group has organized itself in opposition to the dominant group. This self-organization may take the form of trade and labor unions formed along ethnolinguistic lines, or of patriotic and civic organizations. Self-organization often leads to a greater degree of ecological balance between the languages in contact. Formal institutional support, on the other hand, refers to the extent to which minority language groups are represented in the mainstream public affairs of politics, education, and commerce, in relation with this topic Giles et al., mentioned "Of crucial importance for the vitality of ethnolinguistic groups is the use of the minority language in the State education system at primary, secondary, and higher levels" (Giles et al. 1977:316). Religious institutions also play an important role in the institutional support of minority languages. The extent to which the minority language is used in religious activities reveals the level of institutional legitimacy that the minority language has attained in the face of the dominant language. Landry and Bourhis present an additional dimension of formal institutional support. They argue that the extent to which the minority language appears on public signs in a given region also suggests the level of legitimacy that it has attained. They refer to this as the "linguistic landscape" and propose that "the configuration of languages present in the linguistic landscape . . . can provide important information about the diglossic nature of a particular bilingual or multilingual setting. Thus, before communicating interpersonally with a single inhabitant, one can use the linguistic landscape as an indicator of the power and status relationships that exist between the in-group and the out-group" (1997:26).

In nineteenth century South Texas, resistance to cultural absorption was carried out on varying fronts, but it was always associated with communities of individuals whose interests collided with the prevailing *de facto* language policy. These communities afforded Tejano speakers greater degrees of institutional support for the maintenance of their native language and culture. Through the use of Spanish in institutional contexts such as the church, the school, the labor union, and the marketplace, Tejanos would ratify their claim to the native tongue and legitimize its use in certain functional domains.

Ferguson has argued that religion plays a key role in the processes of language maintenance and shift. In general, he notes that voluntary migrants tend to be conservative in their religious affiliations, i.e., they tend to retain their old religion. The retention of the old religion coincides with the retention of the old language, and in this way religious practice itself comes to be a functional support for language maintenance. In colonization scenarios, on the other hand, Ferguson contends that "the role of religion . . . is often extracommunity oriented and aimed at changing the language repertoires of speech communities" (1982:65). Colonized subjects are, therefore, more prone to adopt the religion of the dominant group and this, in turn, comes to be a functional support for language shift. In Texas, however, the role of religion in the maintenance of Spanish did not pattern along the lines of retention of Catholicism and conversion to Protestantism. Instead, both the Catholic and the Protestant churches set up their evangelistic work in a way that was conducive to the maintenance of the native tongue among the Texas Mexican community.

The political changes that swept through Texas in 1836 affected the Tejano Catholic Church in very profound ways. The first major change occurred in 1840 when Pope Gregory XVI moved Texas out of the Mexican diocese of Linares and made it an apostolic prefecture under the diocese of New Orleans. This change spawned a foundational transformation in the clerical make-up of the church and ultimately led to the expulsion of the native clergy in San Antonio. These native ministers were replaced by French clergymen who were commissioned to minister to all of the faithful in Texas. The Catholic Church in Texas, therefore, became a multicultural community of faith very early on. Despite these radical changes, the new Catholic leadership was quite sensitive to the ministerial needs of the Tejano population. In 1840, Jean Marie Odin assumed leadership of the Church in Texas as vice prefect apostolic. Odin was receptive of the Tejano religious customs and often participated in the local religious feasts. Indeed, Odin "learned Spanish and was insistent that those coming to minister in Texas do the same" (Matovina 1995b:43). Proficiency in Spanish had thus become a prerequisite for Catholic clergy wishing to minister in Texas. Of course, the rationale behind learning Spanish did not always reflect a high esteem of the local Tejano population: "Irish Ursuline sister Mary Augustine Joseph wrote from San Antonio in 1852 that 'we are most anxious to speak Spanish, so as to be able to instruct these poor people, and to preserve their children form the danger of imitating the bad example of their parents" (Matovina 1995b:67). Regardless of the Catholic leadership's reasons for learning Spanish, however, the fact that they offered ministerial support in the Tejano's native tongue was a major factor in the legitimization of the language during the Republic and early statehood years.

Anglo Protestants did not turn a blind eye toward the spiritual needs of the Tejano community either. Indeed, Anglo settlers and missionaries went to great lengths to minister to the Spanish-speaking community in Texas during the nineteenth century. These efforts, however, were shrouded in a more global view of evangelism on the part of Protestant missionaries. Protestant proselytism began in Texas as early as 1829 when Sumner Bacon arrived there to minister to the incoming Anglo settlers. Not long after his arrival in Texas, however, "he recognized the necessity to communicate the gospel message to the Spanish-speaking people with whom he frequently came into contact" (Brackenridge & García-Treto 1974:3). Bacon later became a colporteur for the American Bible Society and began distributing Bibles and New Testaments in Spanish throughout the region. Bacon's efforts, however, were never officially recognized by his Protestant denomination and by the time of his death, there was no real interest in continuing his Tejano-oriented ministry. It was not until 1839 that the Presbyterian Church officially commissioned a minister to work with the Spanish-speaking population in Texas. The denomination viewed this population as a possible springboard from which to launch even greater evangelistic efforts in Mexico itself. Rankin expressed this evangelistic strategy in 1850 saying: "Let Texas, then, be the grand lever, and ere the nineteenth century closes, Mexico may be seen 'sitting at the feet of Jesus'" (1966:57). This global view of evangelism propelled Anglo missionaries to meet Tejanos on their own terms and in their own language. Therefore, all of the missionaries who followed Bacon, e.g., William C. Blair, John McCullough, and Melinda Rankin, planted churches and founded schools that operated exclusively in Spanish although Rankin's Brownsville school did offer English as an academic subject. Rankin, like Odin, viewed Spanish, as a necessary tool for ministering in Texas.

O, how much good could a missionary do amongst the people of the valley of the Rio Grande! But, he must be acquainted with the Spanish language and he must be willing to go from ranche to ranche and fare hard. Will not some of the young men from our seminaries go to this region and try to bring these poor benighted ones under the Protestant and heavenly influences? (1966:178)

During the nineteenth century, then, Protestant religious efforts also served to symbolically legitimize the Spanish language.

By 1900 there was a sharp divide between Anglo and Tejano communities of faith. The division was drawn more along cultural and linguistic rather than doctrinal lines, however. Presbyterians, Methodists, Baptists, and Catholics had both English- and Spanish-speaking congregations in any given town. The segregation along ethnolinguistic lines heightened the vitality of the subordinate tongue because it constituted a legitimate domain away from the home for the sustained use of the language. In this way, then, communities of faith, both Protestant and Catholic, served as an institutional support for the maintenance of the Spanish language among nineteenth century Tejanos.

The use and legitimization of a subordinate language in educational institutions is also a crucial factor in its maintenance. Anglo schools in Texas and throughtout the Southwest had frowned upon Spanish language use since their inception. However, these institutions had little effect on the vitality of the language during the first three quarters of the century because Tejano children often attended their own Spanish language schools. Another factor that dimished the influence that Anglo schools may have exerted on language maintenance is that school attendance rates among Tejano children were low. In the final quarter of the nineteenth century, however, Anglo schools began to exert more pressure on Tejano language maintenance because public schools and compulsory attendance laws were established.

During the years prior to the Texas Revolution, education was largely in the hands of the individual *ayuntamientos* or city councils. Each *ayuntamiento* was responsible for providing adequate education for the children of the town. Funding for these schools was secured primarily by taxes levied on parents of school-aged children and secondarily by fundraising initiated and administered by the *ayuntamiento* (Tijerina 1994:58). Securing funds for local education, however, was no easy task. "José Antonio Gama y Fonseca, the first teacher of the [San Antonio de Béxar] school, entered into a four-year contract at a salary of five hundred pesos a year; the *ayuntamiento* did not raise sufficient funds to pay even this meager salary, however, and he left within a year" (Evans 1955:29). Another problem affecting the early educational endeavors in the Tejano community were the low attendance rates. In 1833, only 60 of 631 school-aged children enrolled at the San Antonio school (Evans 1955:28). Notwithstanding the practical problems associated with schooling in the *ayuntamientos*, the philosophy of independent and locally funded schools spread well into the Republic and early statehood years. Several religious and secular private schools were established for Tejano children with greater degrees of success during this period. San Miguel points out that as early as 1853 the Incarnate Word parochial school was admitting students in Brownsville. In 1852, as mentioned above, Presbyterian missionary Melinda Rankin founded the Rio Grande Female Institute for the education of Tejana girls. Secular Spanish language schools prevailed in some of the rural areas of South Texas such as Martin's Ranch and Hebronsville up until the 1870s. Thus, San Miguel writes that "the availability of educational facilities spurred school attendance with the [Mexican American] community" (1988:12). School attendance in Laredo reached almost 50% in 1850 with 186 children attending school and 185 not attending (Hinojosa 1983).

After 1870 several developments led to lower school attendance rates and little availability of private Spanish language schools. The founding of State-controlled public schools in Texas served as an impetus toward a heightened marginalization of Tejano children within educational institutions. In fact, the very definition of public schooling, as proposed by secretary of the State Board of Education, O. N. Hollingsworth, slighted children coming from Spanish-speaking homes both implicitly and explicitly. According to Hollingsworth, a public school should be:

1. A school organized in the manner prescribed by the general school law, and one that recognizes the legal authority of the public school officials.
2. A school taught by a teacher holding a certificate of competency, and under a lawful contract between the teacher and legally approved trustees.
3. A school from which none who desire to participate in benefits are excluded from the organization.
4. A school with no extra charge for tuition from parents for branches prescribed by law and in which public funds are not credited on private tuition rates.
5. A school that is taught in the English language.
6. A school that is non-sectarian in religious matters. (Evans 1955:101)

Such guidelines, while not explicitly exclusive of Tejano students, were implicitly adverse to the cultural background of these students. The condition that the school be taught in English, for example, clearly demonstrates a bias against

Spanish-speaking students relegating them to deficient status even before beginning schooling. Even the expressively egalitarian point, that "a school from which none who desire to participate in benefits are excluded" places the privilege of participation in the institution's perception of those who desire to participate. San Miguel argues that, in fact, it was this interpretation that prevailed in many local school districts:

> The legal basis for the establishment of common schools for all was laid in the third quarter of the nineteenth century . . . Although Spanish-speaking children were never legally excluded from the public schools, many local school districts failed to provide educational provisions for them or else grudgingly promised separate but unequal facilities. Thus because of inadequate finances, political conditions, social instability, and discriminatory school policies, public school availability was limited until the turn of the century. (1988:12)

And while there was no specific legal basis for the exclusion of Tejano children, there was legislation that made English "the language of instruction for all public schools" (Tijerina 1998:93). Therefore, even when separate schools were set up for Spanish-speaking children, the instruction was provided in English. The justification for these separate facilities was often found precisely in perceived deficiencies stemming from cultural and linguistic difference. A common argument of advocates of segregated educational facilities was that "because of (1) social differences between the two races; (2) much higher percentage of contagious diseases (among Mexican children); (3) much higher percentage of undesirable behavioral characteristics; (4) much slower progress in school, and (5) much lower moral standards, it would seem best that . . . Mexican children be segregated" (cited in González 1990:25). The curriculum oftentimes attempted to address all of the perceived deficiencies in one fell swoop. González notes that

> as illustrated by a teacher's guide issued by the state of California, English instruction complemented the cleanliness program. The method of instruction recommended must have been humiliating for the children. In one particular model classroom vignette, the teacher helps a child wash his hands and face and comb his hair. Upon completion of the assignment, the teacher brings him before the class and [comments] favorably upon his accomplishment and looks, as in "Look at José. He is clean." (1990:44)

In light of these new policies, school attendance rates fell dramatically. As early as 1870 in Laredo, for instance, only 69 Tejano children were attending school while 479 were not (Hinojosa 1983).

While it might appear that such policies had little effect upon language maintenance among Tejanos given the fact that the general response was to stop attending school, we would argue that the educational marginalization of Tejanos during the late nineteenth century had far reaching psychological effects. Foley notes that

> the Mexicano perception of schooling is closely related to the problem of language. Since the language at home was Spanish, Mexicano children who did not go to school seldom learned to speak, read, or write in English. Most of the older people regretted learning so little English which they considered crucial for escaping poverty and succeeding in society . . . Schooling generally had little effect upon the language competence of the Mexicano. They did not become bilingual, and their ability to use English effectively was an important restriction upon improving their chances in life. (1977:39)

Once education came to be associated with the English language, the English language came to be associated with the positive effects of education, i.e., "escaping poverty," "succeeding in society," and "improving their chances in life." Thus to be a Spanish-speaker came to be perceived in and of itself as a liability, a hurdle to overcome in the struggle for success. The net result of this new view of education was a sense of urgency in shifting toward the English language. So while the "older people regretted learning so little English," they made sure that their children would not suffer the same fate. It is in this sense, then, that the impact of educational institutions on language maintenance made an about-face in the late nineteenth century. Up until the final decades of the nineteenth century, educational institutions served the Hispanic community as a site of language legitimization in close-knit communities of learning. By the turn of the century, however, the state-controlled institutions became a detriment to language maintenance and laid the foundation for more widespread and accelerated language shift.

The Hispanic community was losing ground on a number of fronts by the close of the nineteenth century. Hispanics were losing their land, they were becoming occupationally displaced, and they were losing control over their children's schools. The response to the rapid decline in socio-economic influence over their homeland was not passive and submissive as many social scientists have previously argued. Instead, as labor historian Emilio Zamora has shown, Hispanics were politically mobilizing in ever greater numbers by the turn of the century (1993). The primary institution through which this mobilization took place was the *mutualista,* a social club formed for the benefit of its members and their community. Workers would join the club and pay dues; these dues would later be used to assist sick and unfortunate members in their time of need. The clubs were formed exclusively along ethnic lines. Indeed, many *mutualistas* set out to serve the entire Spanish-speaking community and not just their own members. The *Memoria dirigida á la Sociedad Española de Protección y Beneficiencia y á los demás Españoles residentes de esta frontera* attests to the policy of offering support to all Spanish (or Spanish-speaking) residents of the region. De León describes some of the additional functions of the *mutualista* as follows:

> Aside from these functions *mutualistas* provided a convenient forum for discussion of political and other matters and served as a fulcrum for organizing the social life of the community. In a familiar setting, poor people exchanged problems with members of *mutualistas*, and as the associations' officers frequently came from the ranks of the moderately-established and the politically minded who understood the American system best, organizers frequently pressed for the amelioration of the Tejano community. At the same time the *mutualistas* acted as organizations that extolled the virtues of the Mexican culture before a white society that insisted Mexicans were degenerate. As such, *mutualistas* operated as institutions committed to the preservation of those things that Tejanos held dear and those other qualities Tejanos thought vital to their existence. (1997:196)

The *mutualista*, therefore, was an important source of informal institutional support for the maintenance of Spanish from the 1880s well into the twentieth century.

Spanish language media had been a strong source of institutional support in the Southwest as early as 1850.

> Numerous Spanish-language newspapers were founded and began to offer an alternative to the flow of information from the Anglo-American sources during the period of transition from Mexican government to United States rule following the Mexican-American War (1846-1848). This was only logical, for it was their specific business mission to serve the interests of the Mexican (American) and Hispanic communities. (Kanellos 1993:109)

The presence of these newspapers offered functional support and a certain degree of legitimization to the subordinate language in South Texas. They served as a functional support simply by virtue of offering a legitimate space for the public use of the language. However, they also played an important role as the vehicle for the expression of cultural consent on the part of the dominant society. Anglo society participated in these newspapers in a number of ways, but the single most important act of ratification of the subordinate language and culture was the financial support it offered through its advertising dollars. Anglo commercial interest in the Hispanic market provided an important functional support for the subordinate language. By seeking out Spanish-speaking customers in their own language, Anglo businesses were implicitly validating the presence and importance of Hispanics in the Texas economy.

Social status within the in-group, institutional support from the church, the *mutualistas*, the media, and the distribution of the Tejano population throughout the region all converged on a sociolinguistic situation that was favorable to the preservation of the subordinate language. Even though other factors such as declining economic status and educational marginalization represented adverse conditions for the continued existence of the language, they were outweighed by other more basic structural factors such as the existence of a steady stream of Spanish speakers from the south, the functional support and legitimization found in their own institutions of faith, of learning, and of labor, and a steadfast resolve and determination to defend their cultural integrity. While adverse factors did not succeed in effecting a wholesale shift of the language, they did succeed in relegating and maintaining the language in a subordinate position.

In this section we have seen how a focus on structural factors supporting ethnolinguistic vitality can shed light on patterns of language maintenance and shift from a diachronic perspective. The demographic, status, and institutional support variables in nineteenth century South Texas converge on a general picture of the language situation faced by Tejanos of that era.

5.3. Census Data

Researchers studying patterns of language maintenance and shift have often relied on the data provided by the U.S. Census Bureau. The U.S. Census is a powerful tool for discovering general patterns of language maintenance and shift over sustained periods of time for a large sample of the population. In recent years, furthermore, the U.S. Census Bureau has refined its language-related questions to yield ever richer data about the patterns of language shift in the United States. In the 1990 census, for example, 15% of all households in the United States received the "long form" of the census questionnaire. This version of the questionnaire contained a three part question designed to elicit specific data about language use among respondents. The questions read as follows:

Does this person speak a language other than English at home?
If so, what is the language?
How well does this person speak English?

Such data allow for fine-tuned analyses of language maintenance and shift patterns in the present and serve as a reliable source for the prediction of future trends. The data on ability to speak English, while not optimal for an investigation of language maintenance and shift, can shed light on the likelihood of language shift from a diachronic perspective. However, these data are not available for all historical periods because the U.S. Census Bureau has not always included such questions in its surveys. Census data up until 1890, for example, did not register any information with respect to language. After 1890, however, the U.S. Census Bureau did begin to inquire as to whether or not respondents were able to speak English. In fact, much of the language data available through the census today did not come into being until the 1970s.

An analysis of census data available from 1900–1910 in Texas, for example, shows that non-English speaking Tejanos out-numbered English-speaking Tejanos by margins of as much as four to one. These data underscore the fact that in most parts of Texas during the nineteenth and early twentieth centuries, Spanish was a viable language and that, despite the perception of English as a unifying national language, many Tejanos remained unable to speak it. In periods of intense immigration to South Texas, such as the late nineteenth and early twentieth century, however, this type of scenario is to be expected. A straightforward explanation might be that the rate of immigration was simply outpacing the rate of language shift. If this were the case, however, we would also expect to find that most non-English speakers were foreign born. Census data, however, do not support this interpretation, for even though foreign-born residents accounted for greater proportions of the non-English speaking, the percentage of native born residents claiming inability to speak English was still substantial. In fact, well over half of the native-born segment of the Tejano population was non-English speaking. It was not uncommon for the children of immigrants to retain the native tongue of their parents. What does seem surprising with respect to the Tejano population, however, is the fact that these children were continuing to report monolingualism in the subordinate language.

Census data from 1900-1910 demonstrate that upward mobility and the possession of wealth through land holdings correlated rather strongly with ability to speak English. Home ownership was generally on the rise among the Hispanic population in Texas between 1900 and 1910. In San Antonio, home ownership rose from 16% to 47% in the ten-year period, and in Corpus Christi from 24% to 38%. The rise in home ownership in the towns of San Antonio and Corpus Christi suggest the existence of an upwardly segment of the Hispanic population. An analysis of the census data reveals that Hispanic homeowners were almost twice more likely to speak English than non-homeowners.

The examples given in this section reveal that one-dimensional approaches to the study of language maintenance and shift are insufficient for the historical sociolinguist. In order for the historical researcher to uncover a holistic view of the causes, the mechanisms, and the results of language maintenance and shift in the past, it is necessary to adopt multiple perspectives and methodologies that can be woven together to form a picture of the language situation that faced Spanish-speakers during the formative years of the United States.

6. Organization of the Volume

The next section of the volume presents focused historical sociolinguistic studies that exemplify the various methods and approaches described in this introductory section. All of the papers included in the next section deal with aspects of the historical sociolinguistics of Spanish in the United States Southwest. Alejandra Balestra presents a quantitative sociolinguistic analysis of address forms in a corpus of 100 letters written in New Mexico and California during the nineteenth century. This analysis demonstrates that as the nineteenth century progressed, changes in power relations and solidarity were reflected in linguistic changes in the pragmatics of address forms. Magdalena Coll, on the other hand, presents a textual analysis of the defense of Doña Teresa de Aguilera y Roche, New Mexico's first lady between 1659 and 1661. Accused by the Spanish Inquisition of witchcraft, adultery, and heresy, Doña Teresa de Aguilera y Roche presents a defense that at once vindicates her reputation and that serves as a window on daily life and language practices in seventeenth century New Mexico. Deb Cunningham's contribution also engages the reader in close textual analysis. She examines errors in the existing English translations of Fray Isidro Félix de Espinosa's diary of his 1716 expedition into Texas as compared to its original source. In doing so, she demonstrates the unique contributions of historical sociolinguistic textual analysis for historical research and interpretation. Patricia Gubitosi presents a quantitative sociolinguistic analysis of passivity in Spanish newspaper discourse in nineteenth century California. Her analysis sheds light on the emergence of passivity as a common rhetorical device in news stories in nineteenth century California Spanish and the dual expression of passivity through the use of *se* and the periphrastic formation. Glenn Martínez turns our attention from linguistic expression to language ideologies and beliefs in nineteenth century Texas. Based on memoirs, letters, and newspapers editorials from Spanish and English sources, he demonstrates how Spanish was constructed as an inferior language during the nineteenth century in Texas. He also shows how the Spanish-speaking community at the time resisted these discursive constructions through the development of a counterdiscourse that emphasized the European origins of the language and the importance of additive bilingualism. Irene Moyna and Wendy Decker study a corpus of letters exchanged between members of a nineteenth century *californio* family. By examining the specific patterns of bilingual use in three families, they shed new light on how the relationship between Spanish and English played out in everyday life. Their analysis provides information not just about the language choices authors made depending on their addressee, but also about the types of code mixing employed in discourse and their awareness of their linguistic output. Finally, Comfort

Pratt's contribution addresses the language of the lost community of Los Adaes. By locating descendants of the founders of this eighteenth century Spanish Texas community, Pratt uncovers the linguistic features of this unique dialect of Spanish and thereby illuminates a clouded chapter in the history of Texas. Together these essays signal the important contributions of historical sociolinguistics to the continued discovery and recovery of the social, cultural, and political history of the Spanish-speaking peoples of the United States Southwest.

References

Acevedo, Rebeca. 2000. Perspectiva histórica del paradigma verbal en el español de California. In A. Roca (Ed.), *Research on Spanish in the U.S.* (pp.110-120). Somerville, MA: Cascadilla P.

Alonzo, Armando. 1998. *Tejano Legacy: Rancheros and Settlers in South Texas, 1734-1900.* Albuquerque: U of New Mexico P.

Amate Blanco, Juan José. 1992. La filología indigenista en los misioneros del siglo XVI. *Thesaurus,* 47:3, 504-531.

Balestra, Alejandra. 2002. *Del futuro morfológico al perifrástico: un cambio morfosintáctico en el español de California, 1800-1930.* Unpublished doctoral dissertation, University of Houston.

Balestra, Alejandra. 2006. El tiempo futuro en el español de California (1800-1930): Incidencia del género en un cambio lingüístico en marcha. *Spanish in Context* 3:1, 25-47.

Bannon, John F. 1970. *The Spanish Borderlands Frontier, 1513-1821.* New York: Holt, Rinehart and Winston.

Barrera, Mario. 1979. *Race and Class in the Southwest.* Notre Dame: U of Notre Dame P.

Beebe, Rose Marie, & Robert M. Senkewicz (Eds.) 2001. *Lands of Promise and Despair. Chronicles of Early California, 1535-1846.* Berkeley: Heyday Books.

Bernal-Enríquez, Ysaura. 2000. Factores socio-históricos en la pérdida del español del suroeste de los Estados Unidos y sus implicaciones para la revitalización. In A. Roca (Ed.), *Research on Spanish in the U.S.* (pp. 121-136). Somerville, MA: Cascadilla P.

Bills, Garland D., Alan Hudson & Eduardo Hernández-Chávez. 2000. Spanish home language use and English proficiency as differential measures of language maintenance and shift. *Southwest Journal of Linguistics*, 19, 11-28.

Bills, Garland D., & Neddy A. Vigil. 1999. Ashes to Ashes: The Historical Basis for Dialect Variation in New Mexican Spanish. *Romance Philology,* 53:1, 43-67.

Bolton, Herbert E. 1921. *The Spanish Borderlands.* New Haven: Yale UP.

Brackenridge, R. Douglas, & Francisco García-Treto. 1974. *Iglesia presbiteriana: A history of presbyterians and Mexican Americans in the Southwest.* San Antonio: Trinity UP.

Brooks, David C. 2001. *The linguistic conquest of Spanish America: First-contact interpreters and translator acquisition strategy as primary cause of military conquest, 1492-1565.* Unpublished doctoral dissertation, Auburn University.

Brown, Cecil. 1994. Lexical acculturation in native american languages. *Current Anthropology* 35:2, 95-108.

Brown, Cecil. 1996. Lexical acculturation, areal diffusion, lingua francas, and bilingualism. *Language in Society* 25:2, 261-282.

Carver, Rebecca. 1982. *The Impact of Intimacy.* El Paso: Texas Western P.

Castañeda, Antonia. 1993. Presidarias y pobladoras: Spanish-Mexican women in frontier Monterey, Alta California, 1770-1821. In N. Alarcón (Ed.), *Chicana Critical Issues* (pp. 73-94). Berkeley: Third Woman P.

Chambers, Jack K. 1995. Sociolinguistic theory. Linguistic variation and its social significance. *Language in Society.* Oxford and Cambridge, MA: Blackwell.

Cifuentes, Bárbara. 1992. Language policy in Mexico. *International Journal of the Sociology of Language* 96, 9-17.

Craddock, Jerry R. 1998. Juan de Oñate in Quivira. *Journal of the Southwest* 40, 481-540.

Craddock, Jerry R., & Barbara De Marco (Eds). 1999-2000. Documenting the colonial experience, with special regard to Spanish in the American Southwest. *Romance Philology* 53.

Cutter, Donald, & Iris Engstrand. 1996. *Quest for empire. Spanish settlement in the Southwest.* Golden, Co.: Fulcrum Publishing.

De León, Arnoldo. 1997. *The Tejano Community, 1836-1900.* 2nd Printing. Dallas: Southern Methodist UP.

De León, Arnoldo. 1983. *They Called Them Greasers.* Austin: U of Texas P.

De León, Arnoldo, & Kenneth Stewart. 1989. *Tejanos and the Numbers Game: A Socio-Historical Interpretation from the Federal Censuses, 1850-1900.* Albuquerque: U of New Mexico P.

Duignan, Peter J., & L. H. Gann. 1998. *The Spanish Speakers in the United States.* Lanham, MD: UP of America.

Espinosa, Aurelio. 1975. Speech mixture in New Mexico: The influence of the English language on New Mexican Spanish. In E. Hernández-Chávez, A. D. Cohen, & A. F. Beltramo (Eds.), *El lenguaje de los Chicanos* (pp. 99-114). Arlington, VA: Center for Applied Linguistics.

Evans, Cecile Eugene. 1955. *The Story of Texas Schools.* Austin: The Steck Co.

Faulk, Odie B. 1968. *Land of Many Frontiers. A History of the American Southwest.* New York: Oxford UP.

Ferguson, Charles. 1982. *Sociolinguistic Perspectives: Papers on Language and Society.* Oxford: Oxford UP.

Foley, Douglas, Clarice Mota, Donald Post, & Ignacio Lozano. 1977. *From Peones to Políticos: Class and Ethnicity in a South Texas Town, 1900-1987.* Austin: U of Texas P.

Francis, Jessie Davis. 1976. *An Economic and Social History of Mexican California, 1822-1846: Volume I: Chiefly Economic.* New York: Arno P.

Gal, Susan. 1979. *Language Shift: Social determinants of Linguistic Change in Bilingual Austria.* New York: Academic P.

Giles, Howard, Richard Bourhis, & David Taylor. 1977. In H. Giles (Ed.), Towards a theory of language in ethnic group relations. *Language, Ethnicity, and Inter-group Relations* (pp. 307-348). New York: Academic P.

Gonzales-Berry, Erlinda. 1987. Enmienda del inglés. *La Opinión,* Los Angeles, April 9.

Gonzales-Berry, Erlinda, & David R. Maciel, Eds. 2002. *The Contested Homeland. A Chicano History of New Mexico.* Albuquerque: U of New Mexico P.

Gonzales-Berry, Erlinda, & David R. Maciel. 2002. The Nineteenth Century Overview. In E. Gonzales-Berry & D. Maciel (Eds.), *The Contested Homeland: A Chicano History of New Mexico* (pp. 12-22). Albuquerque: U of New Mexico P.

Gonzales-Day, Ken. 2006. *Lynching in the West, 1850-1935.* Durham: Duke UP.

González, Gilbert. 1990. *Chicano Education in the Era of Segregation.* London: The Balch Institute P.

González, Jovita. 1997. *Dew on the Thorn,* Ed. by José Limón. Houston: Arte Público P.

González, Jovita, & Eve Raleigh. 1996. *Caballero: A Historical Novel.* College Station: Texas A&M UP.

González, Juan. 2000. *Harvest of Empire: A History of Latinos in America.* New York: Viking.

Griswold del Castillo, Richard. 1979. *The Los Angeles Barrio, 1850-1890: A Social History.* Berkeley: U of California P.

Griswold del Castillo, Richard. 1984. *La Familia: Chicano Families in the Urban Southwest, 1848 to the Present.* Notre Dame: U of Notre Dame P.

Griswold del Castillo, Richard, & Arnoldo De León. 1996. *North to Aztlán: A History of Mexican Americans in the United States.* New York: Twayne Publishers.

Guinn, J. M. 1903. *History of the State of California and Biographical Record of Santa Cruz, San Benito, Monterey and San Luis Obispo Counties: An*

Historical Story of the State's Marvelous Growth from its Earliest Settlement to the Present Time. Chicago: Chapman Pub. Co.

Haarmann, Harald. 1986. *Language in Ethnicity: A View of Basic Ecological Relations*. Berlin: Mouton de Gruyter.

Haas, Lisbeth. 1995. *Conquests and Historical Identities in California*. Berkeley: U of California P.

Hausberger, Bernd. 1999. Política y cambios lingüísticos en el noroeste jesuítico de la Nueva España. *Relaciones* 20, 41-77.

Hernández-Chávez, Eduardo. 1993. Native language loss and its implications for revitalization of Spanish Chicano communities. In B. Merino, H. Trueba, & F. Samaniego (Eds.), *Language and Culture in Learning: Teaching Spanish to Native Speakers of Spanish* (pp. 58-71). Washington, DC: Falmer P.

Hernández-Chávez, Eduardo. 1994. Language policy in the United States: A history of cultural genocide. In T. Skutnabb-Kangas, & R. Phillipson (Eds.), *Linguistic Human Rights: Overcoming Linguistic Discrimination* (pp. 143-158). Berlin: Mouton de Gruyter.

Hinojosa, Gilbert. 1983. *A Borderlands Town in Transition: Laredo, 1755-1870*. College Station: Texas A&M UP.

Hollon, William E. 1967. *The Southwest: Old and New*. New York: Knopf.

Hudson, Alan, Eduardo Hernández-Chávez, & Garland Bills. 1995. The many faces of language maintenance: Spanish language claiming in five Southwestern states. In Carmen Silva-Corvalán (Ed.), *Spanish in Four Continents* (pp. 165-183). Washington, D.C.: Georgetown UP.

Imhoff, Brian (Ed.). 2002. *The Diary of Juan Domínguez de Mendoza's Expedition into Texas (1683-1684): A Critical Edition of the Spanish Text with Facsimile Reproductions*. Dallas, TX: William P. Clements Center for Southwest Studies, Southern Methodist U.

Jackson, Robert H. 1994. *Indian Population Decline. The Missions of Northwestern New Spain, 1687-1840*. Albuquerque: U of New Mexico P.

Jackson, Robert H., & Edward Castillo. 1995. *Indians, Franciscans, and Spanish Colonization*. Albuquerque: U of New Mexico P.

Jaramillo, June. 1995. The passive legitimization of Spanish. A macrosociolinguistic study of a quasi-border: Tucson, Arizona. *International Journal of the Sociology of Language*, 114, 67-91.

Kanellos, Nicolás (Ed). 2002a. *Herencia: The Anthology of Hispanic Literature of the United States*. Co-editors: K. Dworkin y Méndez, J. B. Fernández, E. Gonzales-Berry, A. Lugo-Ortiz & C. Tatum. Coordinator: A. Balestra. Oxford: Oxford UP.

Kanellos, Nicolás (Ed.) 2002b. *En otra voz. Antología de la literatura hispana de los Estados Unidos*. Co-editors: K. Dworkin y Méndez, J. B. Fernández, E. Gonzales-Berry, A. Lugo-Ortiz & C. Tatum. Coordinator: A. Balestra. Houston: Arte Público P.

Kanellos, Nicolás, 1993. "A Socio-historic study of Hispanic newspapers in the United States." In R. Gutiérrez, & G. Padilla (Eds.), *Recovering the U.S. Hispanic Literary Heritage* (pp. 107-28). Houston: Arte Público P.

Kessell, John L. 2002. *Spain in the Southwest*. Norman: U of Oklahoma P.

Killea, Lucy. 1977. The True Origins of Spanish Colonial Officials and Missionaries. *The Journal of San Diego History* 23:1, 1-7.

Kloss, Heinz. 1977. *The American Bilingual Tradition*. Rowley, MA: Newbury House Pub.

Labov, William. 1966. *The Social Stratification of English in New York City*. Washington, D.C.: Center for Applied Linguistics.

Landry, Rodriguez, & Richard Bourhis. 1997. Linguistic landscape and ethnolinguistic vitality: An empirical study. *Journal of Language and Social Psychology*, 16, 23-49.

León Portilla, Miguel. 2000. *La California mexicana. Ensayos acerca de su historia*. México D.F.: Instituto Nacional de Investigaciones Históricas, Universidad Nacional Autónoma de México - Universidad Autónoma de Baja California.

Luca, Francis X. 2004. *Re-Interpreting the Conquest: European and Amerindian Translators and Go-betweens in the Colonization of the Americas, 1492-1675*. Unpublished doctoral dissertation, Miami: Florida International U.

Luebke, Frederick C. 1980. Legal restrictions on foreign languages in the Great Plains states, 1917-1923. In P. Schach, (Ed.), *Languages in Conflict: Linguistic Acculturation on the Great Plains* (1-19). Lincoln, Nebraska: U of Nebraska P.

Marschner, Janice. 2000. *California 1850: A Snapshot in Time*. Sacramento: Coleman Ranch P.

Martínez, Glenn. 2000a. A sociohistorical basis of grammatical simplification: The absolute construction in nineteenth-century Tejano narrative discourse. *Language Variation and Change* 12:3. 251-266.

Martínez, Glenn, 2000b. *Topics in the Historical Sociolinguistics of Tejano Spanish, 1791-1910: Morphosyntactic and Lexical Aspects*. Unpublished Ph.D. dissertation, U of Massachusetts at Amherst.

Mason, William M. 1998. *The Census of 1790. A Demographic History of Colonial California*. Menlo Park, CA.: Ballena P.

Matovina, Timothy. 1995. *Tejano Religion and Ethnicity: San Antonio, 1821-1860*. Austin: U of Texas P.

McKevitt, Gerald. 1979. *The University of Santa Clara: A History, 1851-1977.* Stanford: Stanford UP.

McKevitt, Gerald. 1990/1991. Hispanic Californians and Catholic higher education. The diary of Jesús María Estudillo, 1857-1864. *California History* 69:4, 320-331.

McWilliams, Carey. 1990 [1948]. *North from Mexico: The Spanish-Speaking People of the United States.* Westport, CT: Greenwood P.

Mejías, Hugo, Pamela Anderson-Mejías, & Ralph Carlson. 2003. Attitude update: Spanish on the South Texas border. *Hispania*, 86, 138-150.

Milanich, Jerald T. 1998. *Florida's Indians from Ancient Times to the Present.* Gainesville, FL: UP of Florida.

Milroy, Leslie. 1978. *Language and Social Networks.* Second Edition. Language in Society, 2, London and New York: Blackwell.

Montejano, David. 1987. *Anglos and Mexicans in the Making of Texas, 1836-1986.* Austin: U of Texas P.

Moreno de Alba, José G. 1993. *El español en América* (2nd ed.). Mexico D.F.: Fondo de Cultura Económica.

Nevalainen, Tertu, & Helena Raumolin-Brunberg. 1996. *Sociolinguistics and Language History. Studies Based on the Corpus of Early English Correspondence.* Amsterdam, Atlanta, GA: Rodopi.

Nichols, Steven Philip. 1989. *The Official English Movement in the United States with Special Reference to New Mexico and Arizona.* Unpublished doctoral dissertation, U of New Mexico.

Paredes, Américo. 1993. *Folklore and Culture on the Texas-Mexican Border.* Austin: U of Texas P.

Perissinotto, Giorgio. 1992. El español de los presidios y misiones de California en 1782. *Estudios de Lingüística Aplicada*, 10 (15-16), 35-47.

Perissinotto, Giorgio (Ed.) 1998. *Documenting Everyday Life in Early Spanish California.* Santa Barbara: Santa Barbara Trust for Historic Preservation.

Perrigo, Lynn I. 1960. *Our Spanish Southwest.* Dallas: Banks Upshaw.

Piñera Ramírez, David (Coord.). 1994. *Visión histórica de la frontera norte de México.* Mexicali, B.C.: Universidad Autónoma de Baja California / Editorial Kino / El Mexicano.

Pitt, Leonard. 1966. *The Decline of the Californios: A Social History of the Spanish-speaking Californians, 1846-1890.* Berkeley: U of California P.

Portes, Alejandro, & Rubén Rumbant. 1996. *Immigrant America: A Portrait.* Berkeley: U of California P.

Raumolin-Brunberg, Helena. 1996. Forms of address in an early English correspondence. In T. Nevalainen & H. Raumolin-Brunberg (Eds.), *Sociolinguistics and Language History. Studies Based on the Corpus of Early English Correspondence* (pp. 167-181). Amsterdam, Atlanta: Rodopi.

Rankin, Melinda. 1966. *Texas in 1850*. San Antonio: Texian P.

Richardson, Rupert N. 1934. *The Greater Southwest*. Glendale, CA: The Arthur H. Clark Company.

Romaine, Suzanne. 1982. *Socio-historical Linguistics. Its Status and Methodology*. Cambridge: Cambridge UP.

Rosales, F. Arturo. 2000. *Testimonio: A Documentary History of the Mexican American Struggle for Civil Rights*. Houston: Arte Público P.

Rosenbaum, Robert J. 1981. *Mexicano Resistance in the Southwest*. Austin: U of Texas P.

San Miguel, Guadalupe. 1988. Culture and education in the American Southwest. *Journal of American Ethnic History*, 7, 5-21.

Silva-Corvalán, Carmen. 1994. *Language Contact and Change: Spanish in Los Angeles*. New York: Oxford UP.

Stewart, Kenneth, & Arnoldo De León. 1993. *Not Room Enough: Mexicans, Anglos, and Socio-economic Change in Texas, 1850-1900*. Albuquerque: U of New Mexico P.

Swadesh, Mauricio. 1959. *Mapas de clasificación de México y las Américas*. México: UNAM.

Tijerina, Andrés. 1998. *Tejano Empire: Life on the South Texas Ranchos*. College Station: Texas A&M UP.

Tijerina, Andrés. 1994. *Tejanos and Texas under the Mexican Flag, 1821-1836*. College Station: Texas A&M UP.

Trujillo, Juan Antonio. 2000. Socioeconomic identity and linguistic borrowing in pre-statehood Mexico legal texts. *Southwest Journal of Linguistics*, 19: 2, 115-128.

Veltman, Calvin. 1991. Theory and method in the study of language shift. In J. R. Dow (Ed.), *Language and Ethnicity: Festschrift for Joshua Fishman on the Occasion of his 65th Birthday* (pp. 148-65). Amsterdam: John Benjamins.

Weber, David J. 2003 [1973]. *Foreigners in their Native Land: Historical Roots of the Mexican Americans*. Albuquerque: U of New Mexico P.

Wellman, Paul I. 1954. *Glory, God, and Gold. A Narrative History*. Garden City, N.Y.: Double Day.

Zamora, Emilio. 1993. *The World of the Mexican Worker in Texas*. College Station: Texas A&M UP.

Part II

Analyzing the U.S. Hispanic Linguistic Heritage

Formas de tratamiento en correspondencia en español: California y Nuevo México, 1800-1900

Alejandra Balestra
Independent Scholar

1. Introducción

Los estudios realizados sobre las fórmulas de tratamiento utilizadas en distintas comunidades lingüísticas han puesto de manifiesto que uno de los ámbitos de mayor interés para el análisis de este aspecto del uso de la lengua es el de las relaciones familiares (Rigatuso 1994). En el espacio familiar se entrecruzan vínculos de sangre, de solidaridad y de poder, además, se manifiestan roles de género que, en cierta forma, son un reflejo de lo que sucede en la sociedad en general. También resulta de interés estudiar la correspondencia que se intercambie con amigos, con miembros del gobierno o con comerciantes porque en estos ámbitos las personas ponen de manifiesto relaciones de clase y la conformación del espacio social de una época.

Este estudio se enfoca en dos tipos de formas de tratamiento: nominales y pronominales y su uso en una situación particular de contacto social y lingüístico. En este trabajo se analiza los cambios lingüísticos producidos en las formas de tratamiento de las familias y otros corresponsales de cartas escritas en español en el marco temporal del siglo XIX en un área, California y Nuevo México, que a partir de 1848 sufrirá la influencia del contacto con otra lengua, el inglés, y con una cultura que se impone sobre la hispana, la anglosajona.

En esos dos tipos de fórmulas se analiza, por una parte, el proceso de pragmatización y, por otra, las relaciones de poder y de solidaridad. Raumolin-Brunberg (1996) define pragmatización como "linguistic developments leading to the creation of new conventionalized pragmatic elements in language. Pragmatization differs from grammaticalization in the sense that it does not

75

involve any change in the grammatical character of the elements, which is the main issue in grammaticalization" (167).

Brown y Gilman (1960), en su estudio del uso de pronombres de segunda persona estudian relaciones de poder y solidaridad. Los autores encuentran que el poder estaría asociado con el uso de formas pronominales no recíprocas (tú-usted), mientras que la solidaridad se asociaría con el uso de formas pronominales recíprocas (tú-tú, usted-usted). El poder gobierna relaciones asimétricas donde una persona estaría subordinada a otra, mientras que la solidaridad maneja relaciones simétricas donde se observa que no existen diferencias sociales entre los interlocutores.

Definimos formas de tratamiento nominales a las fórmulas que se usa como apertura de la correspondencia. Por ejemplo:

1) Mi venerado Padre Sr. y Dueño (Vicente Francisco de Sarría a José Señán, San Carlos, CA, 1822[1])

2) Mi apreciable hijo (María Antonia Pico a Manuel Castro, Monterey, CA, 1852)

3) Sobrino que hapresio (Pío Pico a Manuel Castro, San José, CA, 1853)

4) Hermanita (Concepción Ruiz, Las Cruces, NM, Septiembre 1863)

Se observa las motivaciones sociales que promueven el uso de determinadas fórmulas y pronombres de tratamiento. Para este estudio es particularmente importante tener en cuenta el poder relativo que existe entre las personas que mantienen correspondencia y la distancia social entre los remitentes.

La hipótesis de este estudio es que a medida que avanza el siglo XIX y debido al contacto lingüístico y a los cambios en la estructura económica, en las relaciones sociales y familiares en la región de los Estados Unidos analizada, cambian también las convenciones de formalidad debido a que se transforman las relaciones de poder y de solidaridad. Esos cambios en las convenciones de formalidad se analizarán en el marco de la pragmatización que se produce en el uso de fórmulas de tratamiento y en el de las relaciones de poder y solidaridad del modelo de Brown y Gilman.

2. Metodología

Se utiliza la metodología de la sociolingüística histórica, es decir se analiza aspectos lingüísticos en documentos escritos en el pasado y se correlaciona con aspectos histórico-sociales predominantes en la comunidad durante la época que se estudia. Los documentos utilizados son cartas familiares, correspondencia entre amistades y correspondencia oficial escrita en California y Nuevo México

---

[1]Las cartas se citan de la siguiente forma: Nombre y apellido del autor de la carta, lugar donde se escribió, estado, año en que fue escrita. En el Apéndice aparece la lista de cartas usadas en los ejemplos y archivos donde pueden hallarse.

entre los años 1800 y 1900. El corpus contiene 100 cartas que fueron recolectadas en archivos de Nuevo México y de California. Las variables lingüísticas que estudiamos en este ensayo son las formas pronominales de segunda persona. En la correspondencia, se considerará que se utiliza *tuteo* o *usted* teniendo en cuenta los pronombres en posición de sujeto, término de preposición o como posesivo. Los ejemplos ilustran las formas pronominales de segunda persona ya sea como sujeto (5), como término de preposición (6) o como forma posesiva (7):

5) . . . *tu* recibirás cien pesos que te quiero regalar de mi parte, no como valor de dicho Piano, sino como un cariño de tu hermano. (Ezequiel Soberanes a su hermana, Monterrey, CA, 1883)

6) Tome la pluma para saludarte a *ti* y a Lili tu esposa para los dos es esta carta. (Benicia de Vallejo a su hijo Platón Vallejo, Sonoma, CA, 1869)

7) Adios recibe tú y las muchachas el cariño de *tu* esposo. (Mariano Guadalupe Vallejo a Benicia de Vallejo, México[2], 1877).

Se preparó una base de datos con todas las formas nominales y las pronominales de segunda persona, para observar cómo evoluciona su uso a lo largo del siglo XIX. Las variables extralingüísticas son: período histórico-social y género de los corresponsales. Se realiza tres cortes temporales que corresponden con acontecimientos históricos que se produjeron en la región estudiada: 1800-1831 época del gobierno español, que termina aproximadamente en 1828 con la secularización de las misiones; 1832-1848: época mexicana, antes de la culminación de la guerra México-Americana con la firma del Tratado de Guadalupe Hidalgo, cuando México otorga a los Estados Unidos casi el 51% de su territorio; 1849-1900: afianzamiento del poder angloamericano en la región. Los acontecimientos históricos afectarán de manera diferente a California y a Nuevo México debido a la demora y falta de interés de la Unión en convertir a Nuevo México en uno de sus Estados. Además de considerar el marco histórico, por último se utiliza la variable sociolingüística de género.

La hipótesis que se plantea es que a medida que avanza el siglo XIX y debido a los cambios en la estructura económica, en las relaciones sociales y familiares en la región de los Estados Unidos que estamos estudiando, cambian también las convenciones de formalidad. Esos cambios se reflejarán en las formas de tratamiento nominales y pronominales.

3. Revisión de bibliografía

La bibliografía sobre las formas de tratamiento es extensa. Podemos encontrar numerosos estudios acerca de la evolución de esas formas en obras

---

[2]Si bien la carta la envía Vallejo desde México, a él se le considera californio, ya que se encontraba de visita en México por un negocio y desde allí escribe a su esposa.

literarias (Ferreira Blayer 2002) y en correspondencia o en documentos (Williams 2004, Raumolin-Brunberg 1996, Rigatusso 1993, Fontanella de Weinberg 1970). Sin embargo, nada se ha escrito acerca de las formas de tratamiento usadas en la correspondencia escrita en el español en los Estados Unidos en el siglo XIX. El presente estudio trata de completar ese espacio vacío y de observar si los cambios sociales que se producen durante el siglo XIX y principios del XX en el sudoeste de los Estados Unidos y en particular en California y Nuevo México influyen en las relaciones familiares y, por consiguiente, en las fórmulas de tratamiento utilizadas en la cartas.

Ferreira Blayer (2002) analiza la evolución de las formas pronominales de tratamiento en el español peninsular en noventa y seis piezas dramáticas escritas entre los siglos XV al XIX. Encuentra que *tú* tiene dos posibilidades semánticas que mantiene a lo largo de todos los períodos: forma de respeto usada por inferiores para dirigirse a superiores o tiene connotación de igualdad entre miembros de la familia, e indica un criterio de inferioridad en relaciones donde primaba la noción de poder. *Usted*, sustituye a *vos* y mantiene la característica de respeto y lejanía entre los interlocutores. Considera la autora que es difícil aplicar el esquema de Brown y Gilman (1960) quienes plantean que "the dimensions of power and solidarity" (253) son dos factores fundamentales en la elección de las formas de tratamiento. En las obras analizadas más antiguas se manifiesta un predominio de la noción de autoridad sobre la de solidaridad. En la actualidad, la autora considera que hay un predominio de los tratamientos solidarios.

Williams (2004) estudia las formas de tratamiento en la corte de Felipe IV de España. Muestra la complejidad y rigurosidad en el empleo de formas de tratamiento en la alta sociedad española y europea del siglo XVII donde usan un sistema multipolar en oposición al sistema bipolar de tratamiento que mencionan Brown y Gilman (1960). Este sistema multipolar obliga a ser riguroso en el uso de formas de tratamiento dependiendo de si se trata con un inferior o con un superior, y es tan estricto que si no se respetan los usos adecuados los hablantes pueden recibir castigos. También muestra la dificultad para tratar a personas excluidas de la sociedad, porque pierden su estatus social: ¿Se puede ser rey sin reino?

Por su parte, Raumolin-Brunberg (1997) estudia un amplio corpus de correspondencia en inglés y encuentra un proceso de pragmatización que acompaña los cambios en la sociedad inglesa desde 1420 hasta 1680. En el artículo muestra que las formas de tratamiento, si bien pueden ser relativamente fijas, cuando se las observa en períodos de tiempo extensos manifiestan cambios: aparecen formas nuevas para reemplazar a las que se vuelven obsoletas o estereotipadas, sin embargo no se producen cambios en la estructura de las fórmulas, por eso se trata de un caso de pragmatización y no de gramaticalización. Los avances en la alfabetización habrían favorecido el incremento en el uso de estrategias de cortesía positiva. Finalmente encuentra que el marco teórico de Brown y Levinson puede aplicarse a estudios históricos, sin embargo la cuantificación directa como la proponen Brown y Gilman (1960) es imposible de usar en comparaciones cronológicas porque cambian los prototipos de las formas de tratamiento.

Rigatuso (1994) estudia un corpus de documentos compuesto de epistolarios, memorias, obras literarias y periódicos. La autora analiza los cambios que se produjeron en la sociedad durante el siglo XIX y primeras décadas del siglo XX en Buenos Aires. Encuentra que en concordancia con el proceso de modernización que vivió la Argentina a fines del siglo XIX que afectó también las relaciones familiares, las formas de tratamiento también cambiaron, produciéndose cada vez con mayor frecuencia pautas de trato simétricas y abandonando las asimétricas. Concluye la autora que se pasa de la primera etapa estudiada (1800-1880), que se "caracteriza por la vigencia de una pauta de empleo asimétrico en la que predomina el criterio de poder, al uso de esquemas simétricos con un peso cada vez mayor del criterio de solidaridad" (17). Los cambios sociales se reflejan en el uso de fórmulas de tratamiento más modernas, que acompañan el proceso de modernización del país. Esto coincide con lo hallado en este estudio de las fórmulas usadas en el español utilizado en cartas escritas en California y Nuevo México. Veremos cómo las sociedades nuevo mexicana y californiana irán cambiando su estructura social y con ella el grado de formalidad de las relaciones entre las personas.

4. California y Nuevo México en el siglo XIX

La lengua española llega a California y Nuevo México con los primeros misioneros. Ambos estados pasan por tres gobiernos durante el siglo XIX, uno español, uno mexicano y, finalmente, la colonización angloamericana. Durante el gobierno español, la iglesia es la que impone la mayor parte de las pautas económicas y sociales. En general los espacios se organizan alrededor de las misiones y mucha de la población vive y trabaja en ellas. En la misión se cultiva la tierra siguiendo las prácticas traídas de España, se alfabetiza a la población indígena y ésta queda a cargo de los misioneros o de personas que ellos convocan para alfabetizar a los indígenas y aculturarlos y, así, integrarlos a la religión católica. Este tipo de alfabetización sólo tiene como objetivo el adoctrinamiento religioso. Durante la época española y mexicana de California y de Nuevo México no se desarrolla una educación formal separada de la iglesia. El objetivo principal de los misioneros es la implantación de la doctrina de la iglesia y convertir los productos naturales mediante la labor de los indios[3]. Definitivamente esta educación influirá en la constitución de la familia y en las normas que regulan las relaciones familiares.

Con la independencia de México, España pierde su poder en California y en Nuevo México, aunque en este último el cambio de gobierno no lo afecta demasiado porque siempre fue considerado como un lugar remoto al norte de México sin demasiado interés para la cabecera del Virreinato de Nueva España. En California el proceso de secularización representó una ruptura importante, ya que da comienzo a la época de oro de los rancheros, quienes toman las tierras que habían pertenecido a las misiones y desarrollan sus propias formas económicas. Al final, tanto nuevomexicanos como californianos se verán afectados por estos cambios políticos. Los angloamericanos llegan a la región con ambiciones económicas y culturales que afectarán de alguna manera el espacio social del sudoeste de los Estados Unidos.

Los años de influencia de la iglesia católica en California y Nuevo México se percibirán en los valores que conserva la población hispana, donde prevalecen las relaciones asimétricas con respecto a los padres y, cuando se trata de relaciones entre personas de diferente sexo, el tratamiento de respeto es hacia los varones y más aún hacia los varones mayores. La esposa trata de *usted* al esposo, mientras que el esposo puede dirigirse a ella de *tú*. Estas formas de tratamiento en esa época se hallan asociadas a una relación de poder donde un inferior usa *usted* para dirigirse a un superior y *tú* es usado por alguien que está en una escala superior para tratar a un inferior.

Como se menciona más arriba, la llegada masiva de los angloamericanos a la región producirá cambios en la estructura económica que afectará la conformación de las familias (en muchos casos los hombres dejarán a su familia al cuidado de la esposa para ir en busca de oro o para trabajar en la instalación del ferrocarril, entre otros factores). En California estos cambios se produjeron antes que en Nuevo México. La invasión angloamericana fue resistida por la población que hablaba español en Nuevo México, en 1848 se produce la revuelta de Taos donde se asesina al gobernador angloamericano (Espinosa 1975:99). Además de la oposición de los que se denominaban mexicanos, Nuevo México no era un territorio que le interesara a la Unión: un estado pobre, sin oro, gran parte del territorio es un desierto y poblado mayoritariamente por hablantes de español (Hernández-Chávez 1994:147). Sin embargo, al final los angloamericanos se imponen en ambos estados y esto debilitará las características sociales, culturales de los hispanos y, lo que es más importante, la lengua española.

---

[3] Señala Griswold del Castillo en *The Los Angeles Barrio*, 1850-1890, refiriéndose a Los Ángeles en particular que "During the Mexican period, the pobladores had to rely on the sporadic efforts of ex-soldiers whom the *ayuntamiento* periodically appointed as schoolmasters . . . and the attendance was limited to boys" (86). Rosaura Sánchez agrega, citando a Semo, que "Indians, previously forcibly relocated to work in given tasks (mining, public works, agriculture, and the like) as result of a system of *repartimiento* (distribution of labor to different sites) or a system of leasing, would become subservient to a patriarchal family within a new worksite, the *hacienda*" (1995:54).

5. Análisis y discusión

Algunas de las fórmulas de tratamiento halladas en la correspondencia analizada han sido agrupadas en la Tabla 1 por épocas y por región en que fueron escritas a manera de ejemplos. Esto nos permitirá observar el tipo de estructura y léxico usado en las cartas para determinar el proceso de pragmatización y además ver las diferencias que surgen entre dos regiones del sudoeste de los Estados Unidos. La Tabla 1 muestra las distintas formas usadas en California y en Nuevo México en los cuatro períodos estudiados. Decidimos presentarlas de esta forma para ilustrar de forma clara lo que estamos analizando.

	California	Nuevo México
1800-1830	Mui Sr. mio Mi mui estimado amigo Mi mas Estimado Amigo Mui sor. mío de mi más distinguido aprecio	Mui señor mio y venerado amigo Mui estimado y apreciable hijo
1831-1848	Mi estimada Madre Muy hapreciable Schana Muy señora mia Amigo y muy señor mío Mi estimado Sr. y Dueño	Nuestro muy querido hijo Mi apreciable y querido sobrino
1849-1900	Francisca Sobrino que hapresio Querido Platon Querida Ma. Ignacia Querido primo Estimado hermano Estimado primo Estimado hijo Muy Sr. mío Mi estimado sobrino Estimado sobrino de mi apresio Nuestro muy querido Ermano Comadre Dna. Antonia	Hermanita Querida mamá Queridísima mamá Mi idolatrada hijita Mi querida hermanita Mi querida mamacita Mi queridísima hermanita Refugio Mi siempre querida hermanita Mi queridísima y linda mamacita
1901-1930	Estimado amigo Muy señor mío Mi apreciable prima Lola	Querida Julia Querida hma. mía Mi querida Güerita Mi queridísima Julieta Muy estimada amigita Mi muy querida Julieta Muy querida amiguita Julieta

Tabla 1. Formas de tratamiento en los cuatro períodos y en las dos regiones estudiadas.

Mostraremos a continuación el cambio lingüístico que se produce por la pragmatización de las formas de tratamiento relacionada con los cambios en la sociedad hispana de California y Nuevo México. Las trasformaciones en las formas de tratamiento ocurren en dos niveles: una es en el vocabulario utilizado y el otro es en la conformación de la estructura gramatical. A medida que los eventos históricos van cambiando la fisonomía social y económica de las dos regiones esto se verá reflejado en las relaciones familiares y por este motivo las fórmulas de tratamiento irán simplificándose de dos formas: con menos cantidad de vocabulario y con un vocabulario nuevo y con estructuras menos elaboradas. Esto afectará también las cuestiones de cortesía, ya que cambiarán las relaciones de poder, de relaciones asimétricas se pasará a relaciones más simétricas.

En el período de 1800 a 1830, la cantidad de palabras usadas en la fórmula es mayor que en el último período (1901-1900). Sin embargo no se producen grandes cambios en cuanto a los sustantivos y a los adjetivos utilizados. Por ejemplo el adjetivo *estimado/a* puede rastrearse desde la primera hasta la última época. Lo mismo sucede con el sustantivo *amigo* y con los sustantivos que se refieren a relaciones familiares: *primo/a, hermano/a, sobrino/a*. Sin embargo la palabra *mamá* pareciera que recién empieza a extenderse en el período de 1849-1900, antes de ese período la palabra más frecuente era *madre*. Desde la segunda época estudiada, además, se extiende el uso del primer nombre para dirigirse a familiares o amigos: *Francisca, Mi muy querida Julieta*; y el uso de diminutivos o de sobrenombres: *mamacita, amiguita, Güerita, hermanita*. Es evidente que se está produciendo en la sociedad un cambio en las relaciones familiares y entre desconocidos. Las relaciones asimétricas que se producían entre padres e hijos se van perdiendo para convertirse en una relación más simétrica. El trato de *mamá* o *mamacita* en vez de *madre*, está mostrando que la distancia impuesta entre padres e hijos se va diluyendo y es un cambio en las relaciones familiares que se ha impuesto en la sociedad contemporánea.

En la selección de adjetivos, intensificadores y sustantivos también se puede analizar los patrones de cortesía. Brown y Levinson (1987) plantean un sistema bipolar con estrategias de imagen positiva y de imagen negativa. Raumolin-Brunberg (1996) incorpora una escala de valores que van de los más negativos a los más positivos y que resulta más útil para analizar las estrategias usadas por los corresponsales. La escala de Raumolin-Brunberg presenta en el extremo negativo las formas de tratamiento que apelan al rango en la sociedad y, en el extremo positivo, los sobrenombres, apelativos cariñosos, nombres de pila. Sin embargo, todos estos valores son relativos. En nuestro corpus encontramos superposición de adjetivos e intensificadores *Mui sor mío de nuestro más distinguido aprecio* que ponen de manifiesto una relación distante y asimétrica, mientras que en las formas posteriores la relación es más cercana y simétrica *Muy estimada amiguita, Mi querida Güerita*.

La tendencia innovadora que se ve en el léxico de las fórmulas de tratamiento, se refleja también en la estructura de las mismas. Las estructuras sintácticas mantienen el formato de la frase nominal, pero van reduciéndose en cuanto al número de modificadores que recibe el sustantivo núcleo de la frase. Así tenemos en la primera época formas de tratamiento como *Mui sor. mío de nuestro más distinguido aprecio* en el segundo período analizado ya vemos frases como *Mi estimado señor y dueño*, y en el tercer período *Estimado amigo*, *Querida Julia*, donde se combina un sustantivo con un adjetivo que lo modifica. Sólo para enfatizar una relación afectiva y como una estrategia de cortesía positiva se utilizan intensificadores: *Muy querida amiguita Julieta*, el uso de diminutivos es también en estos casos un marcador de cortesía. Vemos con la incorporación de palabras como *mamá*, diminutivos y nombres propios que se produce un proceso de pragmatización, es decir que las fórmulas de tratamiento se adaptan a los nuevos tiempos, donde las relaciones familiares y amistosas pierden parte de la distancia asimétrica que se imponía al comienzo del siglo XIX, sin embargo conservan su estructura y los elementos que componen la fórmula de tratamiento no sufren cambios gramaticales.

En cuanto a las relaciones solidarias y de poder, la primera época se caracteriza por el predominio de pautas de uso asimétrico en las que prevalece el criterio de poder, en las cuales el pariente de menor autoridad trata de manera más formal al pariente de mayor autoridad. Por ejemplo en la carta que un hijo dirige a su padre utiliza: *Mui sor mío de mi más distinguido aprecio*, mientras que el padre se dirige a un hijo con: *Mui estimable y apreciable hijo*; en el segundo período encontramos *Mi estimada madre*, mientras que en el tercero hallamos *Querida mamá, Mi querida mamacita*. Debemos tener en cuenta que durante el primer período que analizamos todavía se imponen las normas de conducta importadas de España, poco a poco irán modernizándose y volviéndose menos rígidas con el cambio en la sociedad del sudoeste de los Estados Unidos y como indicó también Rigatuso (1994), en otras sociedades americanas.

Además de lo mencionado hasta ahora sobre el proceso de pragmatización de las fórmulas de tratamiento nominales, se encuentra una relación entre los pronombres utilizados por los escritores para dirigirse a sus corresponsales y el género, el papel que tienen los participantes en la sociedad y el uso de pronombres de segunda persona.

Los hombres usan con mayor frecuencia que las mujeres el *tuteo* para dirigirse a las mujeres, mientras que las mujeres usan el *ustedeo* con mayor frecuencia para dirigirse a los hombres, sin embargo vamos a ver que esta generalización debe interpretarse a la luz de las relaciones de poder y solidaridad que se da entre miembros de la familia o con amigos o con desconocidos. La Tabla 2 muestra los porcentajes de uso de *tuteo* y *usted* en la correspondencia entre hombres y mujeres, o entre personas del mismo sexo.

Género del autor/receptor	Cantidad	Forma de tratamiento			
		tuteo	%	usted	%
M a M	24	18	75	6	25
M a H	33	7	21	26	79
H a H	26	8	31	18	69
H a M	17	11	65	6	35
Total	**100**				

Tabla 2. Correlación entre género del autor, género del receptor y sistema pronominal utilizado.

El *tuteo* entre los hablantes hispanos de esa época se utiliza en las relaciones de poder y en las de solidaridad. En las relaciones de poder, una persona que estaba ubicada en una escala socioeconómica, familiar u oficial de más poder, usaba el *tuteo* para dirigirse a otra persona que se encuentra en un rango social inferior. En cuanto a la forma *usted* se utiliza con personas que se sentía se hallaban en una posición de respeto o de poder: ya sea por diferencia de edad o por su condición social.

Para interpretar de una forma más completa los resultados tenemos que observar cuál es la relación entre el remitente de la carta y el receptor de la misma. Los datos con que se cuenta pueden dar una idea de las relaciones y las estrategias de cortesía usadas en el siglo XIX por los escritores de estas cartas. A continuación se presenta las formas de tratamiento utilizadas en la correspondencia dependiendo de la relación entre los participantes.

5.1. Usos de usted

Se usa *usted* para dirigirse a la madre o al padre, a tíos y tías, sin importar el género del que escribe. Este uso se extiende hasta comienzos del siglo XX en Nuevo México y California, y según datos recogidos a través de una observación etnográfica, este uso continúa en muchos lugares entre los hablantes de español de California y Nuevo México. A continuación se incluye algunos ejemplos:

8) Ya es noche y me levante muy temprano tengo sueño. Recuerdos á cada uno besos de Julieta y mira a las chiquitas, y Ud. reciba muchos abrazos de su hija que desea verlos. (María Amador a su madre, El Paso, 25 de enero de 1896)

Las mujeres usan *usted* para dirigirse a varones, inclusive en correspondencia dirigida a hermanos o primos, donde se podría pensar que la relación sería más simétrica por la afinidad de edad, y teniendo en cuenta que se trata de cartas escritas en la segunda mitad del siglo XIX. En estudios realizados en otros países, para esa época las relaciones familiares asimétricas estaban desapareciendo. Los siguientes son algunos ejemplos:

9) Querido hermano:
Resibi su carta en la cual me dise que Carolina esta bastante enferma lo siento demasiado pobre Carolina hermana escribame y digame como sige. (María Ignacia Soberanes a su hermano, Monterey 1880)

10) Estimado primo,
Un tal Manuel Ruiz, (. . .) a quien Pio, mi hermano, tenía bajo un contrato en Sta. Margarita, se ha fugado de aquel rancho, usurpando como dos mil pesos de varios intereses que le fueron confiados, y sabiendo que ha tomado el camino de la frontera para irse al sur, (. . .) quisiera que V. hiciese cuantos pudiera por que ese Sr. sea detenido por el juez de esos puntos. (Tomasa Pico Alvarado a Manuel Castro, San Diego, 24 de febrero de 1851)

Con respecto al *tuteo*, las mujeres usan *tuteo* en correspondencia dirigida a los hombres cuando se trata de sus hijos varones:

11) Sor. D. Manuel Castro.
Mi apreciable hijo: Hay algunas noticias de los comisionados de quienes hiciste encarge que desde el mes pasado han llegado á la ciudad de San Fran^co. que han principiado ha trabajar en su comision. (María Antonia Pico de Castro a su hijo Manuel Castro, Monterey, 15 de febrero de 1852)

5.2. Uso de *tuteo*

Los hombres usan el *tuteo* para dirigirse a las mujeres cuando se trata de hermanas y algunas veces con amigas:

12) Querida Hermana
. . . te escribo estos ringlones con el objeto de saber como te incuentras de salud tu y Carolina y toda tu familia escribeme y dime como sigue Carolina. (Ezequiel Soberanes a su hermana, María Ignacia Soberanes, Monterrey 1891)

También se usa *tuteo* para dirigirse a miembros de la familia, pero el que usa el *tuteo* se halla en una posición de más autoridad con respecto al hombre que recibe el *tuteo*, lo usan los tíos para dirigirse a los sobrinos:

13) Sor. Dn. Manuel Castro
Sobrino que hapresio:
Estoy asiendo todo empeño el rebisar los archibos deste pueblo para comprobar que los titulos del Rincón son legales pues ala bes que nuestro amigo Pimentera no á querido arreglarse conmigo, es mi deber el ber por mi interes. ay te mando unos puntos de la Ley dada el 6 de Eno. de 1831 por echandia figeroa firmada de Dn. Jose María Padres te impongo desto para que sepas que tengo alguna esperansa de ganar la cuestion. (Antonio María Pico a Manuel Castro, 30 de agosto de 1853)

14) Sor. Dn. Manuel Castro
Estimado sobrino de mi apresio, encargo muchisimo arregles con Mariano Romero que por medio de la Justicia de una escritura de benta allegandote el pagare. (Antonio María Pico a su sobrino Manuel Castro, San José, 15 de marzo de 1853)

El análisis de las formas de tratamiento nominales y pronominales, muestra que las relaciones de poder y de solidaridad son relevantes para los escritores en el momento de elegir la forma que usan en su correspondencia. En el caso de relaciones más solidarias usarán formas simétricas (entre hermanos hacia fines del siglo XIX), como el *tuteo*; en cambio, en el caso de relaciones de poder, usarán formas asimétricas como el *usted* (los hijos o hijas para dirigirse a su padre y/o madre, sobrinos/as para escribir a tíos y tías) o el *tuteo* usado por alguien que se halla en un nivel superior en la sociedad (padre o madre para dirigirse a sus hijos/as, tía o tío para escribir a sobrina/o). Ese estatus superior está dado muchas veces por la diferencia de edad, como es el caso del uso del *tuteo* por los padres y las madres cuando se dirigen a sus hijos. En la correspondencia oficial o comercial, siempre primará la relación de distancia y formal, y sólo usan ustedes.

6. Conclusiones

En este estudio se encuentra que durante el siglo XIX en las dos regiones estudiadas se produce un proceso de pragmatización que se relaciona con los cambios en la sociedad debido al contacto con el inglés y con la cultura anglosajona: las frases nominales que sirven de introducción a las cartas se vuelven más breves, cambia el léxico, sin embargo las cartas mostrarían una relación de poder entre los miembros de la comunidad, manifestada a través de las formas de tratamiento pronominales que no cambia de la forma esperada para fines el siglo XIX.

Predomina el uso del *tuteo* entre los hombres para dirigirse a mujeres pertenecientes a la familia y de edades similares, sin embargo cuando hombres y mujeres escriben a mujeres amigas del mismo rango social, en general utilizan la forma de tratamiento *usted*. Esto se relaciona con el deseo de preservar la imagen de los corresponsales. Los padres tratan de manera más familiar y afectiva a los hijos y sobrinos debido a la estructura de poder de la sociedad, los mayores pueden tratar a hijos y sobrinos con más familiaridad. Los hijos continúan con un trato distante y asimétrico. En correspondencia formal, se utiliza únicamente *usted* (con comerciantes o en cartas oficiales). Este estudio es otro ejemplo, que se suma a los de Balestra (2002, 2006), Moyna y Decker (2005), Martínez (2000, 2001), que analiza algunos fenómenos lingüísticos del español en el pasado teniendo en cuenta el contexto social, económico y político en que se produjeron.

Bibliografía

Balestra, Alejandra. 2006. El tiempo futuro en el español de California en el siglo XIX: incidencia del género en la selección de las formas de futuro. *Spanish in Context* 3:1, 25-47.

Balestra, Alejandra. 2002. Del futuro morfológico al perifrástico: un cambio morfosintáctico en el español de California: 1800-1930. (Doctoral dissertation, University of Houston, 2002). *Dissertation Abstracts International, 64, 1622.*

Brown, Roger, & Albert Gilman. 1960. The pronouns of power and solidarity. En P. P. Giglioli (Ed.), *Language and Social Context* (pp. 252-282). Harmondsworth: Penguin Books.

Espinosa, Aurelio. 1975. Speech mixture in New Mexico: The influence of the English language on New Mexican Spanish. En E. Hernández-Chávez, A. D. Cohen, & A. F. Beltrano (Eds.), *El lenguaje de los Chicanos. Regional and Social Characteristics Used by Mexican American* (pp. 99-114). Arlington, VA.: Center for Applied Linguistics.

Ferreira Blayer, Irene M. 2002. Las formas de tratamiento en el español peninsular, un estudio diacrónico. *Boletim, 42,* 29-58.

Fontanella de Weinberg, Beatriz. 1970. La evolución de los pronombres de tratamiento en el español bonaerense. *Thesaurus: Boletín del Instituto Cano y Cuervo,* 25(1), 12-22.

Gonzales-Berry, Erlinda, & David R. Maciel (Eds.). 2002. *The Contested Homeland. A Chicano History of New Mexico.* Albuquerque: U of New Mexico P.

Griswold del Castillo, Richard. 1979. *The Los Angeles Barrio, 1850-1890. A Social History.* Berkeley: U of California P.

Hernández-Chávez, Eduardo. 1994. Language policy in the United States. A history of cultural genocide. En T. Skutnabb-Kangas, & R. Phillipson (Eds.), *Linguistic Human Rights. Overcoming Linguistic Discrimination* (pp. 143-158). Berlin, New York: Mouton de Gruyter.

Martínez, Glenn. 2000. Topics in the Historical Sociolinguistics of Tejano Spanish, 1791-1910. Morphosyntactic and Lexical Aspects. (Doctoral dissertation, University of Massachussets-Amherst, 2000). *Dissertation Abstract International, 61/09.*

Martínez, Glenn. 2001. Política lingüística y contacto social en el español méxico-tejano: La oposición -ra y -se en Tejas durante el siglo XIX. *Hispania,* 84, 1, 114-125.

Moyna, María Irene, & Wendy Decker. 2005. A historical perspectiva on Spanish in the California borderlands. *Southwest Journal of Linguistics,* 24(1) (In print.)

Raumolin-Brunberg, Helena. 1997. Forms of address in early English correspondence. En T. Nevalainen, & H. Raumolin-Brunberg (Eds.), *Sociolin-*

guistics and Language History. Studies Based on the Corpus of Early English Correspondence (pp. 167-181). Amsterdam, Atlanta: Rodopi.

Rigatuso, Elizabeth. 1994. Familia y tratamientos. Aspectos de la evolución de las fórmulas de tratamiento en el español bonaerense (1800-1930). En M. B. Fontanella de Weinberg (Ed.), *El español en el Nuevo Mundo*. Colección INTERAMER 30. Biblioteca Digital de INEAM.

Sánchez, Rosaura. 1995. *Telling Identities: The Californio Testimonios.* Minneapolis: U of Minnesota P.

Williams, Lynn. 2004. Forms of address and epistolary etiquette in the diplomatic and courtly worlds of Philip IV of Spain. *Bulletin of Spanish Studies* LXXXI, 1, 15-36.

Apéndice: Cartas incluidas en los ejemplos

Antonio María Pico a Manuel Castro, San José, 15 de marzo de 1853, Manuel de Jesús Castro Papers, 1836-1863. BANC MSS C-B 483.

Antonio María Pico a Manuel Castro, San José 30 de Agosto 1853, Colección Manuel de Jesús Castro, 1836-1863. BANC MSS C-B 483 Box 2.

Ezequiel Soberanes a su hermana, María Ignacia Soberanes, Monterrey 1891, Bale Family Papers, 1841-1899. BANC MSS C-B 746.

Tomasa Pico Alvarado a Manuel Castro, San Diego, 24 de febrero de 1851, Manuel de Jesús Castro Papers, 1836-1863. BANC MSS C-B 483.

Vicente Francisco de Sarría a José Señán, San Carlos, 14 de abril de 1822. Guide to the Archivos de las Misiones, 1769-1856. BANC MSS C-C 4-5, Folder 552.

María Ignacia Soberanes a su hermano, Monterey 1880. Bale Family Papers, 1841-1899. BANC MSS C-B 483.

Mariano Guadalupe Vallejo a Benicia de Vallejo, México, 1877. Guerra Family Papers, 1752-1955. Huntington Library and Museum, San Marino, California.

María Antonia Pico a Manuel Castro, Monterey, 1852, Manuel de Jesús Castro Papers, 1836-1863. BANC MSS C-B 483.

Concepción Ruiz a su hermana, Las Cruces, New Mexico, Septiembre 1863, Amador Family Papers, 1836-1949, Archives and Special Collections, New Mexico State University Library.

Benicia de Vallejo a su hijo Platón Vallejo, Sonoma, CA, 1869. Guerra Family Papers, 1752-1955 (bulk 1806-1886). Huntington Library and Museum.

María Amador a su madre, El Paso, Enero 25 de 1896. Archives and Special Collections, New Mexico State University Library.

Doña Teresa de Aguilera y Roche: una mujer en la Inquisición en Nuevo México, una voz en la historia del español del Sudoeste de los Estados Unidos

Magdalena Coll
Universidad de la República, Uruguay

1. Doña Teresa de Aguilera y Roche nos deja su defensa

Existen manuscritos coloniales cuyo valor sociolingüístico histórico es irremplazable. Tal es el caso de la defensa que doña Teresa de Aguilera y Roche, esposa de quien fuera gobernador de Nuevo México entre 1659 y 1661, escribe desde las cárceles secretas de la Inquisición. doña Teresa busca refutar la evidencia presentada en su contra en el proceso titulado *El Señor Fiscal del Santo Oficio contra Doña Teresa de Aguilera y Roche, muger de Don Bernardo López de Mendizabal, por sospechosa de delictos de Judaísmo* (Archivo General de la Nación, México, Inquisición, Vol. 596) y, de esa manera, nos brinda una de las pocas manifestaciones escritas pertenecientes a una mujer de la época colonial y una de las únicas escritas por una mujer sobre Nuevo México.

2. Los manuscritos de Doña Teresa como fuente para la lingüística histórica

Los manuscritos de doña Teresa surgen como una fuente de inigualable valor para una lingüística histórica que ha comenzado a andar un camino parcialmente común con la sociolingüística. La lingüística histórica —que sólo puede trabajar con documentos escritos que la historia ha conservado— reconoce las limitaciones de trabajar con fuentes de archivo, pero no por ello se paraliza. Por el contrario, busca trabajar con manuscritos que le permitan hacer un análisis sociolingüístico de quien los escribe. El objetivo de esta sociolingüística histórica es, entonces, realizar estudios diacrónicos de la lengua tomando en cuenta la variación sociolingüística existente en la comunidad que la emplea, tal como señala S. Romaine (1988:1453).

Para ello es imprescindible identificar la procedencia geográfica y principalmente el nivel socio-educativo del autor de los documentos con que se trabaja. Una causa inquisitorial como la que aquí nos ocupa presenta toda la información social que necesita una lingüística histórica sensible a las condiciones sociales de los autores de los documentos con que trabaja. Ya en la primera audiencia de su juicio, doña Teresa aporta sus datos genealógicos, información sobre la ocupación y el rango de su familia y sobre su nivel de instrucción, como veremos más adelante.

Aunque escrito, este documento nos muestra un mundo oral, mundo en el que se movían las mujeres de la época. Doña Teresa cruza la frontera entre la oralidad y la escritura que también es, en la época colonial, un límite entre el mundo femenino y el mundo masculino, ya que la lengua escrita se usaba para funciones a las cuales no accedían las mujeres. Es excepcional que doña Teresa supiera leer y escribir y es excepcional, también, que decidiera escribir de su puño y letra parte de su defensa. Los textos de doña Teresa nos muestran —sin el filtro de un notario o un escribiente— la cotidianeidad de un mundo oral y las ideas, creencias y esperanzas de esta mujer del siglo XVII.

La gran expresividad y espontaneidad con que fueron escritos hacen de estos manuscritos una mirilla a través de la cual podemos conocer a los protagonistas de la vida cotidiana en Nuevo México en el siglo XVII. Doña Teresa deja traslucir los usos y costumbres de la época, las pautas sociales, la rivalidad entre la autoridad religiosa y la civil, los conflictos entre los vecinos, el rol de los indígenas y de los esclavos de origen africano, el funcionamiento de la casa del gobernador, el papel de las criadas, la infidelidad conyugal, etc. Asimismo estos escritos brindan información sobre el habla de esta mujer excepcional y también —a través de las continuas y frecuentes citas directas al discurso de otras personas—, sobre el habla de la comunidad de Santa Fe. Doña Teresa es una mujer que no nació en Nuevo México pero que supo contar lo que allí vivió en los cruciales años de 1659-1662.

Por otra parte, los lingüistas históricos han visto como una necesidad que su corpus se integre con documentos que, en la forma más fiel posible, reproduzcan el vernacular de la época estudiada. Así, las cartas familiares, los diarios íntimos y los testimonios de testigos de causas criminales o penales surgen con un valor singular. El caso de la defensa escrita por doña Teresa también cae dentro de este tipo de documento, ya que es un manuscrito que carece de rigideces propias de la lengua escrita, de formalismos y de formulismos. No se trata de un texto cuidado, de tipo literario o de origen administrativo o burocrático sino de un documento de una autora semialfabetizada, en el sentido de que si bien doña Teresa leía con absoluta facilidad, manejaba bastante mal la escritura por no haber tenido nunca ocasión de adquirir lo que era, después de todo, un oficio manual propio de escribanos, notarios y letrados, es decir, de hombres. En otras palabras, se trata de un documento escrito por una persona que, si bien era capaz de leer y escribir, no dominaba este arte en toda su complejidad. Este factor cobra suma importancia porque determinó que la escritura de doña Teresa se acercara mucho a su modo de hablar. Se trata de una autora "semiculta", según la definición de Oesterreicher:

> Los fenómenos específicos del español en los textos de autores semicultos no corresponden muy a menudo a la modalidad ejemplar de la lengua común que, por supuesto, es la que utilizan los autores profesionales. Por el contrario, éstos emplean más bien un material gráfico y fonético, morfosintáctico y léxico muy marcado dentro del diasistema, es decir, hacen uso de variantes del subestándar que normalmente no se emplean en textos de escrituralidad . . . nos abren el acceso al español variacional del español americano y nos permiten una visión parcial de la diasistemática del español [de la época de la conquista]. (1994:172-173)

La pluma incierta de doña Teresa permite la permeabilidad de cambios, modismos, vacilaciones e innovaciones populares de la época. Además, el propio estilo de doña Teresa y el objetivo apremiante de su escritura hacen que este documento se destaque por su riqueza en cuanto a giros coloquiales y expresiones cotidianas. Es un documento que puede caracterizarse por su espontaneidad e informalidad, a pesar de las condiciones en que fue escrito.

Ya Marquilhas (2000) había destacado el valor de ciertos "escritores inexpertos" que, tratándose de individuos poco familiarizados con la lengua escrita, por presión de las circunstancias, pasan a ser autores materiales de algunos de los textos archivados en los legajos inquisitoriales. Es la misma idea que había presentado Blanche-Benveniste (1993) cuando recurrió a la expresión "scripteurs maladroits" para referirse a los autores materiales de un texto en cuanto hablantes estacionados en una fase incipiente de adquisición de la escritura.

El manuscrito de este tipo de "escritor inexperto" tiene una apariencia física particular que fue definida por Petrucci (1978:167-188) como aquella que caracteriza a la "escritura elemental de base". Tiene un trazo inseguro, el alineado es imperfecto, las mismas letras pueden tener una apariencia diferente, se recurre a letras mayúsculas incluso en el interior de palabra y hay una ausencia casi total de abreviaturas. La mayoría de estos rasgos caracterizan la caligrafía de doña Teresa.

El hecho de que esta defensa pertenezca a un legajo inquisitorial es lo que le ha dado la posibilidad de que se haya conservado hasta nuestros días, dado que el aparato judicial del Santo Oficio mantenía una fuerte preocupación por almacenar y conservar sus materiales, pruebas y documentos. Otras mujeres de la época —muy pocas sin dudas— podrían saber escribir, pero sólo si lo hacían en ámbitos oficiales, de dominación masculina, sus escritos tendrían posibilidades de conservarse. Paradójica —aunque lógicamente— la voz de una mujer como doña Teresa llega a nuestros días porque estuvo involucrada en una causa inquisitorial, entablada y desarrollada por y para hombres.

2.1. La lengua española en la época de doña Teresa

Es de destacar la época en que doña Teresa escribe estos folios. Por un lado, es un período de consolidación del español en la región. Se trata de un documento escrito en la primera centuria de la colonización española en Nuevo México, a poco más de 60 años de la fundación de los primeros establecimientos de españoles en la región. La extensa defensa de doña Teresa es uno de los pocos testimonios de la época, que sobrevivió a la Rebelión de 1680.

Por otro lado, el español del siglo XVII da testimonio de los últimos coletazos de una época de fuertes cambios lingüísticos. Si bien la crisis de la lengua española comienza un siglo antes de que doña Teresa tomara su pluma para escribir su defensa, los cambios no están aún consolidados cien años después y estos escritos dan cuenta de las variaciones, alternancias y confusiones propias de esa crisis. Manifiestan —principalmente a nivel fonético/fonológico, morfosintáctico y léxico— ciertas tendencias reveladoras del momento histórico por el que atravesaba la lengua española, como veremos más adelante.

3. Lejos de todo y de todos: Nuevo México en el siglo XVII

La clave en la historia de Nuevo México en el siglo XVII es el aislamiento respecto al resto de los territorios de la Corona Española. Lejos de todos y de todo crecía, con mucha lentitud, una región que tenía muy pocos atractivos para los colonizadores. Sometidos a un duro clima, los primeros colonos describían Nuevo México como "ocho meses de invierno y cuatro de infierno" (cfr. Kessell 1987:90).

Dos hechos básicos explican la historia de Nuevo México. El primero es la dilación con que la provincia fue colonizada. La ciudad de México cae en manos españolas en 1522 pero la conquista hacia el norte no se concretó hasta finales del siglo XVI y la fundación de la villa de Santa Fe tiene lugar recién en 1610. No es una colonización de carácter prioritario para la Corona: una y otra vez fue postergada por diferentes motivos como la falta de recursos económicos, la dificultad en alcanzar un número razonable de colonos para emprender la empresa, las urgencias bélicas de la Corona en otras regiones del Imperio, etc. Es evidente también que la falta de riqueza de esta región no impulsó a los españoles a invertir en ellas, por lo menos, en un principio. Los recursos naturales de Nuevo México eran insignificantes en comparación con aquellos hallados en el corazón de la civilización azteca. La provincia cobra, sin embargo, un valor estratégico en términos de fronteras del Imperio. Entre 1598 y 1680, la provincia cumplió la función de detener los posibles avances ingleses y franceses en la región. También adquirió importancia expansiva dado que constituía la base de la exploración española de las llanuras centrales y Tejas, al este, del actual Colorado, al norte, y del actual Arizona, al oeste.

El segundo hecho es la gran distancia que esta provincia tenía con el centro cultural más próximo —y en definitiva, con la metrópoli— y las dificultades de comunicación reinantes en la época. Nuevo México estaba unido al resto del Imperio español por un simple camino que descendía por el valle del Río Grande desde Santa Fe, a través de la puerta natural de El Paso, y que se dirigía hacia las provincias del Virreinato de Nueva España y a la Ciudad de México. Este camino unía la Ciudad de México —capital del virreinato de Nueva España— y la villa de Santa Fe, a través de 3.000 km de desiertos, cañones, ríos caudalosos y montañas. Usualmente una caravana tardaba, en un viaje de ida y vuelta, un año y medio, en el mejor de los casos.

Un corolario de la situación descrita es el nivel socio-cultural de los pobladores de Nuevo México. Se trata, por lo general, de personas con escasa instrucción o, en muchos casos, de analfabetos. France V. Scholes (1930) define la provincia como una zona de elevado analfabetismo, escaso refinamiento cultural y un alto grado de monotonía y aislamiento. La mayoría de los colonos de Nuevo México vivían y morían en la provincia sin salir de sus límites. Pocos colonos tenían algún tipo de preparación académica. Cierto número de escuelas se crearon en la provincia, especialmente durante las primeras décadas de la colonia, con el propósito de enseñar la doctrina cristiana a los niños indígenas, pero no existía ningún otro tipo de educación formal. Los niños de las familias más prominentes recibían sólo instrucción elemental.

Las investigaciones de Adams y Scholes (1942) ilustran el panorama sociocultural de la época. Dichos historiadores hallaron, en las fuentes documentales para el período anterior a 1659, sólo referencias a libros en posesión de tres gobernadores de la provincia: Pedro de Peralta (1610-1614), Juan de Eulate (1618-1625) y Juan Manso de Contreras (1656-1658). Para el período posterior a 1659, destacan los libros que aparecen en las listas de pertenencias de los gobernadores don Bernardo López de Mendizábal y don Diego de Peñalosa. En ellas aparecen libros como *Don Quijote*, la *Gramática* de

Nebrija, *Marcos de Obregón* de Espinel, un libro de comedias de varios autores y algunas obras religiosas. Del juicio a la esposa del gobernador Mendizábal, doña Teresa, se desprende también información sobre los libros que poseía y que leía, como veremos más adelante. Aun cuando el número de libros seculares listados como propiedad de don Bernardo y doña Teresa no es muy amplio, ellos tenían algunos de los trabajos más sobresalientes e influyentes de la época.

El escaso número de libros —en términos generales— que existía en la colonia y el hecho de que la primera imprenta llegara a Nuevo México recién en la primera mitad del siglo XIX muestran un nivel sociocultural bastante pobre y limitado. Scholes (1976:133) describe la situación diciendo: "(. . .) sin ningún grado de refinamiento social, la vida en Nuevo México se caracterizaba por su aspereza, una falta de lujo y refinamiento, una ordinariez y un asombroso grado de ignorancia, que se refleja en todos los documentos".

También los datos respecto a los sobrevivientes de la Rebelión de los Pueblos brindan importante información acerca del nivel de instrucción de los colonos. En 1680 cuando se hacían planes para intentar recuperar la provincia después de los trágicos sucesos acontecidos, el gobernador convocó a una asamblea general a todos los hombres disponibles. En una de las listas se encuentran los nombres de 147 hombres capaces de portar armas: 86 de ellos no sabían firmar (Scholes 1976:134).

Con respecto a las mujeres, se dispone de información acerca de aquellas que dieron testimonio ante el representante de la Inquisición durante los años 1626 a 1680. Más del 90 por ciento de ellas no pudo firmar sus declaraciones. En 1631, cuando atestiguaron 33 mujeres, ninguna de ellas pudo firmar (Scholes 1976:134). En este contexto, doña Teresa resalta —sin dudas— como una excepción.

Otra característica fundamental de la historia de Nuevo México —y que explica en cierta manera la existencia del manuscrito que aquí nos ocupa— es el grave, e incluso violento, conflicto de poder entre las autoridades eclesiásticas y las civiles. La raíz de este conflicto es una cuestión de supremacía de una autoridad sobre la otra y, en general, la controversia creció a causa de motivos económicos y religiosos que existían en toda la América colonial española.

La situación era más grave en Nuevo México que en otras provincias, explica W. Beck (1962:64), por el aislamiento que caracterizaba la región, el cumplimiento dificultoso de las leyes españolas relativas al tratamiento de los nativos, y, al mismo tiempo, por la disputa entre frailes y gobernadores a causa de la mano de obra indígena, única fuente de riqueza en una tierra tan pobre.

La pugna entre Estado e Iglesia comenzó en la primera administración, cerca de 1610, y creció en intensidad hasta llegar casi a una guerra civil en la década del 30. El conflicto no disminuyó después de esa fecha y continuó hasta la Rebelión de los Pueblos. La autoridad franciscana logró tener suficiente apoyo de los colonos y de los altos mandos en la Ciudad de México como para arrestar y encarcelar a cuatro gobernadores: Pedro de Peralta, Luis de Rosas, Bernardo López de Mendizábal y Diego de Peñalosa.

4. Don Bernardo López de Mendizábal

Fuertes conflictos surgieron (a partir de 1659) entre el nuevo gobernador de Nuevo México, don Bernardo López de Mendizábal, y el nuevo jerarca franciscano, fray Juan Ramírez. Hombres inteligentes, tenaces y ambiciosos los dos, pronto resultó que no había espacio en Nuevo México para ambos.

El éxito de la administración del nuevo gobernador en Nuevo México dependía, dice Scholes (1936:150), del tacto, habilidad y firmeza con que éste manejara su relación con los franciscanos y los colonos. Desafortunadamente, la administración de Mendizábal no se caracterizó por estas cualidades, convirtiéndose en uno de los períodos más violentos.

La confrontación con los franciscanos se da por un tema de jurisdicciones, situación que se venía repitiendo a lo largo del siglo en Nuevo México. Mendizábal se enfrenta a problemas en torno a las misiones y su disciplina, a la inmunidad y los privilegios eclesiásticos y a la autoridad y jurisdicción genérica de los prelados (Scholes 1940:400-406).

El resentimiento en contra de las políticas gubernamentales de Mendizábal se acentuó debido a su conducta personal y a su negligencia en la observancia de las obligaciones religiosas. Este conflicto derivó en una serie de denuncias presentadas tanto al Virrey de México como al Tribunal de la Inquisición en dicha ciudad.

En abril de 1663 los esposos Mendizábal ingresaron en las cárceles de la Inquisición en la ciudad de México. La acusación formal fue presentada por el fiscal el 28 de noviembre de 1663. Decenas de cargos recayeron sobre Mendizábal (Scholes 1937:420 y ss.); la denuncia más grave era aquella que lo inculpaba de ser judío.

Tiempo después el abogado de Mendizábal presentó la defensa del acusado. El 16 de septiembre de 1664 Mendizábal, tras una larga enfermedad, muere en su celda y es enterrado en tierra no santa.

5. La Inquisición contra doña Teresa de Aguilera y Roche

La esposa de Mendizábal fue arrestada por los agentes del Tribunal de la Inquisición en octubre de 1662 en Santa Fe, al tiempo que arrestaban a su marido. Es la única mujer de Nuevo México enjuiciada por la Inquisición durante el período colonial.

A principios del siglo XVII, en la década del 30, Fray Esteban de Perea había juntado evidencia sobre varias denuncias hechas contra mujeres en Nuevo México pero no se llegó a concretar ningún juicio. Los testimonios por él recogidos hablan de casos de superstición, hechicería, infidelidad conyugal y uso de la planta alucinógena conocida como "peyote". Algunas mujeres, esposas de colonos, comparecen ante el comisario, admitiendo haber usado ciertos polvos para atraer a sus maridos. Además, dos mujeres fueron acusadas de brujas y hechiceras: Beatriz de los Ángeles, india mexicana, y su hija mestiza, Juana de la Cruz. Ellas mismas prestaron testimonio ante Perea, pero el caso no pasó a mayores.

La situación de doña Teresa es, entonces, excepcional en varios sentidos. En primer lugar, son los hombres los que generalmente son enjuiciados por la Inquisición: las mujeres no representan más del 30% del total de trámites inquisitoriales en México en la época colonial (Alberro 1989:17). Este rasgo, que seguramente se encontrará en cualquier actividad, sólo expresa la condición objetiva de la mujer en la sociedad; su menor participación en la vida pública la protegía en cierta medida de eventuales denuncias.

También es excepcional el caso de doña Teresa en cuanto al tipo de cargos que se levantan contra ella. En los registros inquisitoriales, las mujeres son ante todo hechiceras, acusación que no recae sobre doña Teresa, aunque sí hay una alusión al uso de ciertos polvos mágicos. La magia erótica y la utilización de hierbas y procedimientos de origen indígena o africano son los principales motivos por los cuales son acusadas las mujeres y, entre ellas, las mujeres mestizas y de clase social baja (Alberro 1989:17). Doña Teresa no cabe dentro de esta categoría y no puede ser agrupada junto a otras mujeres de Nuevo México acusadas de hechiceras como la india Beatriz de los Ángeles o su hija mestiza, Juana de la Cruz, ya mencionadas. Tampoco se trata de una mujer "alumbrada", "ilusa", beata o poseída por el demonio, categorías frecuentes entre las mujeres enjuiciadas por la Inquisición en Nueva España. Y no puede ser agrupada junto a las mujeres acusadas de judaísmo, como aquellas del tristemente célebre clan Carvajal en México.

El caso de doña Teresa responde a una trama de tipo político, pero esta trama no estaba tejida en torno a ella sino en torno a su esposo. En este sentido, podrá ser vista como víctima pero también como cómplice de su propio marido.

5.1. Los cargos

Cuarenta y un cargos recaen sobre la persona de doña Teresa (AGN, Inquisición, vol.596, ff. 86r-99vbis), muchos de ellos coincidentes con los de su esposo quien está siendo paralelamente juzgado por la Inquisición. Del cargo número 1 al 34, los inquisidores intentan probar que doña Teresa no sólo era sospechosa de "delitos de fe" sino que presumiblemente fuese judía, al igual que su esposo. Las acusaciones acerca de haber "apostatado de nuestra Santa fee catholica y lei euangelica, pasandose a la obseruancia de la muerta y caduca ley de Moises guardando los ritos y ceremonias Judaicas" (f. 86r/87r) constituyen la parte central de los cargos levantados en su contra. Paralelamente se le acusa de no respetar las prácticas dictadas por la Iglesia Católica. Fue denunciada, junto a su esposo, por no confesarse y no predicar esta costumbre entre sus criados. También recae sobre ella la acusación de no ir a Misa: "esta rea y su marido jamas, se apearon de la carroça en que iban [de camino a Nueuo Mexico] para oir missa, sino que se estaban acostados en ella" (f. 89r/90r). Cuando iban a Misa lo hacían como "violentos y forçados" (f. 92v/93v). Se le imputa también el no bendecir la mesa: "se noto y adbirtio por los asistentes a esta rea y su marido que ni bendeçian la mesa ni al alçarla, quando quitando los manteles los criados deçian: sea loado el Santisimo Sacramento jamas se oio, que esta rea ni su marido, dijese; por siempre" (f. 90r/91r). Según sus sirvientes el ayuno tampoco era respetado por el matrimonio. No invocaban a Dios pidiendo ayuda ni siquiera cuando estaban enfermos: "Y en las ocasiones que esta rea y su marido estubieron enfermos jamas se les oio llamar a Dios nuestro señor, ni a su Santissima madre, ni a Santo alguno" (f. 92r/93r). No se les veía rezar "ni se les vio jamas rosario en la mano" (f. 94v/95v). Ni ella ni su esposo acudieron, "so pena de excomunion maior", a oír el edicto general de la fe el 25 de septiembre de 1661.

Tampoco se salva de cargos de blasfemia y de injuria; Doña Teresa, según los acusadores, tenía el "vicio de hablar mal de los saçerdotes, que no solo injuriaba a los que asistian en el Nueuo Mexico, sino que deçia que un benefiçiado rico . . . hauia muerto con onçe o doçe hijos y su amiga a la caueçera" (f. 94v/95v).

Se le imputan también cargos de superstición que sirven como evidencia adicional para indicar un comportamiento no cristiano. Una sirvienta atestigua que en una ocasión "le dieron [a doña Teresa] unos poluos, para que su marido don Bernardo la quisiese" (f. 85r/86r). Otra criada cuenta que "esa rea recogia la sangre del mestruo, y la guardaba en una taça de plata, sin saberse para que fin, y no puede congeturarse otro, que alguno supersticioso o de hechiço" (f. 95v/96v). Generó sospecha también el hecho de que doña Teresa usara "en los pies cascos de çeuolla" (f. 95v/96v).

Se levantan contra ella cargos de herejía por leer libros "en lengua extrangera, e inteligible . . . que contendria algunas cosas contra nuestra santa fee catholica, o es por deuoçion, o diuersion, y podia usar de libros comunes y en lengua castellana, y de ser el que asi tenia en lengua incognita juntamente con la poca charidad y mal obrar desta rea se ocasiono presumir, seria de hereges" (f. 88r/89r). Los cargos 34 al 41 se basan en el comportamiento de doña Teresa posterior a su arresto en Santa Fe.

5.2. El proceso

El juicio contra doña Teresa sigue a grandes rasgos los pasos de todos los procesos llevados a cabo por la Inquisición. Comienza con la denuncia y querella criminal contra doña Teresa por parte del fiscal del Santo Oficio, fechada el 14 de marzo de 1662 (f. 1r-1v). Luego aparecen compiladas las denuncias de los testigos del caso.

Los votos de prisión contra doña Teresa, con el consiguiente secuestro de bienes, tienen lugar el 29 de agosto de 1662. Cuando ingresa a las cárceles secretas de la Inquisición en México el 11 de abril de 1663 se hace un inventario de sus bienes (ff. 46r-49v) que pone en evidencia que se trata de un mujer rica que poseía ropa y joyas de fina calidad (f. 46r). Llama la atención también la extensión del inventario, que comprende 112 artículos.

Doña Teresa mantiene algunos de sus privilegios aun en las cárceles de la Inquisición dado que, atendiendo a su pedido, es trasladada a una celda de mejores condiciones. Además de la ración diaria, se le asigna medio real de vino cada día durante la Cuaresma, por hallarse "achacosa" (f. 53v). Conserva con ella, mientras está en la cárcel, una de sus esclavas para su servicio personal.

Luego del inventario, se suceden tres audiencias regulares. La primera es del 2 de mayo de 1663, la segunda del 9 de mayo y la tercera del 12 de junio del mismo año (ff. 56r-64v). A dichas audiencias les corresponden la primera, segunda y tercera amonición respectivamente.

La primera audiencia aporta los datos genealógicos de doña Teresa. Sabemos, entonces, que tiene alrededor de 40 años en el momento del juicio, que nació en la Ciudad de Alejandría, "ultra el Po", que es vecina de la ciudad de México, que es casada sin hijos y "que no tiene ocupacion alguna" (f. 56r).

Su padre fue el Maestre de Campo don Melchor de Aguilera "que tubo muchos puestos honrosos" en Europa y fuera de ella. Fue gobernador de Cartagena, ciudad en la que doña Teresa más tarde conociera y se casara con don Bernardo. Su madre es doña María de Roche, natural de Irlanda y era, en tiempos del juicio, viuda. Sus abuelos, tíos y hermanos han ocupado cargos de importancia en la Corte del Rey o en el Ejército. También hay sacerdotes y religiosas en su familia.

Sobre su nivel de instrucción dice que "saue leer bien; pero escriuir no saue tan suelto y que le enseñaron maestros que tenian sus padres y en el combento de San Olderiq en Milan adonde estubo algum tiempo y no ha estudiado facultad alguna" (f. 60r).

5.3. Doña Teresa se defiende

Después de las tres audiencias de rigor, con sus respectivas amoniciones, doña Teresa, aconsejada por su abogado, solicita audiencias extras. En la primera "audiencia pedida de su voluntad" (15 de junio de 1663) doña Teresa entrega un papel en el cual ha escrito 14 renglones y que se guardó, probablemente, con los autos del secuestro de bienes. Lamentablemente no lo hemos podido localizar. Ésta sería la primera de cuatro oportunidades en que doña Teresa escribe al Santo Tribunal. El 27 de septiembre de 1663 doña Teresa vuelve a pedir papel y tinta (f. 75v) y consigue dos pliegos de papel en los cuales escribe parte de su defensa y la de su marido. Con el encabezado "Aqui es escripto", entonces, se introducen los folios 80r-83v, los primeros de su puño y letra que constan en el volumen 596 del AGN.

En ellos doña Teresa básicamente se dedica a plantear sus críticas con respecto a los frailes de Nuevo México y la manera en que éstos han recogido los testimonios contra ella y su marido. Además describe un Nuevo México turbulento y caótico. Ella y su marido se enfrentan tanto a autoridades civiles como religiosas. Tienen graves conflictos con el gobernador don Diego de Peñalosa por el tema de la residencia de don Bernardo, y con los frailes que, según opinión de doña Teresa, habían levantado falsos testimonios para denunciarlos frente al Tribunal de la Inquisición. Estos primeros folios que escribe doña Teresa relatan con mucho sentimiento lo que había vivido en los últimos tiempos en Nuevo México y su desamparo en las cárceles secretas. Repetirá la estrategia de escribir ella misma en el transcurso del juicio; retoma la pluma en los folios 117v-121v para seguir escribiendo en su defensa.

En esta oportunidad doña Teresa centra su defensa en rebatir capítulo por capítulo las acusaciones que recaen sobre ella. Comienza refutando la acusación de judaísmo y, en particular, el cargo en que se le acusa de lavarse los días viernes. A su vez, explica que no se vestía ni se peinaba de forma particular ese día de la semana. A la acusación de no escuchar Misa, responde "que diga frai Diego Rodrigues, predicador apostolico, como quien siempre nos digo la misa si don Bernardo gamas la oio en la caroca" (f. 118r). También afirma que ella y su marido se preocupaban de que los criados fueran a Misa y se confesasen.

Declara que siempre bendecían la mesa "aunque algo quedo" (f. 118v) y que agradecían a Dios. Pone como testigos de esto a aquellos que solían comer en su casa (f. 118v). Siempre respondían al "alabado" en el entendido de que "bastaua acerlo con el coracon quando no lo icieramos sienpre uocalmente" (f. 119r).

Además pone de manifiesto su devoción cristiana, las cofradías a las cuales pertenece, las bulas que posee y cómo guiaba a sus criados en la fe. Niega haber blasfemado contra los religiosos. Su conducta, explica doña Teresa, nunca ha sido la de una mujer supersticiosa; usaba cáscaras de cebolla sólo cuando le "apretauan los callos (. . .) i que no era menester cada dia i esto era porque alla no auia otro remedio para el efeto" (f. 119v).

Doña Teresa presenta sus refutaciones de manera desordenada pero logra abarcar las acusaciones más importantes.

También se ocupa de aclarar que el libro que estaba leyendo nada tenía de herético:

> i en quanto al 6 cargo que se me ace del libro de mas de ser señor el que tengo dicho i que no era el tenerle ni leer en el para mas que por no acauar de oluidar la lengua que fue el fin para que me le dio mi padre en el qual estando el preso en el castillo de Santa Crus de Cartagena me hacia le leiera algunas ueces por diuertir sus quidados i una que no tenia gana de acerlo le dige que sino sauia ablar la lengua i leerla i me respondio ai hija no saues tu que ua de ablarla leerla o entenderla io anque la oigo leiendola io no la pronuncio porque no es la lengua materna i aciendolo tu lo aces i por esa causa la entiendo quanto tu la lees i gusto de diuertirme un rato = i si el fuera malo no me lo pirmitiera leer a mi no lo iciera el como tan christiano i este libro sigun a el lo oi i a otras personas le ai traducido en nuestra lengua castellana como el Petrarca del qual es conpañero aunque en diferente estilo. (f. 120r)

Describe además en estos pliegos la situación de la servidumbre de la casa. Desacredita el testimonio de varios de sus criados porque solían tomar demasiado vino y andar "con vaidos de caueca". Declara que el testimonio de sus sirvientes "es tan falso como es uerda ser ellos enemigos" (f. 119v).

Finalmente, el 20 de diciembre de 1663 se le vuelve a dar tintero, pluma y cuatro pliegos de papel. Doña Teresa, quien ya tenía en su poder otros cuatro pliegos en blanco, entrega al Tribunal, el 9 de enero de 1664, 7 pliegos escritos (y uno en blanco) que conforman los 14 folios que van desde el 147r hasta el 161v incluido.

Doña Teresa había recibido una copia de la Publicación de Testigos a los efectos de escribir una respuesta a la misma y esto es lo que hace en estos siete pliegos. La acusada tiene el derecho, en el marco de su defensa, de nombrar a las personas que a su entender podrían tener razones para acusarla falsamente. Esta defensa de doña Teresa se hace conociendo lo que declararon los testigos pero sin conocer sus nombres, es decir, sin poder identificar concretamente a aquellas personas que declararon en su contra. Doña Teresa debe procurar imaginar quiénes pueden haberlo hecho y por qué causas. Su defensa está estructurada de la forma siguiente: "Juan Manso por si ubiere jurado es enemigo por aver sido don Bernardo su gues de residencia por cuia causa tubo con el diferencias sobre ello grandes" (f. 147r) o "don Juan Griego (. . .) es enemigo desde que fuimos por que le quito don Bernardo el ser interpete cosa que sintio el i todos los suios muchos i dello se dieron por agrauiados" (f. 148r).

De los 26 testigos que declaran contra doña Teresa, 20 son nombrados por ella como personas que tienen enemistad con ella y/o su marido y que tienen razones subjetivas para, en su opinión, atestiguar en su contra y levantar falsos testimonios. Sus acusaciones recaen sobre gobernadores, religiosos, colonos y criados, mostrando de manera elocuente los conflictos que se vivían en la sociedad novomexicana.

Don Bernardo se ganó varios enemigos mientras ejerció el cargo de gobernador; para doña Teresa los enemigos de su marido pasaban a ser sus propios enemigos. La enemistad de Juan Griego, y toda su familia, por ejemplo, nace del hecho, como dijimos anteriormente, de que "le quito don Bernardo el ser interpete (. . .) quera delo que todos ellos comian" (f. 148r). Además, Catalina Bernal, hermana de Juan Griego, y sus hijas habían sido reñidas en varias oportunidades por don Bernardo a causa de su "mal vivir" y porque "por engañar a un onbre fingieron un mal parto de una dellas" (f. 148v). Los dos primeros folios (148r al 150r) están dedicados a acusar al clan Griego-Bernal.

Miguel de Noriega "por si ubiere gurado es enemigo no ostante auerle mi marido dado una placa en esta ciuda" (f. 149v). Al parecer Noriega informaba ilícitamente a Juan Manso sobre la residencia que don Bernardo le estaba realizando. Álvaro de Paredes y Tomé Domínguez de Mendoza son enemigos porque don Bernardo les sacó algunos de sus privilegios. Los Chaves y los Granillos, que están emparentados con Domínguez, también son enemigos. Francisco de Trujillo y su familia "son i an sido desde el primero dia todos mortales enemigos (. . .) porque le quito el alcaidia maior de Moqui de donde era quando fuimos i todos ellos se dieron por ofendidos" (f. 154r). Francisco de Valencia "tiene la quega ordinaria de escoltas i gornadas" (f. 154r). El maese de campo Pedro Lucero de Godoy "le tubo [a don Bernardo] desde que fuimos malisima voluna porque le digo no se que el dia que nos salio a encontrar a causa de auer sauido del algunas cosas" (f. 154v). Diego Romero y su esposa se dieron por agraviados "por las quegas que dimos de auer gurado mal i contra uerda en la residencia" (f. 155r).

La vida en casa del gobernador era desordenada y caótica; en ella los rumores, las calumnias y las traiciones estaban a la orden del día. Doña Teresa deja entrever que sus peores enemigos vivían, en realidad, bajo su mismo techo. El robo era una actividad frecuente entre los criados: "los cogimos muchas ueces con las raciones que enbiauan a las casas que sustentauan fuera i no auia dellos siguras troges ni despensas i asta los carneros atados con sogas echauan de noche por las paredes sin que se contentaran con 4 que matauan cada semana i 2 uacas que todas las consumian" (f. 150r).

Doña Teresa no acusa sólo a vecinos y criados sino también a las autoridades. Acusa tanto al ex-gobernardor de Nuevo México, don Juan Manso, como a don Diego de Peñalosa, quien ejerce tal cargo en el momento del juicio. Así como don Juan Manso "a sido sienpre i es mortal enemigo" dado que, entre otras cosas, fue don Bernardo quien estuvo encargado de realizar su residencia, Peñalosa es también enemigo porque, entre otras cosas, fue el encargado de realizar la residencia de don Bernardo.

Doña Teresa prosigue su escrito acusando a los religiosos de la región: "frai Juan Ramires es i a sido grande enemigo nuestro por causas que se ofrecieron antes de salir desta ciuda quando fuimos los quales son sauidas i fuera deso engaño a mi marido en algunas cosas faltandole a algunas palauras que le daua i promesas que le hacia" (f. 158r). El Padre Custodio fray Alonso de Posada también es considerado como enemigo por doña Teresa.

Termina estos escritos haciendo referencia a las prácticas cristianas que eran parte de su vida diaria:

> i por quanto lo que dicen de que no me uieron recar ni supieron tenia deuocion alguna i para que se uea esto i como christiana que por la gracia de dios nuestro señor e sido soi i sere asentada en las cofradias sigientes primeramente en San Pedro i San Pablo = en la de Jesus Maria i Jose = tenia la bula = i asi mesmo en San Juan de Leteran i la tenia = i la de San Anton = i la de San Roque = i en San Agustin . . . = i en Santo Domingo . . . ademas e recado sienpre el rosario del decenario de la pasion de Nuestro Señor Jesuchristo . . . i sienpre e recado estas i otras deuociones i ademas el oficio menor de la Uirgen Santisima i en el a muchos dias reco los salmos penitenciales i graduales i otras deuociones i por ellas mediante la misericordia de Dios Nuestro Señor su Santisima Madre, mi señora, fiome a de librar su misericordia santan de mis falsos acusadores i me a de sacar por quien es a puerto siguro de tantos tormentos para maior seruicio suio = (f. 161v).

Como hemos visto, aparecen en el juicio contra doña Teresa varios grupos de folios escritos de su puño y letra: ff. 80r-83v, 117v-121v y 147r-161v. Al defenderse, presenta una viva imagen de la sociedad novomexicana del siglo XVII, utilizando palabras cargadas de emotividad, rabia y angustia y que carecen del barniz estandarizador de un notario. Son escritos llenos de espontaneidad, únicos por su carácter y por provenir como ya dijimos, de la mano de una mujer.

El último grupo de folios (ff. 148r-161v) compone la base del presente trabajo de investigación. Ha sido elegido porque es el más extenso y porque constituye un discurso autosuficiente en sí mismo.

6. Análisis lingüístico de los manuscritos de Doña Teresa

La ortografía utilizada por doña Teresa demuestra cierta arbitrariedad y los usos específicos no son siempre predecibles. Dada la época en que fue escrito este documento y dada la escasa instrucción recibida por doña Teresa, estos rasgos de su escritura no nos deben sorprender. Este documento no puede presentar un sistema ortográfico estable, puesto que este no existía en el siglo XVI y aún tardaría en establecerse hasta el siglo XVIII. Aún tardaría más en establecerse en Nuevo México, una región alejada de los centros de cultura, y en una persona poco expuesta al uso de la escritura como lo fue doña Teresa.

En cuanto a la representación gráfica de los fonemas, destacamos en estos manuscritos la de los grupos consonánticos. El español áureo puede caracterizarse como época de alternancia, al menos en la escritura, entre el respeto a la forma latina y la tendencia a adoptar fórmulas simplificadoras. Esto lleva a pensar a Fontanella de Weinberg (1987) y a García Carrillo (1988) que, en la mayoría de los casos, los grupos consonánticos no se pronunciaban en la lengua oral. Esto mismo puede verse en el caso de doña Teresa. Su lengua se caracteriza no por una alternancia de formas sino, lisa y llanamente, por una simplificación de las mismas. Las consonantes implosivas de los cultismos \<pc>, \<pt>, \<nct>, \<mpt>, \<ct>, \<cc>, aparecen siempre reducidas; *concecion* (161v32), *efetivamente* (154r11), *protetor* (155v3), *efeto* (157r16), *editos* (159v43), *aciones* (148v22), *acidente* (150v28). El sonido [ks] pierde el oclusivo velar; *espresar* (148r14), *esplicar* (148r21), *estrane* (148v5), *espresadas* (149v34), *pretesto* (153r15), *escusar* (153v53), *esperiencia* (156r7), *estenso* (157v30), *estremo* (161r11). El grupo \<bs> también se simplifica; *ostante* (149v46), *asoluto* (155v7). Cae también /g/ delante de nasal y de dental; *inorauan* (154v24), *sinificando* (154v44), *Madalena* (161v45) y el grupo \<ns> aparece también simplificado en *istancias* (148v48), *estancias* (154r20), *istante* (149r8).

En doña Teresa no hay seseo ni yeísmo. Esta tendencia se contrapone a aquella presente en otros documentos de su época y, a su vez, es llamativa en un texto en el cual se dan otros fenómenos de tipo andalucista como la caída de /-d/ en *cantida* (148r8), *ciuda* (148r11), *uerda* (148r35), *mita* (150r39), *pieda* (150v22), etc.; la aspiración de /s/ en *los grande ruido* (148v37), *las cosa* (152v42), *los suio* (148v51), *lo hijo* (155v4), *gornadas (. . .) forcosa* (156v6), etc.; el refuerzo velar del diptongo [we] en *Guerta* (148v5) en lugar de "Huerta" y la confusión de los fonemas líquidos /r/ y /l/ en *Bernar* (149r41) en lugar de "Bernal" y *Gabiel* (148v31) en lugar de "Javier."

En la categoría verbal de doña Teresa[1], hay muestras de un español perteneciente a una variante tardía, arcaica y conservadora, que se diferencia de aquel hablado en el centro de poder más próximo, la ciudad de México. Donde encontramos una clara superposición de lo innovador o moderno sobre lo arcaico o medieval, hecho que se concreta para México en el siglo XVI (cfr. Parodi 1995). No se nos escapa el hecho de que el español que llegó a América lo hizo cargado de múltiples fluctuaciones y vacilaciones que perduran, de alguna manera, hasta nuestros días. Llama particularmente la atención la fuerza con que se da dicha oscilación en estos manuscritos del XVII cuando ya se estaba diluyendo en la capital virreinal desde el XVI.

Se registran ciertos fenómenos de corte antiguo como el pretérito del verbo "traer": *mi marido trugo al suio* (150v47), *la trugeron presa* (152r13-14), *las truge mui coridas* (154v18) o como los infinitivos asimilados al pronombre enclítico del tipo *escalalle* (156r15), *adulalle* (158v37), *llevalles* (160v51). También se encuentran en doña Teresa formas de futuro con /rn/; *no se si esta terna (. . .) algunos* (149v34), *que otro uerna* (154v42).

Pero esta tendencia hacia lo arcaico en los verbos doña Teresa, sin embargo, no es tajante dado que no aparecen ni perfectos simples como "uido" ni imperativos del tipo "dalde".

En lo que a las construcciones con "haber" se refiere, hemos podido encontrar un solo caso en el cual posee el significado de "obtener, conseguir", un resabio arcaizante y formulaico: *no an menester mas que tener uno una quegita para que (. . .)* (159v38). No puede decirse, entonces, que "haber" compita con "tener" en este sentido y tampoco lo hace en el contexto de la auxiliaridad. Los únicos casos que se registran de "tener" como auxiliar son perífrasis resultativas en las cuales el verbo "tener" marca el matiz aspectual que se quiere expresar. Son todas estructuras con el participio del verbo "decir" y en todas se respeta la concordancia de género y número; *lo que dicho tengo* (148v37), *querella que tengo dicha* (156r12), *los escritos que dichos tengo* (161v14).

Presenta un resabio arcaizante la construcción, bastante frecuente, "infinitivo + de + haber"; *le habia de dar con un cuchillo* (151v8), *auia de uenir preso* (151v33), *auia de acotar* (148r41). Doña Teresa, por otra parte, al igual que otros escritores de la época, y siguiendo un modelo medieval, emplea "haber" como núcleo de construcciones impersonales con significado temporal, en las cuales hoy usaríamos el verbo "hacer"; *por auer poco que se auia ido* (148v6), *poco a* (150r10), *a muchos dias* (161v40).

---

[1]Un análisis más extenso de las formas verbales de este manuscrito fue presentado en el 83rd Annual Meeting of the Association of Teachers of Spanish and Portuguese (San Francisco, California—5 al 9 de julio de 2001), en una ponencia que titulé "Variación en el español de la Provincia de Nuevo México y de la Banda Oriental".

En otro orden de cosas, en el manuscrito de doña Teresa aparece gran cantidad de formas verbales no flexionadas, hecho que se relaciona con la prosa medieval. Fontanella de Weinberg (1987:36), Bravo García (1987 y 1989) y García Carrillo (1988:64) también han encontrado en sus investigaciones una fuerte presencia de formas no flexionadas del verbo en manuscritos americanos, aunque mayoritariamente en manuscritos fechados en épocas anteriores al que aquí nos ocupa.

Abunda el infinitivo, en su forma simple y en su forma compuesta, en contextos en que hoy usaríamos una forma conjugada: *callo por auer gente* (150v9) [porque había gente], *por quanto auer dicho el diferentes ueces* (151v32) [por cuanto él dijo diferentes veces].

Abundan también las perífrasis modales del tipo "deber de + infinitivo" (*no deuio de sauer* (161v5) y las aspectuales como "dar en + infinitivo" (*dieron en traer* (151r13), *dieron en sustentar* (151r19), "venir a + infinitivo" (*vine a tener tantos disgustos* (153r18), *uino a perder la uerguenca* (153r22) y "quedar + infinitivo" (*este nos quedo a deuer algunos pesos* (158r21-22).

Se destaca, además, en los escritos de doña Teresa, la alta frecuencia de gerundios —con diferentes valores— aparecen tanto en su forma simple como en su forma compuesta. Se destacan estructuras del tipo *me digo en la siesta don Bernardo pidiera una llaue de una despensa por que **auiendo** aquel traido cantida de mantas (. . .) **mandandole** a ellos los que entraron (. . .) al almacen (. . .) i estando el aca fuera (. . .) le parecio que el uno estaua en espia i el otro en otro aposento **sospechando** mal (. . .) i **abiendosele oluidado** (. . .) **acordandose** dello me lo digo i sali i pedile a Diego la llaue* (150v4-8).

Llama la atención, además, el uso de la construcción "en + gerundio" para indicar una acción inmediatamente anterior a la que desarrolla el verbo en la oración principal; *en llegando a la uilla le abia de hacer don Bernardo muchos males* (156r55-56).

Se multiplican también los participios. Muchas veces aparecen en frases absolutas para significar, fundamentalmente, una circunstancia de tiempo anterior a la del verbo de la oración principal: *ido Penalosa (. . .) la agrego a esta* (153r47), *ido don Diego i estando el mundo rebuelto (. . .) lo llamaron* (153v6). Esta estructura es resabio de una sintaxis latinizante y ha perdido su vitalidad en el español actual con verbos intransitivos.

A estos rasgos arcaicos, se contrapone el hecho de que no se registra falta de delimitación del uso de los verbos "ser" y "estar" ni supervivencia del primero en funciones que modernamente corresponden al segundo. El uso de "ser" y "estar" es básicamente de tipo moderno.

En términos generales, entonces, la vacilación ente los polos moderno y arcaico que encontraron Bravo García (1987 y 1989) y Parodi (1995), entre otros, para textos mexicanos pertenecientes al siglo XVI, aparece aquí en un documento perteneciente a la segunda mitad del siglo XVII.

El léxico que encontramos en este documento se relaciona con la vida doméstica y es, en términos generales, de uso coloquial, hecho que se vincula estrechamente con el tipo de documento en cuestión y con el estilo de la autora. Doña Teresa retoma y transmite las palabras que los primeros españoles dieron a la nueva realidad hispanoamericana. Utiliza varias voces de origen indígena. Entre ellas se destacan *enaguas* y *tamales*, pero también se destaca la forma en que doña Teresa introduce estas voces en su discurso. Recurre a la coordinación de un término indígena con otro patrimonial poniendo en relación significados próximos. Tal es el caso de *enaguas o pollera* (148r59) y *tamales o pastel* (158v36-37) en los cuales se da una duplicación de vocabulario a través de la conjunción disyuntiva *o* que no expresa exclusión sino simple alternancia de elementos léxicos más o menos coincidentes (cfr. también Enguita Utrilla 1979:289 y ss.).

Doña Teresa recurre a la estructura preposicional "de la tierra" para referirse a los indígenas de la región: *los de la tiera* (151v21-22) o *gente de la tiera* (160r29). También utiliza el prodecimiento sintagmático "nombre + complemento de lugar" en *manta de Ciuola* (150r6), *mantas de Moqui* (150v51), *estriuos i cueros de Ciuola* (157v15). Son interesantes en estos escritos las designaciones etnolingüísticas americanas como *gumana* (159r50), *emes* (152r48), *(^lengua) teguas* (148v22), *apachas* (150r53).

El manuscrito de doña Teresa aporta una interesante muestra del léxico utilizado por una mujer que escribe sobre Nuevo México en el siglo XVII, mostrando una lengua española en proceso de adaptación a la nueva realidad hispanoamericana.

7. Desenlace del juicio

El abogado de doña Teresa cierra su defensa el 29 de noviembre de 1664 y casi un mes más tarde el Tribunal da por concluida la causa de doña Teresa y decreta su suspensión. Doña Teresa es puesta en libertad el 20 de diciembre de 1664, después de un año y ocho meses de prisión, aunque en ningún momento se le declara inocente.

Poco se sabe de doña Teresa después que abandonó la cárcel; sin demasiado éxito siguió un juicio contra el tribunal, reclamando los bienes que le habían sido embargados. En lo que sí tuvo éxito —aunque sin proponérselo— fue en dejarnos un manuscrito original de época, que nos trae a nuestros días —a través de un habla espontánea, sin censuras— la lucha de una mujer por lo que consideraba justo. Testimonio de un español tardío, el texto de doña Teresa es un documento colonial único. La sociolingüística histórica solo puede crecer y enriquecerse en el análisis de un manuscrito de este tenor.

Fuente manuscrita

Archivo General de la Nación (México), Ramo Inquisición, Vol. 596.

Referencias bibliográficas

Adams, Eleonor B., & France V. Scholes. 1942. Books in New Mexico. 1598-1680. *New Mexico Historical Review* 17, 226-70.

Alberro, Solange. 1989. El Tribunal del Santo Oficio de la Inquisición en Nueva España: algunas modalidades de su actividad. Inquisición y sociedad en América Latina. *Cuadernos para la historia de la evangelización en América Latina* 4, 9-31.

Beck, Warren. 1962. *New Mexico. A History of Four Centuries*. Norman: U of Oklahoma P.

Blanche-Benveniste, Claire. 1993. Les unités: langue écrite, langue orale. En C. Pontecorvo & C. Blanche-Benveniste (Eds.), *Proceedings of the Workshop on Orality vesus Literacy: Concepts, Methods and Data* (pp. 133-194). Siena, Italia, 24-26 de septiembre de 1992. Estrasburgo: European Science Foundation.

Bravo García, Eva María. 1987. *El español del XVII en documentos americanistas*. Sevilla: Alfar.

Bravo García, Eva María. 1989. *Transcripción y estudio lingüístico de la Historia de los descubrimientos de Nueva España de Baltasar de Obregón*. Tesis doctoral, Universidad de Sevilla, Facultad de Filología.

Coll, Magdalena. 2000. 'fio me a de librar Dios Nuestro Señor . . . de mis falsos acusadores': defensa de Doña Teresa de Aguilera y Roche al Tribunal de la Inquisición (1664, México). *Romance Philology*, Spring, 289-361.

Enguita Utrilla, José María. 1979. Indoamericanismos léxicos en el Sumario de la Natural Historia de las Indias. *Anuario de letras* 17, 285-304.

Fontanella de Weinberg, María Beatriz. 1987. *El español bonaerense. Cuatro siglos de evolución lingüística (1580-1980)*. Buenos Aires: Hachette.

García Carrillo, Antonio. 1988. *El español en México en el XVI. Estudio lingüístico de un documento judicial de la Audiencia de Guadalajara (Nueva España) del año 1578*. Sevilla: Alfar.

Kessell, John. 1987. *Kiva, Cross and Crown: the Pecos Indians and New Mexico*. Washington, DC: National Park Service, U.S. Department of the Interior.

Marquilhas, Rita. 2000. *A faculdade das letras. Leitura e escrita em Portugal no século XVII*. Lisboa: Imprensa Nacional, Casa da Moeda.

Oesterreicher, Wulf. 1994. El español en textos escritos por semicultos. Competencia escrita de impronta oral en la historiografía indiana. *El español de América en el siglo XVI. Actas del Simposio del Instituto Ibero-Americano de Berlín.* Comp. Jens Lüdtke, 155-91. Madrid: Vervuert—Iberoamericana.

Parodi, Claudia. 1995. *Orígenes del español americano.* México: Universidad Nacional Autónoma de México, Publicaciones del Centro de Lingüística Hispánica.

Petrucci, Armando. 1978. Scritura, alfabetismo ed educazione grafica nella Roma del primo cinquecento: da un libretto di conti di Magdalena Pizzicarola in Trastevere. *Scrittura e Civiltà* 2, 163-207.

Romaine, Suzanne. 1982. *Socio-historical Linguistics: Its Status and Methodology.* Cambridge: Cambridge UP.

Scholes, France. 1930. The Supply Service of the North Mexican Missions in the Seventeenth Century. *New Mexico Historical Review* 5, 93-115, 186-210, 386-405.

Scholes, France. 1936-1937. Church and State in New Mexico. 1610-1650. *New Mexico Historical Review* 2, 1 (1936):9-76, 2:145-78, 3:283-94, 4:297-349 y 12, 1 (1937):78-106.

Scholes, France. 1937-1941. Troublous times in New Mexico. En 1659-1670. *New Mexico Historical Review* 12, 2 (1937):134-74 y 12, 4:380-453; 12, 1 (1938):63-85; 15, 3 (1940):249-69 y 15, 4:369-418; 16, 1 (1941):15-41, 16, 2:184-206 y 16, 3:313-328.

Scholes, France. 1976. La sociedad en el siglo XVII en Nuevo México. En D. J. Weber (Ed.), *El México perdido: ensayos escogidos sobre el antiguo norte de México (1540-1821).* México: Secretaria de Educación Pública, Dirección General de Divulgación.

Espinosa's Diary Chronicling the 1716 Ramón Expedition into Texas: Notes on the Translations*

Deb Cunningham
Texas A&M University

This article presents the unique contributions of historical sociolinguistic textual analysis for historical research and interpretation. The article will highlight the errors in the existing English translations (1930:339-361) of Fray Isidro Félix de Espinosa's diary of his 1716 expedition into Texas, as compared to its original source (1716: vol. 81, folios 405v-411v). Both translations are problematic, though for different reasons. Through the analysis of various problems with existing translations, unedited transcriptions, and microfilm sources, I will argue that scholars' reliance on secondary source material can contribute to inconsistencies in the historical literature. I emphasize the need for critical, paleographic examination of the original Spanish documents on which the translations and narrative accounts of this expedition and, by extension, of similar colonial expedition diaries, are based. Before analyzing the translations, however, it is necessary to discuss the historical background of the expedition.

Prior to 1716, the Spanish and French had battled for control of the lands north of the Río Grande. European exploration and colonization of Mexico laid the foundation for subsequent exploration and attempts at colonization of areas far removed from the capital city in northern Mexico and what is now the southwestern United States. The Spanish and French had sent expeditions into the area in an attempt to establish and maintain control; however, both had failed. (Bolton 1996:218) The Spaniards made frequent expeditions into the outlying country, (Bolton and Marshall 1936:292) most of which can be characterized as

* The author would like to thank Professor Brian Imhoff for reviewing this article and for his continued support and guidance with all research related to this expedition.

exploratory in nature, though there had been attempts prior to the Ramón expedition to colonize New Spain, particularly in response to what the Spaniards perceived as a French threat. One expedition sent in response to this threat of French encroachment was that of Alonzo de León, who raised the Spanish flag at the Nabedache village in May 1690 and founded the mission of San Francisco de los Tejas, the first in East Texas (Bolton 1996:17). This period of Spanish occupation of East Texas was short-lived. On October 25, 1693 Father Damian Massanet torched the mission and fled (Bolton 1996: 217; Foster 1995:109).

While the French focused mainly on commerce, the intent of the Spanish was primarily that of christianization of the Indian population and settlement of the territory leading to permanent occupation. In the eighteenth century the presence of the French in the Mississippi Valley, both in the Illinois country and in Louisiana, was a dominant force in shaping Spanish policy in the northern frontier (Bannon 1997:108). Spanish officials in Mexico kept a watchful eye on French activity in the region.

While Texas was unoccupied by Spaniards for more than two decades between 1694 and 1715, it was not entirely forgotten or unvisited. It especially remained on the mind of Father Francisco Hidalgo, who made unfinished work among the Tejas Indians a consuming passion (Chipman 1992:105). According to Donald Chipman, the "mission effort in East Texas had familiarized Spaniards with the geography and Indians of Texas and convinced both church and government officials that future missions must be sustained by presidios and civilian settlements" (17). This interest, coupled with reports of new French activity in the region, sparked renewed concern on the part of Spanish officials. The catalyst that would force them to take action, rather than monitor French activity, was the arrival of the Frenchman Don Luis de St. Denis at San Juan Bautista.

According to Elizabeth West, (1904:3-78, 21) St. Denis and Don Medar Jalot, with two other Frenchmen, arrived at San Juan Bautista in July 1715. St. Denis declared that he was captain of the presidios of San Juan (Biloxi) located on a small stream of that name, which ran from the Mississippi to Lake Pontchatrain. He reported that he had left Mobile with twenty-four French Canadians. Upon finding the missions abandoned, he headed to San Juan Bautista. St. Denis emphasized the "natural affections" which the Indians had for the Spaniards and their great desire to have the Fathers return and establish missions among them (Castañeda 1936:33-34). St. Denis's appearance was a shock to the Spaniards, even though there had been rumors of Frenchmen among the tribes to the east for several previous years (Bolton 1996:110). A report of the arrival of the Frenchmen was given to the Viceroy Fernando de Alencastre Norona y Silva Duque de Linares (West 1904:24).

The issue of why St. Denis, a Frenchman, would be hired to work on an expedition, the purpose of which was to counter French expansion, has been the topic of discussion among historians for some time (Phares 1975:112). Castañeda best sums up St. Denis's agenda by stating that "St. Denis's mission was a purely commercial venture" (40). Since he had arrived from a departure point that was even more distant than the current expedition's destination, he was qualified to serve as a guide. He had also declared his intention to settle on the Spanish frontier and go into business there; he would later marry Ramón's niece (John 1975:203-5). In response to the new French presence, Spanish officials called a general *junta*, which met August 22, 1715, and endorsed the recommendations to have Spanish missionaries return to the land of the Tejas Indians and reestablish missions (Archivo General de la Nación México, Provincias Internas, vol. 181, fs. 370r-375r.). Approval of the expedition was the first step in permanent Spanish occupation of lands northeast of the Río Grande, and it represented Spain's commitment to the permanent occupation of the Province of the Tejas Indians (Hadley 1997:360). The Viceroy officially appointed the commander of the expedition and drew up a set of instructions for the proposed *entrada.* He appointed Domingo Ramón leader of the expedition and St. Denis conductor of supplies for as long as his services would be required (Chipman 1992:111). Domingo Ramón was the son of the Captain of San Juan Bautista, Diego Ramón, and had lived his entire life on the frontier (Chipman 1997:111).

Religious interests on the expedition were divided equally between friars from the missionary colleges of Querétaro and Zacatecas (Chipman 1992:112, Weddle 1968:117). Father Isidro Félix de Espinosa was the president of the missionaries from the College of Querétaro. The fathers who accompanied him from this college included: Francisco Hidalgo, Benito Sánchez, Gabriel de Vergara, and Manuel Castellanos. The fathers from the College of Zacatecas included: President Antonio Margil de Jesús, who was unable to make much of the journey due to illness, Agustín Patrón, Francisco de San Diego, Matías Saenz de San Antonio, Pedro de Santa María y Mendoza, Javier Cubillos, and Domingo de Vrioste (Espinosa, Archivo General de la Nación México, Provincias Internas, vol. 181, 406 r 9-16). Espinosa had been present on previous expeditions and "was qualified to serve not only as a diarist but, more significantly, as a guide" (Foster 1995:112). Spanish expansion interested Espinosa due to his previous experience in the region and his religious agenda; his standing on the expedition was reflected in his authority to name campsites and streams (Kessell 2002:112). Despite the extensive frontier experience of the three key players involved in the 1716 expedition, neither Ramón, Espinosa, nor St. Denis were familiar with the territory north of the Colorado River (Foster 1995:112).

After the *junta* authorized the expedition and appointed leaders, the expedition from the Río Grande to modern day East Texas was quickly planned and organized. The journey of the entire expedition party lasted from April until July 1716. Ramón spent February to April preparing his expedition party, gathering supplies, and making the trek to the Presidio San Juan Bautista, where he met with Espinosa and other religious leaders to begin the journey together (391r-401v). As the march got under way, Ramón listed seventy-five persons in the caravan, including eight priests, two lay brothers, twenty-five soldiers, three Frenchmen, and several dozen civilians (393r32-303v29).[1] Seven of the soldiers were married and brought along their wives and families. Ramón also lists a six-year-old boy and a four-year-old girl among the expedition party members, as well as a black man, and five Indians (two guides and three who were in charge of the goats) (Ramón, 393v17-29).

The combined expedition party of military, religious, and civilian members left San Juan Bautista on April 27, 1716 (Ramón, Untitled Diary 393v29). The expedition party usually traveled in a northeasterly direction, covering anywhere from one to twelve leagues per day (Ramón 385v; 395r16). They camped near springs, streams, lagunas, and lakes when possible. Father Espinosa and Captain Ramón provide detailed descriptions of flora and fauna encountered, as well as the names of camp sites, stopping places, posts where they camped, and the names of rivers and streams they crossed. The rivers the expedition party crossed during their trek from the Río Grande to East Texas include: the Nueces, the Frío, the Hondo, the Medina, the San Antonio, the Guadalupe, the San Marcos, the Colorado, and the Trinity.[2]

Within a month of arriving in East Texas, four missions stood in settlements designated by the Tejas leaders. According to Espinosa, the founding of the first mission, Nuestro Padre San Francisco de los Tejas, for the Neche Indians, occurred on July 5, 1716. The second mission, the Mission of the College of Nuestra Señora de Guadalupe de Zacatecas, for the Nacogdoches Indians, was also founded later this day. The priests from Zacatecas established their mission for the Hainai Indians, Mission of Purísima Concepción, on July 6. The priests from the College of Querétaro established their third mission, Mission San José

---

[1] Ramón, Untitled Diary, 393r32-393v29. The number of expedition party members has been a source of debate among historians. See the discussion below on Note 2.

[2] Ramón, Untitled Diary, 394r33-34 *al rio que llaman | de las Nuezes*; 394v24 *el Rio Frio*; 394v33 *del Rio Ondo*; 395r18 *el Rio de Medina*; 395r37-38 *el Rio de S<a>n | Antonio*; 395v2 *el Rio de Guadalupe*; 395v36 *el Rio de S<a>n Marcos*; 396r8 *al Rio Colorado*; 397v16-17 *al Rio de la | Trinidad*; Espinosa, Diario Derrotero, 406v34 *el Rio de las Nuezes*; 407r11 *el paso de Rio Frio*; *el Arroyo Hondo*; 407v5 *el Rio de Medina*; 407v16-17 *del Ri[o] | de San Antonio*; 408r2 *el Rio de Guadalupe*; 408r27 *el Rio de S<an> Marcos*; 408v3 *el Rio del Espiritu Santo o Colorado*; 409v23 *el Rio de la Trinidad*; cf. note 125.

de los Nasonis, for the Nasoni Indians on July 8 (John 1975:208). Each group for whom the missions were established elected its captain general, to whom Ramón presented a cane of office (John 1975:208). According to Chipman, "the new missions in East Texas were set up in the very locale where two had failed in the 1690s" (1992:113). They were extremely isolated, as San Juan Bautista, the nearest Spanish settlement, was over four hundred miles away. Even so, this venture was worth the risk. The Tejas were the strongest and most influential Indians between the Río Grande and the Red River, and if the Spanish could gain influence over them, the activities of the French in East Texas might be thwarted (Chipman 1992:18). The reestablishment of missions and a presidio in East Texas gave Spain a claim to lands north of the Río Grande, did much to determine that Texas would be Spanish, not French, and helped advance the eventual boundary between Texas and the United States to the Sabine River (Chipman 1996:18).

Historians of the Southwest have typically relied on English translations of expedition diaries as their source, which has resulted in discrepancies in the historical literature. William C. Foster documents problems stemming from reliance upon translations and warns that "any dependence on Spanish diary accounts requires not only a review of the English translation of the diaries, but a careful study of manuscript and typescript versions, where available" (1995:7-8). Jerry R. Craddock calls for scholars to "make serious efforts to gain access to the Spanish originals or at least support the efforts of those who are attempting to make the Spanish texts available to a wider audience" (1998:481-540). With respect to this expedition, I argue that only the systematic comparison of all known sources of the original manuscript can provide scholars with an accurate account of events.

The extant sources for the Espinosa expedition diary include: the original diary,[3] located in the Archivo General de la Nación México, Provincias Internas, vol. 181, fols.405v-411v, from which I have made a semi-paleographic transcription, and will hereafter refer to as "O";[4] and what appears to be a contemporary copy of the diary made by Franciscan monks, located in the Biblioteca Nacional de México, Archivo Francisco, caja 1/1.24, f. 46v-57v.[5] Neither trans-

---

[3] Espinosa, Diario Derrotero, folios 405v-411v. The original is signed by Espinosa and his signature and rubric appear at the end of the diary on folio 411v.

[4] A typescript of this diary is available in the Center for American History at the University of Texas at Austin; box 2Q250 in a collection titled "Spanish Material from Various Sources." I will show that Tous relied on this transcript when making his translation.

[5] This document is titled "Derrottero del viage q<u>e fue escriviendo con ttoda individual<idad> Pr<esident>e el P<adr>e Fr<ay> Ysidro Feliz Espinosa, desde 25 de abril h<as>ta 30 de julio de 716 [sic]." A photostat copy of this document (hereafter cited as CAH) is available at the Center for American History at the University of Texas at Austin, box 2Q250.

lator cites this copy as a source for their translation, and paleographic variants between the original and this copy supports these authors' assertion. There are two extant translations of the Espinosa diary: 1) that produced by Gabriel Tous in 1930 and reprinted in 1997; hereafter "Tous"; and 2) that produced by Hadley et al. in 1997;[6] hereafter "Hadley Translation." Hadley et al. provided a Spanish modernization following their translation, which serves as a third source for this article and is hereafter referred to as "Hadley Spanish Modernization."

Errors in the two existing translations relative to O are numerous, and can be categorized as omissions and misrepresentations based on the use of secondary source material.[7] In the passage preliminary to the diary, for example, Tous translates, "The Rev. Father Fray Antonio Margil de Jesús of the College of Zacatecas became seriously ill at the Mission of San Juan Bautista on the Río Grande. The apostolic preacher, Rev. Father Fray Pedro de Santa María y Mendoza, the lay-brother Fray Francisco Xavier Cubillos and Fray Domingo de Vrioste with the habit of Donado remained with him . . . ." (Tous 68)[8] The original manuscript shows "*Del Collegio de Sacatecas que- | do grauem<en>te enfermo el R<everendo> P<adre> Fr<ay> Antt<oni>o Margil de Jesus, en el Rio Grande en | la Mission de San Juan Bapt<ist>a y en su compañia el P<adre> P<rocurad>or Fr<ay> Agustin Pa- | tron y el Herm<an>o Fr<ay> Fran<cis>co de San Diego, los que entraron, el P<adre> P<rocurad>or Fr<ay> Mathi- | as Sans de S<an> Antt<oni>o, el P<adre> P<rocurad>or Fr<ay> Pedro de S<an>ta Maria y Mendoza, el her<man>o Fray | Fran<cis>co Xavier Cubillos, y el her<man>o Domingo de Vrioste con habito de donado . . . ,*"[9] and reveals that only Agustín Patrón and Francisco de San Diego remained with Father Margil, while Pedro de Santa María y Mendoza, Francisco Javier Cubillos and Domingo de Vrioste accompanied the expedition party. This error may have contributed to the discrepancies in the historical literature regarding the number of expedition party members.[10] Carlos E. Cas-

---

[6] Tous made his translation from "from a transcript found among the documents pertaining to the life and memoirs of the Venerable Father Fray Antonio Margil de Jesus in the García Latin-American Library at the University of Texas," 68; The 1997 reprint does not edit or improve upon the 1930 translation.

[7] This analysis does not present an exhaustive account of all the problems or errors encountered in the two translations.

[8] Tous, "Ramón Expedition: Espinosa's Diary," 68. It should be noted that the Center for American History typescript, upon which Tous relied, matches information contained in O.

[9] O 406r11-16

[10] Some scholars have stated that the expedition party was comprised of seventy-five people cf. Weddle. *San Juan Bautista*, 117; Chipman, *Spanish Texas*, 112; John. *Storms Brewed in Other Men's Worlds*, 207; Others propose that there were sixty-five cf. Bolton, *The Spanish Borderlands*, 225; Foster, *Spanish Expeditions into Texas 1689-1768*, 109; Bolton et al., *The Colonization of North America 1492-1783*, 293.

tañeda, who compared the diaries of Espinosa and Ramón in great detail concluded "There are exactly seventy-five persons. Heretofore, everybody has maintained that there were only sixty-five members in the expedition, but a careful count of those listed by Ramón will show there were seventy-five without counting the families of Joseph Maldonado and Pedro Botello. If we take into consideration that two priests and a lay brother joined Ramón before he reached East Texas, the actual number should be between seventy-eight and eighty persons" (Castañeda 1936:47). In his diary, Ramón states that there are seventy-five people.[11] However, the only extant English translation of Ramón's diary states that there are sixty-five people (Foik 1999:129-148). Previous research by this author revealed that the English translation is based on a copy of the Ramón diary, rather than on the original.[12] This evidence further reveals the need to make use of original documents versus relying on faulty translations or unedited transcriptions.

In the diary entry for May 18 the Tous translation shows "melodious songs of different birds. **Omission.** Ticks molested us, attaching themselves to our skin" (Tous 1997:76)[13] The original states "*las vozes canoras de diferentes paxaros. | Puede sin vadearse passar por tierra enjuta subiendo a las lomas medio quarto de legua. | No faltaron garrapatas que nos dieron sus puntadas,*"[14] thus providing information about a river, which could be translated as "One can cross over dry land, without fording [the river], by climbing the hills a quarter of league." Here, in what appears to be a case of homoeuteleuton, Tous omits the location and other information about a river. The CAH typescript includes this information. Another omission occurs in the entry for April 28 when Tous translates "for an **Indian**" (1997:70) where the original shows "*por un yndio gu[ia]*."[15] In this instance, however, Tous is not to blame, for the typescript from which he was working also omitted the information (CAH:96).

Aside from errors of omission, the Tous translation contains a series of mistranslations, some of which are clearly paleographic in nature. In the entry for May 17, for example, Tous mistakenly translated "*guia*" as "*quia*" in "*se adelanto . . . Don | Juan de Medar, frances, y un yndio guia*"[16] which he used as an Indian tribal name: "Don Juan de Medar, Frenchman, and a Quia Indian went ahead" (Tous 1997:75). Similarly, for the June 21 entry, Tous mistakenly translated an adjective as a name: "Captain Francis went ahead . . . , " (Tous 1997:83)

[11] Ramón, Untitled Diary, 393v28-92: *que por todas hazen | setenta y cinco personas.*
[12] cf. Cunningham, 2006.
[13] Tous, "Ramón Expedition: Espinosa's Diary," 76.
[14] O 408r16-18.
[15] O 406v11.
[16] O 407v43-44.

but the original shows "*Adelantose el Cap<ita>n frances,*"[17] referring to the French Captain, St. Denis. Similar examples abound, including "we found **two** springs of water" (1997:80) from "*Encontramos algunos ojos de agua,*"[18] which means that "**some**" springs were encountered, and "Here we beheld many **high hills**," (Tous 1997:83) from "*Aqui hallamos muchos pinos encumbrados,*"[19] which should be translated as "Here we found many towering pines."

Other examples of mistranslation are "language oriented"; one such example, though many could be reported, is found in the May 13 entry where Tous wrote "so much confusion followed, that eighty-two of them (horses) were drowned, and **we were left bewildered**" (73); a more faithful translation would be, "so much confusion followed that eighty-two of them drowned, **constituting a great loss to all of us**," as the original indicates "*se ofreçio tal confusion que quedaron ahogados ochenta y dos de ellos de que | quedamos todos perdidosos.*"[20] In the entry for May 9, this type of mistranslation occurs again, when Tous translates "the great number of people living together on the Colorado River," (72) which does not correspond to the original diary entry "*estar mucha gente | junta en el Rio Colorado,*"[21] as "*junta*" does not indicate that the people were "living" on the River. Although the nature of the examples illustrating stylistic differences may not be as significant as those presented earlier, the errors in translation are completely avoidable by making use of original rather than secondary source material.

The more recent translation completed by Hadley et al. is also problematic, though for different reasons. Here many of the errors resulted from the use of a faulty microfilm copy of the source document in which the right margins of all verso folios were illegible or cut off.[22] Having compared the original document to the Hadley translation and Spanish modernization, I focus here on restoration errors.

In the entry for June 27, the modernization "*treinta y cuatro indios y algunos de ellos capitanes,*"[23] is translated "thirty-four Indians arrived, **several**

---

[17] O 410r13.

[18] O 409r35.

[19] O 410r20.

[20] O 407v8-9.

[21] O 407r23-24.

[22] This is true of two microfilm sources that I consulted: the Nettie Lee Benson Latin American Collection at The University of Texas, Film 22,279, vol. 181, and the South Texas Archive at Texas A&M Kingsville in their holdings of the Provincias Internas. The original at the Archivo General de la Nación, México, Provincias Internas is bound in such a way that the researcher is required to manually separate and carefully lift the pages at the spine of the volume in order to see the text in the verso folios. The awkward manner in which the original is bound has resulted in illegible microfilm and photocopies.

[23] Hadley, Spanish Modernization, 394.

chiefs among them," (Hadley 1997:380) but the original gives the actual number of Indian chiefs: *"treinta y quatro yndios **y cinco** | de ellos capitanes."*[24] Similarly, Hadley's Spanish modernization shows *"**caminaron** al sitio preparado para el recibimiento que era una choza de ramas de árboles **sombreado** con mantas,"* (394) which was translated as "**they walked** to the place prepared for the reception. It was a hut built of tree branches **covered** with blankets" (381). The original states, *"**caminamos** | al sitio preparado para el receuimiento q<u>e era una chosa de ramas de arboles | **alfombreado** con mantas"*[25] in which "we (not they) walked" and "carpeted with blankets" are rendered inaccurately.

Similar examples are found throughout the translation. In the entry for June 18, for example, the Spanish modernization shows, *"En estos medios salieron al camino **tres indios** . . ."*(393) which is translated as "**Three Indians** . . . emerged on the road," (379) but the original diary provides information about the Indian tribe: *"En estos medios salieron al camino **tres yndios Tej[a]s**."*[26] In the entry for June 29, the Spanish modernization shows: *"Vinieron cerca de medio día otros [ilegible] ocho capitanes . . . ,"* (395) which is translated in the following manner: "About midday, eight more **[illegible]** chiefs arrrived" (381). The original document provides the number of the chiefs *"Vinieron cerca de medio dia otros **nueuos con** | ocho capitanes."*[27] A more accurate translation would be "Near midday others [Indians] came with eight chiefs . . . ."

Another incorrect restoration, which contributes to a misrepresentation in translation, can be found in the entry for May 24. The Hadley Spanish modernization shows *"Tiene este rio a una y otra banda descomunales **robles** y parras . . . ."* (390) and is translated as "On both banks, this river has enormous **oaks**, vines . . . ." (374). However, the original diary shows *"Tiene este rio a una y otra uanda decomunales arb[o]— | les y parras . . . . ,"*[28] and does not provide the variety of trees encountered.

Errors regarding directions, distances traveled, and places visited are also plentiful: *"y dista de esta misión de la Concepción **al [norte]** siete leguas,"* (396) is translated as, "This mission is seven leagues **north** of the mission of Concepción;" (384) the original reveals *"dista de esta Mission de la Concepcion **al nordest[e]** | siete leguas."*[29] In the June 14 entry, the Hadley Spanish modernization does not restore information included in the original ". . . *por tierra llana*

---

[24] O 410v3-4.
[25] O 410v8-10.
[26] O 409v40.
[27] O 410v42-43.
[28] O 408v10.
[29] O 411v14-15.

y a otra [ilegible] que se ofreció un arroyo crecido retrocedimos . . . ," (392) translated "over flat land **for a half a league**, but because there was a swollen arroyo, we retraced . . . ." (378). The original provides omitted details: "*por tierra llana media legua y a otra media | q<ue> se ofrecio un arroyo crecido retrocedimos.*"[30] An accurate translation would be: "over flat land about a **half a league. In about another half a league** . . . we turned back because there was a swollen arroyo." Similarly, for the May 27 entry, the Hadley Spanish modernization shows, ". . . *dos leguas al nordeste al este | y para* . . . ," (390) which they translate as ". . . two leagues toward the northeast quadrant. In order . . . ." (375). The original "*dos leg<ua>s al nordeste 4a al este | y para*"[31] provides additional information that is not represented in either of the Hadley documents. A more accurate translation would be ". . . two leagues northeast and a quarter league **to the east** . . . in order . . . ." In the entry for April 28 a place name is omitted. The Hadley Spanish modernization "*Llegamos a la cueva del [ilegible]*" (386) is translated "We arrived at the *Cueva del* **[illegible]**" (369). The original diary reveals that what is missing is "*Cueva del Leon.*"[32]

There are many other examples of problems encountered in the Spanish modernization as a result of usage of a faulty microfilm source, which in turn impact the translation. For example, in the entry for April 30, the Hadley Spanish modernization "*paramos de esta [ilegible] de los charcos*" (386) is translated "we halted at this **[ilegible]** of the pools," (369) while the original reveals the illegible information "*paramos desta vanda | de los charcos,*"[33] which should be translated as "we stopped at this **bank** of the pools." This occurs again in the entry for June 15, where the Hadley Spanish modernization "*estaba crecido y es muy [ilegible]cador en las orillas*" (392) is translated "was high, and it is was very [illegible] on the banks" (378). The original shows "*estaba crecido y es mui at[as] | cador en las orillas*"[34] which can be translated as "it was high and very miry."

In addition to inaccurate restorations based on the use of faulty source material, there are also examples of mistranslations. In the entry for June 27, the Hadley Spanish modernization shows, "*vinieron los indios que nos habían visto*" (394). Their translation, as a result, is: "the Indians who had seen us arrived" (384). However, the original indicates that in fact the opposite occured "*A la tarde vinieron los yndios q<u>e no nos auian visitado,*"[35] or "That afternoon new Indians who had **not** yet **visited** us came . . . ."

---

[30] O 409v17-18.
[31] O 408v19-20.
[32] O 406v10.
[33] O 406v25-26.
[34] O 409v24-25.
[35] O 410v24.

The original diary provides more specific information than Hadley's source. This occurs with regard to misnaming locations, such as *"Beatísimas Animas"*[36] instead of *"Benditas Animas"* or *"Pedro de Alcántara"*[37] rather than "San Pedro de Alcántara"; titles, such as the omission of *"Don"*[38] before a person's name ("Don" Juan de Medar); and changes in the style of Father Espinosa's writing.[39] Some restorations made by Hadley change the meaning of what is contained in the original diary. For example, the Spanish modernization shows, *"De allí como una legua junta con el río de la Trinidad,"* (392) which they translate as "About a league from here [the arroyo] joins the *Río de la Trinidad,"* (378) while the original reveals *"De alli como a una legua dimos con el Rio de la Trinidad,"*[40] which should be translated as "About a league from there **we came** upon the Trinity River."

It is worth noting that the Tous and Hadley translations differ, especially in entries describing the flora, fauna, and geography encountered during the expedition. For example, manuscript O contains *"nogales altissimos, alamos, olmos, parras, morales, sauzes, | madroños y palmitos legitimos,"*[41] which Tous translated as "very tall nopals, poplars, elms, grapevines, black mulberry trees, laurels, strawberry vines and genuine fan-palms" (74) while Hadley et al. translated this as "very tall walnuts, cottonwoods, elms, [grape]vines, mulberry trees, willows, strawberry trees, and palmettos" (372). Discrepancies between the two translations occur in virtually every instance in which the diary contains description of flora. Finally, some mistranslations occur in both translations: *"dimos con el paso de Rio Frio . . . Passado el Rio ^(q<ue> lo es de nombre^) . . . ."* (Tous 1997:72) is translated by Tous as ". . . found the passage of the River *Frío* . . . Beyond the river, **which is one in name only** . . . ," (72) and by Hadley et al. as "*Río Frío* . . . Beyond the river (**which is a river in name only**) . . . ." (370). The information contained in the original: *"que lo es de nombre"* refers to the river being what its name implies: cold.

It should be noted that the fact that two diaries exist has also contributed to discrepancies in the historical literature pertaining to this expedition. Inconsistencies between the accounts provided by Father Espinosa and Captain Ramón have already been documented in the historical literature, principally by Foster (1995) and Castañeda (1936). Foster points out that the conflicting reports made

---

[36] Hadley, Spanish Modernization, 390; Hadley, Translation, 375; versus O 408v24-25.

[37] Hadley, Spanish Modernization, 390; Hadley, Translation, 375; versus O 407v35-36.

[38] Hadley, Spanish Modernization, 388; Hadley, Translation, 373; versus O 407v43-44.

[39] I have limited the focus of this article to substantive errors. The reader should note, however, that the English translations do not, at times, accurately represent Father Espinosa's tone, writing style, or choice of verb tenses.

[40] O 409v22-23.

[41] O 407v21-22.

by Ramón and Espinosa complicate one's understanding of events on certain days throughout the expedition. For example, Foster notes that, "Espinosa blamed five Bozale Indians for stealing some horses that day, but Captain Ramón reported that he recovered the stolen animals from some Pacuache Indians" (114). Castañeda, who documented much more extensively the discrepancies between the Ramón and Espinosa diaries, discovered that while Ramón reported there were "about two thousand Indians, men, and women, and children, some apostates and others who had never been baptized, [who] came and kissed the hand of Ramón and the missionaries," Espinosa stated that "there were about five hundred persons of all ages and fails to mention whether they were apostates or not" (52). Herbert E. Bolton also discussed discrepancies between Ramón's and Espinosa's accounts, focusing on the inconsistencies of the distances reported among the missions during their establishment in East Texas (1908:249-276). Additional research into the paleographic discrepancies between the two accounts provided by the two leaders of the expedition should aid in rectifying some of these inconsistencies.[42]

This article has focused solely on the translations of Espinosa's diary of his 1716 expedition into Texas. The data clearly shows that neither the Tous or Hadley et al. translation is a faithful representation of the original diary. I have focused on those errors that are attributable to translators relying on unedited typescripts, or a faulty reproduction of original sources. Most scholars would agree that the original documents are the foundation of the discipline. It seems reasonable to call for interdisciplinary collaboration with regard to the transcription and translation of colonial texts. The publication of critical editions of colonial documents, based on a philologically rigorous examination of all source material, can contribute not only to rectifying inconsistencies in the historical literature pertaining to these colonial expeditions, but can also provide access to original source material, from which accurate translations can be made. Reliably edited original texts with translations can serve all scholars interested in colonial New Spain, and can contribute to our understanding of the Spanish colonization effort.

Bibliography

Bannon, John Francis. 1997. *The Spanish Borderlands Frontier: 1513-1821.* Albuquerque: U of New Mexico P.

Bolton, Herbert E., and Thomas Maitland Marshall. 1936. *The Colonization of North America 1492-1783.* New York: Macmillian Company.

---

[42] The author is currently compiling a critical edition of both diaries based on all known sources; new translations of the Ramón and Espinosa diaries will be included.

Bolton, Herbert E. The native tribes about the East Texas Missions. *Quarterly of the Texas State Historical Association,* 11, 249-276.

Bolton, Herbert E. 1996. *The Spanish Borderlands.* Albuquerque: U of New Mexico P. Reprint of New Haven: Yale UP, 1921.

Castañeda, Carlos E. 1936. *Our Catholic Heritage in Texas: 1519-1936,* vol. 2. Austin: Von Boeckmann-Jones.

Craddock, Jerry R. 1998. Juan de Oñate in Quivira. *Journal of the Southwest,* 40, 481-540.

Chipman, Donald E. 1996. Spanish Texas. In R. Tyler, D. Barnett, R. R. Barkley, P. C. Anderson, & M. F. Odintz (Eds.), *The New Handbook of Texas.* vol. 6. Austin: Texas State Historical Association.

Chipman, Donald E. 1992. *Spanish Texas 1519-1821.* Austin: U of Texas P.

Cunningham, Debbie S. 2007. Father Isidro Félix de Espinosa's diary of the new entry into the province of the Tejas, year 1716: An annotated translation. *Catholic Southwest,* 18, 9-37.

Cunningham, Debbie S. 2006. The Domingo Ramón diary of the 1716 expedition into the province of the Tejas Indians: An annotated translation. *Southwestern Historical Quarterly,* 110 (1), 38-67.

Domingo Ramón. Untitled diary. Archivo General de la Nación, México, Provincias Internas, folios 391r-401v.

Espinosa, Fray Isidro Félix de. Diario derrotero de la nueva entrada a la prov<inc>ia de los Tejas, año de 1716. Archivo General de la Nación México, Provincias Internas, vol. 181, folios 405v-411v.

Foik, Paul. 1999. Captain Domingo Ramón's Diary. *Wilderness mission.* Austin: Texas Catholic Historical Society, 129-148. Reprint of Austin: Texas Catholic Historical Society, 1933.

Foster, William C. 1995. *Spanish Expeditions into Texas 1689-1768.* Austin: U of Texas P.

John, Elizabeth. 1975. *Storms Brewed in Other Men's Worlds.* College Station: Texas A&M UP.

Hadley, Diana et al., eds. 1997. Espinosa's diary of the 1716 entrada. *The Presidio and Militia on the Northern Frontier of New Spain. A Documentary History.* Tucson: U of Arizona P.

Kessell, John L. 2002. *Spain in the Southwest. A Narrative History of Colonial New Mexico, Arizona, Texas and California.* Norman: U of Oklahoma P.

Phares, Ross. 1952. *Cavalier in the Wilderness: The Story of the Explorer and Trader Luis Juchereau de St. Denis.* Gretna, LA: Louisiana State UP.

Tous, Gabriel. 1997. Ramón expedition: Espinosa's diary of 1716. *Preparing the Way.* Austin: Texas Catholic Historical Society, 66-89. Reprint of Mid-America 12, (1930): 339-361. Page references are to the 1997 edition.;

Diana Hadley et al., eds. Espinosa's Diary of the 1716 Entrada. *The Presidio and Militia on the Northern Frontier of New Spain. A Documentary History.* Tucson: U of Arizona P, 1997. 359-397.

Weddle, Robert S. 1968. *San Juan Bautista. Gateway to Spanish Texas.* Austin: U of Texas P.

West, Elizabeth Howard. 1904. Bonilla's brief compendium of the history of Texas: 1772. *Quarterly of the Texas State Historical Association* 8, 3-78.

La expresión de la pasividad en California en el siglo XIX

Patricia Gubitosi
University of Massachusetts, Amherst

1. Introducción

El objetivo de este trabajo es investigar la expresión de la pasividad en textos epistolares y periodísticos producidos por los hispanos en California durante el siglo XIX. Es una opinión muy difundida entre los estudiosos que la voz pasiva expresada a través de la perífrasis de ser + participio se ve restringida a la lengua escrita y que es de poco uso en la lengua oral. Las siguientes citas son ilustrativas al respecto aunque, como veremos, en ningún caso hacen referencia a un estudio concreto sino más bien parecen estar justificadas por impresiones personales:

"La voz pasiva en español tiene un uso real muy restringido" (Alonso y Henríquez Ureña, 1946:108)

[es evidente] "la creciente sustitución de *se* por la pasiva refleja para la expresión del proceso pasivo" (Roca Pons, 1958:15)

"Ya hemos advertido que es muy poco frecuente en nuestra lengua —y cada vez menos— el empleo de las oraciones pasivas" (Pérez-Rioja, 1971:365)

"La forma pasiva es bastante lenta e inexpresiva, por lo que está en franco retroceso. En la lengua popular no se usa apenas, y poco en la literaria; la pasiva va desapareciendo por su lentitud, monotonía e inexpresividad" (Hernández Alonso, 1971:65)

"Las gramáticas del español señalan a menudo la equivalencia semántica entre oraciones de pasiva con *se* y oraciones de pasiva perifrástica [. . .]

123

Cuando se da esta circunstancia, es inusual que las dos construcciones se mantengan de forma paralela con el mismo *estatus*: bien una de las construcciones acaba por suplantar a la otra, o bien las construcciones 'se especializan' en contextos diferentes. La mayoría de los autores se inclinan por la primera opción al hablar de la coexistencia de la pasiva perifrástica y la pasiva con *se*: el uso extendido de esta última está contribuyendo a la desaparición de la primera" (Mendikoetxea, 1999:1669)

"En lo que atañe al uso, hay que tener en cuenta que en español la pasiva se utiliza principalmente en la lengua escrita; en el habla, en cambio, se prefieren otras construcciones" (Suñer 2003:211)

El propósito de este trabajo es verificar si estas afirmaciones tienen un correlato en el español de California del siglo XIX, antes y después de que California formara parte del territorio de los Estados Unidos en función del Tratado de Guadalupe Hidalgo firmado en 1848.

Plantear un estudio sobre un fenómeno lingüístico que tiene raíces en el pasado presenta algunos problemas metodológicos que necesitan ser considerados. El principal problema que habrá de presentarse es que no tenemos registros hablados anteriores a la invención de las cintas magnetofónicas. Como señala Labov (1994:11) la lingüística histórica es el arte de hacer el mejor uso de malos datos, dado que sólo disponemos de datos que han sido preservados de una manera fortuita y de los cuales debemos "aprender" a extraer información.

En un análisis cuyo marco teórico sea la sociolingüística histórica, como el nuestro, el texto escrito ocupará un lugar importante en nuestra investigación. A este respecto, nuestro trabajo contempla textos epistolares y periodísticos a los cuales hemos clasificado de acuerdo a un continuum de mayor o menor formalidad teniendo en cuenta, además, los diferentes registros; es decir de mayor alejamiento o cercanía con la oralidad. Las cartas personales representan una auténtica comunicación entre los individuos, pudiendo ser consideradas similares a una conversación persona a persona. Por otra parte, coincidimos con Balestra en que las cartas personales son textos "cercanos a las instancias informales de la lengua escrita, y se pueden considerar como proveedores de datos próximos al uso de la lengua oral" (2002:90). También el periódico presenta variaciones estilísticas en un continuum de mayor o menor formalidad: la publicidad representa el estilo más coloquial mientras que el ensayo se ubica en el otro extremo del continuum[1].

Butt y Benjamín señalan la preeminencia en el uso de la pasiva perifrástica sobre todo en el uso del lenguaje periodístico (1988:229). Dado que la afirmación de estos investigadores se refiere al lenguaje periodístico contemporáneo, nuestra hipótesis es que esta afirmación también es válida para el discurso periodístico histórico.

---

[1] Hemos dejado fuera de nuestro análisis las poesías por considerar al lenguaje poético artificial; esto es, que busca determinados efectos artísticos.

En este sentido el periódico, visto como una unidad estructural llena de voces diferenciadas donde cada una de ellas representa una porción de la realidad que trata de describir, y donde la no-uniformidad está planteando, precisamente, la necesidad de dar cuenta de un mundo múltiple y diverso en el cual no existe una única voz, resulta fundamental. El periódico representa, entonces, un microcosmos que reproduce el universo discursivo de la sociedad en la que está inmerso.

En el presente trabajo trataremos de demostrar que: 1) la expresión de la pasividad cobra relieve en el discurso periodístico por sobre el discurso epistolar; 2) dentro de la multiplicidad de voces que representa el universo periodístico, la pasividad es más frecuente en la *noticia* que en el ensayo, el editorial, las cartas de lectores, etc.; 3) a pesar de lo que establecen, en líneas generales, las gramáticas del español, parecería existir evidencias de que ambas formas, la pasiva con se y la pasiva perifrástica son percibidas como equivalentes por el hablante-lector-escritor de las cartas y periódicos analizados; y 4) aunque la pasiva perifrástica mantiene vigencia en el discurso periodístico, la pasiva con se aumenta la frecuencia de uso a expensas de la perífrasis pasiva incluso aún en este tipo discursivo.

2. Sobre la pasividad

La expresión de la pasividad, en español, puede expresarse a través de una frase verbal formada de ser + participio (llamada pasiva perifrástica); o a través de una construcción con se (llamada pasiva con se). Aunque muchas oraciones con se pueden tener una interpretación ambigua, las construcciones pasivas requieren siempre un agente implícito o una causa externa que no se menciona porque no interesa destacarla. Por el contrario, los verbos que representan eventos que no pueden realizarse de manera espontánea sólo admiten una interpretación pasiva: *si se construyesen caminos* (*El Clamor Público,*19 de junio de 1855) no admite más que la interpretación pasiva: "si los caminos *fuesen construidos* [por el gobierno/ por nosotros/ por alguien]".

En nuestro trabajo, por consiguiente, nos ocuparemos de las construcciones de pasiva perifrástica como de aquellas construcciones con se que expresan eventos de causalidad externa utilizadas con sentido pasivo; en ambas el sujeto gramatical se interpreta como el objeto nocional de la acción llevada a cabo por el verbo; es decir que, desde un punto de vista lógico-semántico, podemos decir que ambas expresiones son equivalentes. La diferencia esencial entre ambas es que, mientras en la pasiva perifrástica el agente puede ser indicado por una construcción encabezada por la preposición *por,* en las oraciones con se "el agente no puede, normalmente, aparecer especificado en un sintagma preposicional con *por*"[2] (Mendicoetxea 1999:1637).

---

[2] Aunque existen casos reconocidos por los gramáticos, la presencia del agente introducido por la preposición *por* en oraciones de *pasiva con se*; éstos son considerados "raros" "no-estándar", "incorrectos", etc. (Mello 1978).

Uno de los aspectos que marca la diferencia entre la pasiva perifrástica y la pasiva con se es, según Mendikoetxea (1999) "el marcado carácter intencional" que tiene la pasiva perifrástica aún cuando no aparezca el sujeto explicitado por la preposición por. De este modo, en la pasiva perifrástica se supone la presencia del sujeto concreto mientras que en la pasiva con se, éste aparece diluido; esto es lo que ha llevado a algunos estudiosos a afirmar que las oraciones con se, precisamente, tienen como objeto desfocalizar el agente (García 1975; Bogard 1999).

Sin embargo, en esta investigación hemos encontrado numerosos casos donde la presencia del agente en las oraciones con *se* pasivo demuestran, precisamente lo contrario:

1) **Se ha firmado** un decreto *por la reina* autorizando el establecimiento de telégrafos eléctricos en toda España (*El Clamor Público*, 26 de junio de 1855)

2) Su presencia en Lima **se ha considerado** *por el ministro del Ecuador* como un insulto a su gobierno (*El Clamor Público*, 3 de julio de 1855)

3) Nos informan que **habiéndose dispuesto** *por el jefe de la zona militar* la partida del 5º Regimiento (*El Monitor*, 16 de julio de 1898)

La aceptabilidad o no de construcciones de este tipo, como bien señala Sánchez López (2002), es una de las más debatidas en la bibliografía acerca de las pasivas con se. Gili Gaya (1972:73) con su clásico ejemplo *Se firmó la paz por los embajadores* considera posible la admisión del sujeto. Sin embargo, otros investigadores rechazan la gramaticalidad de este tipo de construcciones (Jordan, 1973:598), o cuestionan su valor agentivo (Cano Aguilar, 1981:281). Por su parte, Sánchez López establece:

Cuando este sintagma aparece lo hace con unas características precisas que reiteran todos los analistas. Se trata en la mayoría de los casos de un plural, muchas veces sin determinar. Cuando denota entes no animados, expresa el medio, instrumento, procedimiento o causa; si son animados, se trata generalmente de nombres colectivos o de referencia generalizada. (60)

Sin embargo, en los ejemplos presentados, los sujetos son perfectamente identificables y determinados: la reina de España en 1855, el ministro de Ecuador y el jefe de la zona militar del 5º regimiento. No como los sujetos que Sánchez López sugiere del tipo *el tribunal, la embajada, la crítica,* etc. Si bien ella señala que no son imposibles sujetos de este tipo, considera "inusual y casi agramatical la presencia de agentes específicos" (2002:60).

A nuestro juicio la aparición de este tipo de construcciones que indican un agente específico, determinado y singular es una señal que podría estar indicando la sinonimia de ambas construcciones.

Si bien es cierto que la elección de las expresiones pasivas tiene que ver con necesidades de cohesión textual (Sepúlveda Barrios 1988:31), ya que la distinción entre pasiva perifrástica y pasiva con se en lo que respecta a la posición del sujeto podría obedecer a la diferente estructura informativa de ambas construcciones (Sánchez López 2002:54), no siempre la elección de la pasiva perifrástica o de la pasiva con se obedecería a estas restricciones —que por otra parte no siempre se respetan— y, en definitiva, parecería quedar en manos del hablante / periodista.

Por otra parte, la voz pasiva es vista como un recurso apropiado del discurso periodístico permitiendo que el objeto de la noticia pase a un primer plano y se convierta así en el sujeto estructural de la oración. El agente en este tipo de oraciones puede o no ser explicitado aunque, frecuentemente, esta información es elidida de modo intencional. Este proceso de inversión sintáctica puede ser explicado pragmáticamente dado que la información que aporta el sujeto-agente encabezado por la preposición *por* es información ya conocida por los lectores[3].

Obsérvese, a modo de ejemplo, la siguiente información: *El gobierno prohibirá en lo sucesivo cualquier diversión bulliciosa los días domingos, y prenderá a cualquiera que abra un establecimiento público tal como teatro, casa de juego, etc.* Esta información sobre algo que, efectivamente, tuvo lugar en California en 1855 (y que fue conocida como *La ley del día domingo*) fue presentada al público haciendo hincapié sobre los efectos de la acción del gobierno y no sobre el gobierno mismo. Esto es, fue presentada a través de perífrasis verbales pasivas que colocan al objeto en la categoría sintáctica de sujeto dándole así relevancia informativa, según podemos ver a continuación:

4) *Toda diversión barbara ó bulliciosa* **será** en lo sucesivo **prohibida** *los días domingos; y todo individuo que abriere o ayudase a abrir en este día un establecimiento público tal como teatro, casa de juego, cuarto o salón* [. . .] **será prendido** *por un delito especificado por la ley y después de convicto* **será condenado** *a una multa. Todo individuo que comprare un billete de entrada a uno de los lugares de las diversiones enumeradas en la segunda sección de esta acta* **será** *igualmente* **castigado** *con una multa.* (*El Clamor Público*, 19 de junio de 1855)

3. Metodología

Nuestro trabajo está enmarcado dentro de la sociolingüística histórica y nuestra principal preocupación será describir la variación que los distintos modos de expresar la pasividad tienen lugar en el español de California del siglo

---

3 Sobre los efectos que la *pasivización* tiene en el manejo de la información, puede consultarse Gregory Ward and Betty J. Birner "Discourse and information Structure", p. 130-131.

XIX. En este sentido, nuestra *variable* será la voz pasiva realizada a través de dos *variantes*: la frase verbal pasiva y la pasiva con se. Una tercera forma es contemplada en nuestro análisis: el participio perfecto pasivo que, lejos de ser usado con valor adjetival, aparece con verdadero valor pasivo acompañado siempre de un agente encabezado por la preposición *por*[4]. En todos estos casos, el valor verbal aparece reforzado por la posición que ocupa el participio que siempre va pospuesto al sustantivo al que acompaña.

Sin embargo, por tratarse de una variable sintáctica es necesario considerar los siguientes problemas a resolver[5]:

a) La variable sintáctica tiene, como en nuestro caso, sólo dos variantes; a diferencia de la variable fonológica que, casi siempre, tiene por lo menos tres variantes.

b) La variación sintáctica es más difícil de cuantificar debido a la poca frecuencia en que se dan los contextos de ocurrencia de una determinada variante.

c) Los contextos de ocurrencia de una variable sintáctica son más difíciles de determinar y de definir.

Según Silva Corvalán (2001:135), en el estudio de la variación sintáctica es importante: tomar como punto de partida variantes cuya sinonimia lógica no es cuestionable y cuya estructura sintáctica o morfosintáctica (o léxica, si es ésta la variación en estudio) varía solamente con respecto al fenómeno considerado variable. La autora considera, entonces, una *variable sintáctica* a "dos o más realizaciones de un elemento común que dicen lo mismo, equivalentes a un elemento común que dice lo mismo". En otras palabras, el elemento común, la *variable sintáctica*, **fuera de todo contexto discursivo** no altera su equivalencia referencial.

Así, para nosotros los ejemplos siguientes son estructuras sinónimas pues el significado que comunican es el mismo: "X recibe **arresto + acusación**"; aunque las estructuras elegidas difieren en ambas oraciones: mientras en 5) la primera acción está expresada por una construcción de pasiva perifrástica, y la segunda con una pasiva con *se*; en 6) aparecen dos estructuras perifrásticas de pasado. Por otra parte, en ninguno de los ejemplos se establece quién es el que actúa sobre X; es decir quién es el agente que arresta y acusa:

---

[4] Aunque esta forma no está en abierta competencia con las otras dos, dado que no puede aparecer como cláusula independiente consideramos necesario, sin embargo, tabularla junto con las otras para ver si su uso disminuye o aumenta; y si este cambio en su frecuencia está ligado, o no, al aumento o disminución de alguna de las dos formas restantes que son objeto de este estudio.

[5] En los problemas que surgen al analizar una variable sintáctica seguimos a Silva Corvalán (2001: 129-130).

5) Frank Guirado **fue arrestado** esta semana. **Se** le **acusa** de haberse robado varios pares de zapatos de una tienda" (*La Unión*, 9 de enero de 1897)

6) Mr. Pierr Gance **fue arrestado** y **acusado** de haber publicado un artículo criminal" (*El Monitor*, 13 de agosto de 1898)

En ese sentido, podemos considerar a nuestras variantes como variantes válidas de ser analizadas puesto que ambas aluden a un mismo objeto nocional constituido en sujeto estructural tanto de la pasiva con se, como de la pasiva perifrástica. Sin embargo, nuestra tarea exigirá un cuidadoso análisis de cada uno de los contextos de ocurrencia para verificar si existen, por el contrario, diferencias de significado más allá del nivel lógico o referencial; es decir, si existen diferencias de matices entre ambas expresiones que tengan que ver con la "especialización" de una forma u otra en determinados contextos. Aunque, como bien señala Menxicoetxea "la especialización puede ser un paso previo a la desaparición, al limitarse una de las construcciones a contextos muy restringidos, que son gradualmente invadidos por la otra construcción, y esto podría ser lo que está ocurriendo en el español actual" (1999:1669).

Nos proponemos, entonces, investigar cuál es el grado de variación existente entre ambas formas y si es cierto que existe una especificación de ellas que esté preanunciando, como Mendicoetxea señala, su desaparición.

Nuestro corpus está integrado por 113 cartas escritas por californios (30 cartas escritas entre 1814 y 1833, período previo a la guerra mexicano-estadounidense; y 83 cartas escritas en los años posteriores a la guerra); y cinco periódicos publicados en la ciudad de Los Ángeles entre 1855 y 1898, a fin de evaluar si el diferente tipo textual utilizado (*discurso epistolar* vs. *discurso periodístico*) resulta sensible a la utilización de expresiones pasivas por parte de los hablantes.

El corpus (tanto periodístico como epistolar) fue dividido en cuatro etapas diferentes con el objeto de evaluar si las condiciones socio-históricas resultantes del contacto lingüístico con el inglés modificaban, o no, los resultados obtenidos.

Un obstáculo importante con el que nos enfrentamos en una investigación de tipo histórico es la conservación de las fuentes; no todos los periódicos publicados en ese período se han conservado; y, más aún, aquellos que se conservaron, no siempre lo han hecho en óptimas condiciones.

En el análisis se han tenido en cuenta además del período histórico, el género del artículo estudiado, y la presencia o no del agente.

Nuestro análisis se basa en la lectura de:

1) *El Clamor Público*: ediciones del 19 de junio al 21 de agosto de 1855.

2) *El Aguacero*: ediciones del 24 de marzo al 31 de marzo de 1878.

3) *El Demócrata*: ediciones del 14 de octubre al 1 de noviembre de 1882.

4) *La Unión*: ediciones del 9 de enero al 15 de mayo de 1897.

5) *El Monitor*: ediciones del 9 de julio al 13 de agosto de 1898.

Además, se analizaron 113 cartas de las familias Guerra, Amador, y de María Amparo Ruiz de Burton (30 anteriores a 1850, y 83 posteriores a dicha fecha).

4. Análisis

4.1. Análisis del discurso epistolar

El análisis de los datos muestra, en primer lugar, que la presencia de expresiones pasivas en el discurso epistolar no es significativa. En las ochenta y tres cartas analizadas que corresponden al período posterior a 1848 sólo encontramos 12 expresiones pasivas: 6 formas pasivas que utilizan el se, 5 pasivas perifrásticas y sólo un participio pasivo con la presencia del agente[6]. Pero si consideramos el período anterior, las cifras se tornan sumamente significativas pues muestran una considerable reducción en el uso escrito de la voz pasiva, ya sea la forma perifrástica o la pasiva con se[7], a la vez que muestran un incremento en el uso del se respecto de la pasiva perifrástica, según se puede observar en la Tabla 1:

Períodos	Cantidad de cartas	Pasiva con se		Pasiva Perifrástica		Participio		Total de formas
Total General	**113**	**9**	**(35%)**	**12**	**(46%)**	**5**	**(19%)**	**26 = 100%**
Previo: 1814-1833	30	3	(21%)	7	(50%)	4	(29%)	14 = 100%
1º período: 1852-1866	36	3	(37%)	4	(50%)	1	(13%)	8 = 100%
2º y 3º período: 1870-1907	47	3	(75%)	1	(25%)	0		4 = 100%

Tabla 1. Uso de expresiones pasivas en el discurso epistolar.

Por otra parte, a pesar de las pocas formas encontradas, es posible observar cómo la pasiva con se supera, en la preferencia de los hablantes, el uso de la pasiva perifrástica. La escasa cantidad de formas encontradas (sólo 4 en el segundo y tercer período) puede deberse al hecho de que las cartas consideradas en este período son cartas personales que corresponden a un estilo informal, próximo a la lengua oral; y, considerando que el español es una lengua activa, no es extraño que las expresiones pasivas tengan una frecuencia de uso tan baja

---

[6] Bosque (1991) considera, en su capítulo sobre el adjetivo y el verbo, que el participio pierde su característica adjetival cuando aparece pospuesto a él la preposición *por* seguida de agente, transformándose en una construcción pasiva con el verbo auxiliar elidido.

[7] Esta confrontación no ha sido posible en el discurso periodístico porque no tenemos registros de periódicos anteriores a 1855.

en este tipo de texto. Lo interesante es el salto que alcanza la pasiva con se en el último período, lo que puede ser mejor observado en el Gráfico 1 donde se muestra el descenso que manifiesta la pasiva perifrástica y las expresiones de participio pasivo.

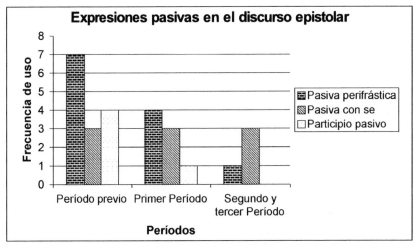

Gráfico 1. *Frecuencia de expresiones pasivas en el discurso epistolar.*

4.2. Análisis del discurso periodístico

El análisis del discurso periodístico muestra, en cambio, una frecuencia de uso mayor que el discurso epistolar; en este tipo de discurso la presencia de la pasividad es significativa. La siguiente tabla muestra la distribución del corpus obtenido:

Nombre del periódico	Año	Período	Total de expresiones pasivas estudiadas
El Clamor Público	1855	Primer	305
El Aguacero	1878	Segundo	11
El Demócrata	1882	Segundo	107
La Unión	1897	Tercer	41
El Monitor	1898	Tercer	71
Total del corpus			535

Tabla 2. *Distribución del corpus.*

Pero lo interesante de los datos analizados es que mientras el uso de participio pasivo con la construcción encabezada por la preposición *por* +

agente se mantiene estable, los datos muestran un descenso importante de la pasiva perifrástica según se puede observar en la Tabla 3:

Período	Pasiva con se		Pasiva Perifrástica		Participio Pasado		Total de formas	
1º Período	72	23.62%	203	66.55%	30	9.83%	305	100%
2º Período	39	32.76%	705	8.82%	10	8.42%	119	100%
3º Período	49	43.75%	53	47.33%	10	8.92%	112	100%

Tabla 3. Tipo de expresiones pasivas por períodos.

Por otra parte, una de las razones que se esgrimen en la preferencia por la utilización de una u otra variable es la posibilidad que tiene el hablante de hacer explícito o no el agente. Sin embargo, la presencia del mismo no se ve obstaculizada por la pasiva con se, según se observa en los ejemplos presentados donde el agente (el sujeto de la acción) se hace expreso a través de la preposición *por*. La siguiente tabla muestra que su incremento a lo largo de los años se da de manera paralela al descenso en la frecuencia de aparición del agente expreso en la pasiva perifrástica:

Período	Pasiva con se		Pasiva Perifrástica		Total de formas	
	Total	Agente Expreso[8]	Total	Agente Expreso		
1º Período	72 (23.62%)	6 (1.96%)	203 (66.55%)	65 (21.31%)	305	100%
2º Período	39 (32.76%)	2 (1,68%)	70 (58.82%)	15 (12.60%)	119	100%
3º Período	49 (43.75%)	3 (2,67%)	53 (47.33%)	9 (8.03%)	112	100%

Tabla 4. Tabla de aparición del agente expreso[9].

Estas cifras de aparición de sujeto expreso con la pasiva con se, a las que la gramática tradicional ha calificado como "sub-estándar", son las que llevan a la investigadora Sheila Corrigan de Fazio a declarar que "the use of *por* plus agent with the *se*-passive construction is not only not unheard of, but may well be increasing in usage" (1971:95).

Resulta significativo, pues, que el "marcado carácter intencional" que Mendicoetxea señala como característico de la pasiva perifrástica, pareciera quedar desdibujado en el corpus estudiado donde tanto la pasiva perifrástica como la pasiva con se son vistas como equivalentes. Obsérvense los siguientes ejemplos de *El Clamor Público*, donde la pasividad del mismo verbo *vender* se manifiesta de diferentes formas:

---

[8] El porcentaje está calculado sobre el total de formas. Este número, obviamente, se elevaría si consideráramos como totalidad porcentual sólo la cantidad de formas con *se*.

[9] El participio pasivo no está en esta tabla pues todas sus apariciones están acompañadas del agente expreso antecedido por la preposición *por*.

7) Los medicamentos de Holloway **son** constantemente **vendidos** en todo el imperio Otomano (26 de junio de 1855)

8) El martes próximo a las 10 de la mañana **se venderá** en pública subasta toda la tienda de joyerías, muebles, &c. del señor R. Josephi (26 de junio de 1855)

9) El viernes pasado **se vendieron** <u>por el sheriff</u> setenta y cinco cabezas de ganado entre chicas y grandes a cinco pesos cada una (26 de junio de 1855)

Mientras en el primer ejemplo la pasividad se expresa a través de la pasiva perifrástica quedando diluido el agente que realiza la venta [el Dr. Holloway es el encargado de fabricar los medicamentos, pero <u>no es el agente de venta de los mismos</u>]; en el segundo ejemplo, la pasiva resulta casi impersonal siendo el agente un desconocido que podría ser reemplazado por un pronombre indefinido: "toda la tienda del señor Josephi será vendida por *alguien*". El tercer ejemplo, sin embargo, la impersonalidad que podría suponer la tercera persona plural más el se es completamente desambiguada al personalizarse la acción a través del agente expreso <u>por el sheriff</u>. El hablante-escritor encargado de redactar la noticia siente esta frase como una clara equivalencia de "setenta y cinco cabezas de ganado **fueron vendidas** el viernes pasado <u>por el sheriff</u>".

Por otra parte, en otros ejemplos, parecería también desdibujarse la diferencia entre las construcciones pasivas y las construcciones medias, absorbiendo el pronombre se un significado totalmente pasivo. Obsérvese las siguientes ocurrencias del verbo *embarcar* tomados de *El Monitor*:

10) En el buque transporte San Louis **ha sido embarcado** el Almirante Cervera y algunos oficiales los cuales van con destino a Nueva York (9 de julio de 1898)

11) El general Miles y un buen número de cañones **se embarcaron** en el transporte Yabe (23 de julio de 1898)

12) Por fin parece que el Septimo Regimiento de Los Angeles, **se embarcará** con rumbo a Manila proximamente (13 de agosto de 1898)

Resulta claro en estos ejemplos que la diferencia entre *embarcarse* y *ser embarcado* aparece desdibujada. En el primer ejemplo, parecería que el Almirante Cervera no subió al buque por propia voluntad, sino que "fue subido"; por otra parte, en el segundo ejemplo se "dota" de voluntad a los cañones, los cuales "se embarcaron" junto con el general Miles.

Obsérvese, por otra parte, la siguiente utilización de *recogerse;* no como verbo de significación media sino con un uso plenamente pasivo:

13) Con motivo del ataque que las columnas americanas dio a los españoles en las inmediaciones de Santiago de Cuba en el cual fueron repulsadas las columnas americanas **se han recogido** 2000 soldados entre muertos y heridos (*El Monitor*, 9 de julio de 1898)

Respecto de cuál es el género periodístico que resulta favorecido por la pasividad; la *noticia* ocupa, ampliamente, el primer lugar, según se puede observar en la tabla 5[10]. Esto parecería indicar que la selección de la expresión de la pasividad tiene que ver con una necesidad metadiscursiva de permitir el flujo de la información priorizando lo *nuevo* por sobre lo *dado* (Hawad: 2004).

Periódico	Noticia		Editorial		Ensayo		Cartas al editor		Publicidad		Total de artículos	
El Clamor Público 1855	217	76.14%	19	6.67%	28	9.82%	10	3.51%	11	3.86%	285	100%
El Aguacero 1878	8	72.73%	—	—	—	—	—	—	3	27.27%	11	100%
El Demócrata 1882	50	46.29%	23	21.29%	14	12.97%	—	—	21	19.45%	108	100%
La Unión 1897	14	35.89%	—	—	15	38.47%	9	17.95%	3	7.69%	39	100%
El Monitor 1898	47	67.14%	1	1.43%	5	7.15%	3	4.28%	14	20.00%	70	100%

Tabla 5. Aparición de expresiones pasivas de acuerdo al género periodístico.

Sin embargo, a pesar de esta necesidad metadiscursiva los siguientes gráficos muestran un abrupto descenso en el uso de la pasiva perifrástica no sólo en lo que respecta al discurso periodístico en general (Gráfico 2) sino, en particular, al género periodístico por excelencia, la noticia, (Gráfico 3).

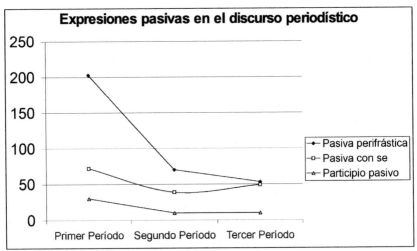

Gráfico 2. Discurso periodístico y pasividad.

---

[10] La única excepción es la que muestra el periódico *La Unión* donde las expresiones pasivas aparecen en los ensayos en una proporción levemente superior a las noticias.

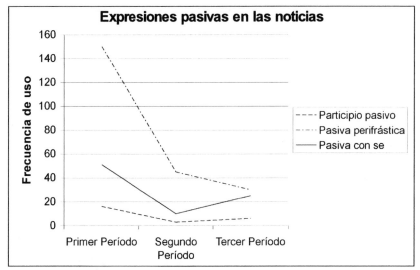

Gráfico 3. La noticia y la pasividad.

5. Conclusiones

A pesar de ser éste un estudio preliminar que amerita una mayor profundización en algunos aspectos, creemos sin embargo que hay indicios suficientes para pensar que efectivamente un cambio en la expresión de la pasividad estaría ocurriendo en el español de California donde la pasiva perifrástica estaría sufriendo un retroceso en beneficio de la pasiva con se.

Por otra parte, si bien la pasiva perifrástica resulta relevante en el discurso periodístico puesto que es funcional al manejo informativo propio de este tipo discursivo, aún en las noticias —género periodístico por excelencia— es posible observar un retroceso de la frase verbal pasiva en beneficio de la pasiva con se. Este retroceso que es más evidente en el discurso epistolar nos lleva a coincidir con Mendicoetxea (1999) quien afirma que este cambio es sentido con mucha más fuerza en la lengua oral.

Además, según hemos visto, y esto tal vez sea lo más importante, existen indicios que parecerían corroborar la equivalencia entre ambas expresiones por parte de los hablantes; entre ellos el más importante es, sin duda, el incremento en la presencia del agente introducido por un sintagma encabezado por la preposición *por*. Esto estaría corroborando las impresiones de Corrigan de Fazio (1971) en el sentido de que el uso del agente con la pasiva con se no sólo no es desconocido sino que ha ido incrementándose en el español del período estudiado.

136 ❖ ❖ ❖ ❖ ❖ ❖ ❖ ❖ ❖ ❖ *Patricia Gubitosi*

Referencias:

Alonso, Amado & Pedro Henríquez Ureña. 1946. *Gramática de la lengua castellana*. Buenos Aires: Losada.

Balestra, Alejandra. 2002. *Del futuro morfológico al perifrástico. Un cambio morfosintáctico en español de California, 1800-1930*. Unpublished doctoral dissertation, University of Houston.

Biner, B. & G. Ward. 2001. Discourse and information structure. In D. Schiffrin, D. Tanner, & H. Hamilton (Eds.). *The Handbook of Discourse Analysis* (pp. 119-137). Oxford: Blackwell.

Bogard, S. 1999. Construcciones antipasivas en español. *Nueva Revista de Filología Hispánica*, vol. 47.

Bosque, I. 1991. *Las categorías gramaticales. Relaciones y diferencias*. Madrid: Editorial Síntesis.

Butt, J. & C. Benjamin. 1988. *A New Reference Grammar of Modern Spanish*. Londres: Arnold.

Cano Aguilar, Rafael. 1981. *Estructuras sintácticas transitivas en el español actual*. Madrid: Gredos.

Corrigan de Fazio, Sheila. 1971. *Separating the uses of* se. Unpublished doctoral dissertation, Georgetown University.

García, Erica. 1975. *The Role of Theory in Linguistic Analysis: The Spanish Pronoun System*. Amsterdam: North Holland Publishing Company.

Gili Gaya, Samuel. 1972. *Curso superior de sintaxis española*. 10ª edición. Madrid: Bibliograf.

Hawad, F. 2004. Verb voice and text informational flow. *DELTA*, 20:1, 97-121.

Hernández Alonso, César. 1971. *Sintaxis española*. 3ª edición. Valladolid.

Jordan, Pablo. 1973. La forma "se" como sujeto indefinido en español. *Hispania*, 56-3. 597-603.

Labov, W. 1994. *Principles of Linguistic Change. Internal factors*. Vol. 20. Oxford and Cambridge, MA: Blackwell.

Mello, G. 1978. On the use of "por" plus agent with "se" construction. *Hispania*, 61.2, 323-327.

Mendikoetxea, Amaya. 1999. Construcciones con *se*: Medias, pasivas e impersonales. En Ignacio Bosque & Violeta Demonte (Eds.), *Gramática descriptiva de la lengua española*; vol. 2, 1631-1723. Madrid: Espasa Calpe.

Pérez-Rioja, José A. 1971. *Gramática de la lengua española*. 6ª edición. Madrid: Tecnos.

Roca Pons, José. 1958. *Estudios sobre perífrasis verbales del español*. Anejo de la *Revista de Filología Española*. Madrid.

Sánchez López, Cristina. 2002. Las construcciones con *se*. Estado de la cuestión. En Cristina Sánchez López (Ed.), *Las construcciones con se* (pp. 18-163). Madrid: Visor Libros.

Sepúlveda Barrios, Félix. 1988. *La voz pasiva en el español del siglo XVII*. Madrid: Gredos.

Silva-Corvalán Carmen. 2001. *Sociolingüística y pragmática del español*. Washington D.C: Georgetown UP.

Suñer, Margarita. 2003. Las pasivas con *se* impersonal y la legitimación de las categorías vacías. En Cristina Sánchez López (Ed.), *Las construcciones con se* (pp. 209-234). Madrid: Visor Libros.

Fuentes documentales:

El Aguacero. 1878 University of Houston: *Recovering the US Hispanic Literary Heritage Project.*

El Amigo del Pueblo. 1861. University of Houston: *Recovering the US Hispanic Literary Heritage Project.*

El Clamor Público. 1855. University of Houston: *Recovering the US Hispanic Literary Heritage Project.*

El Correo Mexicano. 1917. University of Houston: *Recovering the US Hispanic Literary Heritage Project.*

El Demócrata. 1882. University of Houston: *Recovering the US Hispanic Literary Heritage Project.*

El Monitor. 1898. University of Houston: *Recovering the US Hispanic Literary Heritage Project.*

La Opinión. 1941. University of Massachusetts, Amherst.

La Prensa. 1920. University of Houston: *Recovering the US Hispanic Literary Heritage Project.*

La Unión. 1897. University of Houston: *Recovering the US Hispanic Literary Heritage Project.*

Language Wars on the Texas Frontier

Glenn Martínez
University of Texas Pan American

One would expect to find some sort of concerted effort on the part of the Mexican American people to retain their language, some sort of resistance to adopting English, some sort of cultural pride. Or, one would expect to find that the English-speaking dominant group, in its wisdom, had recognized the values inherent in the preservation of the Spanish language and had instituted programs to that end. That is, one would expect to find some laudable and positive cause for the persistence of this beautiful and important language, some wise head, institution, or policy that has conserved this natural cultural resource. Sad as it is to say, the major causal factor is none of these but one which involves factors far less noble, far less intelligent, and much more negative than positive. The conservation of the heritage of the Spanish language is an eloquent illustration that it is indeed an ill wind that does not blow somebody some good! (Sánchez 1970:25)

George I. Sánchez's observations on the survival of the Spanish language in the United States Southwest imbues language maintenance among Mexican Americans with a sense of arbitrary and inadvertent design. Even though I understand language maintenance as depending fundamentally on the interplay and interaction of structural variables within society, I also understand it, at a more basic level, as the result of individual human choice. I take it as axiomatic that individuals make rational and calculated choices with respect to their language behavior. While social structure may in many ways influence and underpin our particular political choices, it does not necessarily determine them. As rational human agents, we are capable of acting on structure, of changing it, of transforming it, of molding and fashioning it as we see fit. At the same time, however, as members of an aggregate of rational human agents who sustain and manipulate power relations through social structure, structure is also capable of acting on us, the agents, of changing us, of transforming us, of molding and fashioning us as it sees fit. The view of language maintenance and shift presented in this chapter attempts to incorporate the dialectics of structure and agency into a holistic view of language history. I recognize that certain structural variables prevalent in society shape the life of a language through the experience of its speakers, and I view these structural variables as important elements of language maintenance and language shift. At the same time, however, I also recognize that rational human agents evaluate these structural variables in conjunction with the languages, cultures, and speakers that they privilege and subordinate. These evaluations converge on ideological formations consisting of ideas, attitudes, and opinions about language; through these ideological formations rational human agents are capable of sustaining or modifying the linguistic behaviors that the structural variables favor.

Language and Power

Whether a minority language thrives or ceases to exist is, at least implicitly, the result of the negotiation of and struggle over societal power between dominating and dominated groups. Power, its definition, and its distribution in society at large determine whether and in what contexts a language will be used. Power also ascribes certain social meaning to those who choose to use one language or the other. Language maintenance and shift, therefore, is not precisely the result of the chance convergence of societal factors. It is not an evolutionary roll of the dice that determines whether or not a language will survive. Rational human beings, overtly or covertly, explicitly or implicitly, express, transmit, and act upon attitudes and opinions about language use that fashion, sustain, and assign it its social meaning. Dorian conveys this idea succinctly stating that "languages have the standing that their speakers have. If the people who speak a language have power and prestige, the language they speak will enjoy high prestige as well. If the people who speak a language have little power and prestige, their language is unlikely to be well thought of" (1998:3-4). Given the intimate connection between the prestige and power of language and the prestige and power of its speakers, I assume that human agents make rational decisions about safeguarding their own language and devaluing that of others in the same way that they make rational decisions about safeguarding their own power and devaluing that of others. In fact, I would argue that decisions made about language are little more than elaborated expressions of more fundamental decisions made about power. Language ideology, in this way, is steeped in questions of power. Silverstein defines language ideology as "a set of beliefs about language articulated by users as a rationalization or justification of perceived language structure and use" (1979:193). In the present discussion, I will adopt this definition, but I will re-orient it to underscore the inextricable ties between language ideology and the propagation and perpetuation of power. It is well known that language ideologies oftentimes fly in the face of language facts. Bourdieu, for instance, refers to this disparity pointing out the misalignments of the "principles of production" and the "principles of evaluation" among the petit bourgeois (1991:83-84). Beliefs about language, therefore, are not restricted to "perceived language structure and use" but they also extend to idealized notions of language structure and use. In my view, then, language ideologies are not simply beliefs about the way things are, they are also beliefs about the way things ought to be. Language ideologies, in this sense, are also language impositions that correspond with the distribution and imposition of power in society.

Language is both an instrument and an institution of power. It is an instrument of power inasmuch as it used to maintain asymmetrical power relations among different social groups. It is an institution of power insofar as it symbolically separates these conflicting social groups. The imposition of power in society feeds on both the institutional and instrumental dimensions of language and power. Bourdieu underscores these inner workings of language and power:

> In order for one mode of expression among others (a particular language in the case of bilingualism, a particular use of language in the case of a society divided into classes) to impose itself as the only legitimate one, the linguistic market has to be unified and the different dialects (of class, region, or ethnic group) have to be measured practically against the legitimate language or usage. Integration into a single 'linguistic community', which is a product of political domination that is endlessly reproduced by institutions capable of imposing universal recognition of the dominant language is the condition for the establishment of relations of linguistic domination. (1991:45-46)

For one linguistic system to attain dominance, according to Bourdieu, other coexistent and competing linguistic systems must be devalued and subordinated.

In connection with Bourdieu's insights, Lippi-Green (1997) proposes a concise model of language subordination. The model hinges on the convergence of ideas and beliefs about language including linguistic mystification, language trivialization, and language-based discrimination. Linguistic mystification is an idea that places language knowledge and authority on a level above communicative functionality. According to this idea, one is not an authority in his or her language simply by virtue of speaking it. True expertise in language use is attained only through expert guidance. The mystified notion of language, then, restricts language authority to an elite group of so-called educated persons. This group, by virtue of its self-proclaimed expertise and authority in language, is capable of determining whose language is correct and whose is incorrect, whose is coarse and whose is refined, whose is logical and whose is illogical. The authority built up in linguistic mystification, then, allows certain elites to segment groups of speakers according to their particular varieties of speech and in this way to, implicitly, separate themselves from all of them. Language trivialization refers to the use of these linguistic differences in stereotyping the subordinate group. Language-based discrimination is also connected with mystification inasmuch as language authorities are the ones who determine the status of the subordinate language in society. Mystification, trivialization, and discrimination together reflect the distribution of power in society through the medium of language.

Fairclough (1989) identifies two interfaces of language and power in society: power in discourse and power behind discourse. Power in discourse is "concerned with discourse as a place where relations of power are actually exercised and enacted" (Fairclough 1989:43). Power behind discourse is concerned with how types of discourse are "themselves shaped and constituted by relations of power" (Fairclough 1989:43). Lippi-Green's model accounts for these interfaces by making a clear distinction between language beliefs and their articulation. Uniform language ideologies may be articulated either implicitly (power in discourse) or explicitly (power behind discourse). In sum, then, Lippi-Green's model of linguistic subordination may be described as a set of beliefs about language articulated in and behind discourse in order to maintain and perpetuate asymmetrical power relations.

But even while language ideologies converge in and behind discourse in order to maintain and perpetuate uneven power relations, I recognize that power and positions of power are constantly challenged and, in connection with this, that language ideologies tend to pattern both offensively and defensively. As Fairclough explains, "power, whether it be 'in' or 'behind' discourse, is never definitively held by any one person or social grouping, because power can be won and exercised only in and through social struggles in which it may also be lost" (1989:43). Because power is attained only through social struggle, agents actively play out power roles and vie for discursive subject positions on a daily basis. The language ideologies that promote linguistic subordination, therefore, face the potential danger of being challenged and defeated through social struggle every time they are expressed. Members of the powerful group must ensure the vitality of their language ideologies through coercion and consent. Coercion has often been identified with overt, violent struggle (Fairclough 1995:219;

1989:3-4) but it need not be played out with physical force. Discourse can also be an instrument of coercion. Language can incite future violence and it can recall and relive past instances of violence. Whether it be oriented towards the future or the past, coercive discourse is meant to discount and subvert the authority and integrity of the minority language community. Consent refers to the discourse that makes language ideologies seem like plain old common sense. It encompasses the discourse that attempts to convince minority language speakers that in order to "get ahead in life" they must speak the dominant language and accept dominant cultural values. It also implicitly and explicitly devalues the minority tongue as a coarse and rudimentary mode of human expression. Consensual and coercive discourse, thus work hand in hand towards one ultimate end, which is to undermine the validity and status of the minority tongue.

In this chapter, I will discuss how language ideology was used to legitimize and effectuate the linguistic subordination of Spanish speakers in Texas during the nineteenth century. I will apply Lippi-Green's model of language subordination to the discourse of Euro-American newcomers and Tejano old timers in South Texas during these often turbulent times. My sources include letters, diaries, travel journals, autobiographical notes, and newspaper editorials. These sources highlight the inter-cultural encounters of Anglos and Mexicans on the Texas frontier, and they evince the emergence of a plethora of negative attitudes about Tejanos. As noted by De León, Anglo attitudes towards Mexicans in the nineteenth century "buttressed the idea that Americans were of superior stock and Tejanos were not, rationalized an elevated place for whites and a subservient one for Mexicans, and justified the notion that Mexican work should be for the good of white society" (1983:103). Embedded in escalating land and labor conflicts, these attitudes resulted in ethnically defined relations of societal power. In this chapter, then, I hope to extend De León's analysis by focusing on the role of language in the construction of power relations in South Texas. I concentrate on explicit and implicit statements about language and show how these attitudes converged on a language ideology that created a privileged space for English and a subordinate one for Spanish and its speakers. At the same time, however, I seek to show how Tejanos rejected this subordination. So, I will also discuss the ways in which Tejanos did, in fact, challenge the dominant language ideologies and struggled to preserve a legitimate space for their own language and culture.

Power and Peace in the South Texas Borderlands

On the eve of victory in the U.S.-Mexico War of 1848, Dr. Ashbel Smith, former Secretary of State of the Texas Republic, proclaimed: "the war in which we are now engaged is comparatively a small matter, except as hastening and preluding to the rivalship of peace" (Montejano 1987:24). On the one hand, Dr. Smith was offering a clear view of the future of Anglo-Tejano relations in Texas. He was, in one fell swoop, proclaiming the Anglo's God given right to the land west of the Mississippi and recognizing the bitterness of those from whom the land was to be taken. On the other hand, however, Dr. Smith was simply echoing the frustrations of a twenty-eight-year-old dispute over land and ethnolinguistic dominance. The "rivalship of peace" began in 1820 as Anglos and Tejanos positioned themselves both in relation to the land and in relation to each other. "Manifest Destiny," in Dr. Smith's eyes, was to be attained not so much by means of military conquest but rather by way of cultural and linguistic hegemony. Only when the English language and Anglo culture and values impregnated and flavored the Texas landscape would manifest destiny be irrevocable. Dr. Smith's statement, in this sense, was more of a warning than a prediction. He was telling his fellow Texans not to be fooled by the illusion of a military victory, and he was calling on them to continue in the struggle to make Texas an Anglo American homeland.

Montejano discusses at great length some of the ways in which this struggle was perpetuated in the post-war years. He argues that the military victory of Anglo Texans set the parameters and fashioned the boundaries for a structure of peace in Texas:

> By "peace structure" I refer to a general postwar arrangement that allows the victors to maintain law and order without the constant use of force. The concept focuses on the manner in which the victors are able to exercise and establish authority over the defeated. In the Texas-Mexico region, such a peace structure was characterized by two major aspects: one, the subordination of Mexicans to Anglos in matters of politics and authority and two, the accommodation between new and old elites. (1987:34)

While the later process of accommodation was carried out through more or less peaceful means such as intermarriage and land loss due to legal trickery or the invisible hand of the market, the former process of subordination seems to have been a continuation of the violence. It was a violence, however, that was effectuated in the theater of discourse rather than on the battlefield. Limón characterizes the move towards a more discursively driven violence in Texas as a shift from a war of maneuver to a war of position, "The war of position had begun in South Texas. In Gramsci's terms, such a phase of struggle begins when one side has achieved nearly complete dominance, making open maneuver nearly impossible" (1994:41).

The "war of position" is fundamentally discursive and is thus played out on the battlefield of signs and symbols. Battles are won by exerting social significance on empirical categories associated with one of the groups. When the in group succeeds in imbuing an out group characteristic such as race, language, religion, or culture with negative social meaning, the possibility of maneuver of members of the out group within in group circles becomes severely constrained. In South Texas, the concept of "race" was clearly a strategic linchpin in the Anglo's war of position against Tejanos. Dr. Ashbel Smith clearly identified "race" as the most powerful weapon in the Anglo Texan arsenal when he stated, "the two races, the American distinctively so called, and the Spanish Americans or Mexicans, are now brought by the war into inseparable contact. No treaties can henceforth dissever them; and the inferior must give way before the superior race" (Montejano 1987:14). The differences between opposing sides in the war of position were racially defined, and race itself was imbued with very specific social meanings. The construct of race itself suggests a reification and rationalization of social difference. Following Omi and Winant, I understand race as

> a concept which signifies and symbolizes social conflicts and interests by referring to different types of human bodies. Although the concept of race invokes biologically based human characteristics (so-called "phenotypes"), selection of these particular human features for purposes of racial signification is always and necessarily a social and historical process . . . indeed, the categories employed to differentiate among human groups along racial lines reveal themselves, upon serious examination, to be at best imprecise, and at worst completely arbitrary. (1994:55)

Looking at race in this way allows for a more transparent understanding of "racial formation" or "racialization" as a historically grounded process in the war of position. Racial formation among Mexicans in the Southwest has been treated extensively in the literature (Almaguer 1994; De León 1983; Garza-Falcón 1998; Limón 1994; Montejano 1987). According to De León, race was construed in nineteenth century Texas in terms of both physical and moral characteristics: Whites were hard-working and Mexicans were lazy, Whites were morally upright and Mexicans were depraved, Whites were trustworthy and Mexicans were deceptive, etc. Viktor Bracht clearly demonstrated this view in his 1848 traveler's guide for German newcomers:

> A passion for gambling is found almost nowhere except among the Mexicans, who are addicted to it in a high degree. Ordinarily the Mexicans are just as polite and agreeable as they could be expected to be. However, many of them are contemptible, untrustworthy, and deceptive. There are, of

course, some most worthy exceptions among them, just as one finds among honorable Americans exceptions of an opposite character—swindlers, rogues, idlers, drunkards, gamblers, and adventurers of various sorts commonly called loafers. Happily, this class of people has decreased every year, and it may be hoped that soon they will have vanished from Texas entirely. The prosperous days for these vagabonds are over, and the Rio Grande, the interior of Mexico and California have greater attraction for them than Texas. (1931:68)

The racial overtones in Bracht's statement betray his contrived sense of social equality. It is an adept sleight of hand that leads one to interpret the "vagabonds" as the deviate Anglo newcomers; however, upon closer reading of the passage, we note that the word "vagabonds" refers to both the deviate Anglo and the average Mexican. Of course, during the Gold Rush, California was the choice destination of unscrupulous Anglos, but the Rio Grande Valley and the interior of Mexico were the choice destinations of vanquished and landless Mexicans. Bracht ultimately constructs his racialized discourse by assigning positive social meaning to Americans in general and to small group of uncommon Mexicans and negative social meaning to Mexicans in general and to a small group of uncommon Americans.

Language plays a central role in racial formation. The use of language difference in order to propagate and perpetuate differential power relations in society has been alternately referred to as "linguicism" and "linguistic imperialism" (Skutnabb-Kangas and Phillipson 1995; Phillipson 1992). As noted by Canagarajah, however, in cases of social and cultural subordination, linguistic imperialism is at the service of both those who racialize and those who are being racialized. On the one hand, language is used by the racializing group in order to produce and reproduce ideologies and policies that are detrimental to the racialized group. On the other hand, however, it is also used by the racialized group in order to resist the effects of structural subordination. Viewed from the perspective of the racializing group, ". . .subjects are passive, and lack agency to manage linguistic and ideological conflicts to their best advantage; languages are seen as monolithic, abstract structures that come with a homogeneous set of ideologies and function to spread and sustain the interests of dominant groups" (1999:2). The view from the vantage point of the racialized group, however, "calls for a different set of assumptions, in which subjects have the agency to think critically and work out ideological alternatives that favor their own empowerment. It recognizes that while language may have a repressive effect, it also has a liberatory potential of facilitating critical thinking, and enabling subjects to rise above domination . . . the intention is not to reject English, but to reconstitute it in more inclusive, ethical, and democratic terms, and so to bring about the creative resolutions to their linguistic conflicts" (1999:2). Throughout this chapter I investigate the interstices of language and racial formation from both vantage points.

In nineteenth century South Texas, the war of position was orchestrated along both racial and linguistic lines. Language differences were used as a pretext for excluding Tejanos from participation and representation in the *polis*. But the simple fact of linguistic difference was not enough to sustain unequal relations of power; instead, the communicative system itself was subordinated and devalued. Anglos were insistent on identifying and demonstrating purported defects in the Tejano tongue, and this devaluation came to be in my opinion, the single most enduring legacy of Texas racism. In the ensuing discussion, I will present a closer look at the development of linguicism in South Texas.

Reproducing Linguicism in South Texas

The expressions of linguicism in nineteenth century South Texas clearly evince a language ideology that held up English as a logical and coherent system of communication and construed Spanish as a deficient and untidy system. Newcomers expressed this ideology in varying forms and to varying degrees. In general, however, Anglo observers in Texas tended to adopt a mystified view of language. They viewed themselves as authorities in matters pertaining to language and consistently exercised their authority by making explicit statements about the languages spoken around them. They also expressed sole ownership of language by blurring the communicative import of speech in subordinated tongues. They trivialized the subordinate language and marginalized its speakers by attributing undesirable characteristics to them such as indolence, deceitfulness, and ignorance. But even though metalinguistic comments generally converged on a uniform ideology of linguistic dominance, the discursive spaces in which the comments appeared differed widely. Some of the comments were expressed in a context of confrontation and others were expressed in a context of observation.

Language ideologies articulated within a context of confrontation manifested the exercise of power in discourse. Speakers used their socially constructed roles within a communicative event in order to actualize their language beliefs. This articulation of language ideology is evident in numerous accounts of interactions between Tejanos and Texas Rangers in nineteenth century South Texas. These accounts show how Rangers laid claim to authority in language by way of the physical authority that they obtained through coercive force. In claiming linguistic authority, furthermore, they also symbolically stripped the subordinate language of communicative functionality.

George Durham, one of Captain McNelly's Rangers, relates an encounter with a Mexican that demonstrates the exercise of power in discourse. He says,

> I had been in my post an hour or so when my field glasses picked up a rider . . . I flew across the opening in a long lope and overhauled my man. He turned out to be a dressed up Mex riding a mule. I couldn't habla Mex and he couldn't habla United States. He wanted to argue by heaving up his shoulders and jabbering and turning up his palms to me. So, I finally shoved my pistol in his ribs and pointed and he got the idea. (Durham 1962:43)

This account reveals the subordination of rational discourse to violent force. The communicative event is successfully actualized only through physical, life-threatening gestures. Even though Durham admits that he could not "habla Mex," he implicitly suggests that the failure of verbal communication was due to the Tejano's inability to "habla United States." It is interesting to note how Durham characterizes the Tejano's initiation of the communicative event. Verbal communication is patently subordinated in the description. The mention of verbal communicative intent is placed in between two physical communicative gestures, "heaving up his shoulders" and "turning up his palms." And even while verbal activity is muffled by the description of physical gestures, it is also contemptuously described as "jabbering." The Oxford English Dictionary defines "jabbering" as "talking rapidly and indistinctly or unintelligibly; speaking volubly and with little sense; chattering, gabbling, or prattling. Often applied, in contempt or derision, to the speaking of a language which is unintelligible to the hearer." One sense of the word, therefore, implicitly blames the speaker and not the hearer for the failure of communication. Given the fact that communication in this encounter is only achieved through Durham's assertion of physical authority, it seems to me that this later sense is the one in which the term is applied.

The term "jabbering" occurs over and over again in the narratives of Anglo-Tejano encounters on the Texas frontier. For instance, Martin Henry Kilgore, an Uvalde Ranger, uses the term in his account of the intrusion of a Mexican sheep herder into a Ranger camp.

> I woke up one night and there stood a man close by. I jumped up with a six-shooter in my hand and he began jabbering. I finally made out that he was a Mexican and he was trying to pray. That woke up all the other boys and they all got up too. The man told us he came into our camp for water, but as it was drizzling rain, we knew that couldn't be right. (Fenley 1939:18-19)

In this account, the term "jabbering" is once again used with the sense of the speaker's inability to communicate and not the listener's inability to understand.

This becomes remarkably clear when we look at the subject position of the next sentence: "I finally made out." Thus, it is the listener who finally gets the credit for the successful actualization of the communicative event, and because of this, the speaker's role in the event is diminished. The term "jabbering," then, suggests that the words uttered by the Mexican were devoid of semantic value, and could achieve it only through the effort and ingenuity of the Ranger. However, even when the Ranger successfully imbued the words with semantic value, we find that they were devoid of truth value: "we knew that couldn't be right." The devaluation of Tejano discourse in this account also served to symbolically strip the subordinate language of communicative functionality.

Ranger cunning and ingenuity was oftentimes discursively reified by blurring the communicative functionality of the Mexican's language. Big Foot Wallace is perhaps the most widely known Ranger for his discursive cunning. One occasion in Big Foot's biography relates an encounter between the Ranger and some Mexican soldiers.

> He [Big Foot] slept all night without rousing once and the [Mexican] soldiers said he would never wake but die that way. When morning came, however, Big Foot waked [sic] up refreshed and hungry, and opening his knapsack began to make a hearty meal of his remaining mule meat. One of the Mexicans said: "Look at that man; he is not dead; watch him eat." Another one came to him and asked what he was eating. "Mule meat," said Wallace, as he looked the Mexican in the face. "Whose mule was it?" was the next question. "My mule," says Wallace. "It was not," said the Mexican. "He belonged to Captain Arroyo." "Why did he not stay with him then?" said Big Foot as he continued to eat, and then resumed: "The coward ran off and left him, and I got him. So then he belonged to me, and when I got hungry, I killed him and ate him. Mule meat is good—better than horse meat."
> (Sowell 1964:71)

In this exchange, Big Foot's cunning is wholly dependent on his subversion of the words and meanings conveyed by his interlocutor. When the truth value of his own words is brought into question by the inquiring Mexican official, he simply turns this value on its head and recasts his words to fit his own conception of truth. While Big Foot's linguistic dexterity is partially accounted for by his peculiar "way with words," it also projects a sense of linguistic backwardness and dysfunctionality on the part of his interlocutors.

There is considerable evidence in the historical record to suggest that certain language ideologies in South Texas construed Tejanos as communicatively impaired. The ideology is a clear mystification of language, contending that there was nothing wrong with the language that Tejanos spoke, the problem was that they were cognitively unable to understand the complexities of their own native language and of any other language for that matter. This ideology is evident in the representations of Tejanos using English. Noah Smithwick, for instance, related the account of a Mexican official visiting Austin's San Felipe colony in the years leading up to the Texas Revolution.

> The Mexicans applied the term "brute" to all non-Catholics. I recall a laughable incident that occurred a way back in the colonial days of San Felipe. A Mexican official came out on some business, having with him as interpreter a Mexican who had spent his life in Texas, and, having been a good deal among the Americans, had adopted their ways and was proud to class himself as an American. Someone asked him if he was a Christian. "Oh, no," said he, "me one brute, same like Mericans." (Smithwick 1935:273)

The characterization of the severely accented English and the Tejano's inability to decipher the semantic nuances of the term "brute" reify an ideology which regarded Tejanos as cognitively incapable of mastering the complexities of any language. Even though the Tejano had admittedly "adopted the ways" of the Americans and had held them in high esteem, he remained an outsider by virtue of his perceived intrinsic, racially construed, inferiority.

Smithwick's language ideology was steeped in his conception of the Mexican's intellectual backwardness. He displayed this prejudice callously in an account of his work as a doctor's assistant in San Antonio.

> Tartar emetic was the doctor's favorite prescription, and his doses were liberal. I looked on the Mexicans as scarce more than apes and could with difficulty restrain my enjoyment at the situation when the medicine got in its work, seemingly turning the poor devils inside out, they meanwhile swearing and praying alternately. And I felt no twinge of remorse for the monstrous imposition we were practicing upon them when they finally emerged from the doctor's heroic treatment looking as dry and shrunken as so many pods of chili Colorado (their favorite article of diet) and loaded him with thanks for his ministrations. I managed to keep down my risible while in attendance on the patients, but I gave full vent to them when I got back to Villar's store and rehearsed the performance for his benefit. (1935:45-46)

Aside from the overtly racializing statements in this fragment, we can also see that the category of "race" is coupled with a series of logically opposed elements, such as "swearing" and "praying," that are symbolically construed as indicators of primitive or lower order cognitive abilities.

The exercise of power in discourse during the nineteenth century reflects the emergence of a historically situated language ideology that at once elevated the position of Americans and subordinated the position of Tejanos. The view that Tejanos were incapable of mastering the complexities of language and that they were communicatively impaired, however, was contradicted in daily experience. Although Tejanos were perceived as linguistically degenerate, they did use their language to communicate effectively among themselves and others. The language ideology was thus forced to work out this internal inconsistency. One way of dealing with the contradiction was to create folk language typologies. In other words, if Tejanos were linguistically degenerate in the sense that they were unable to master the underlying complexity of language, then it stood to reason that whatever language they used was also linguistically degenerate in the sense that it lacked the underlying complexities of other languages. The identification of Tejano Spanish as a defective and dirty tongue is amply demonstrated in my analysis of language-related comments articulated in a context of observation.

Newcomers on the Texas Frontier routinely recorded their observations of the place and its people. The observer's comments, furthermore, oftentimes betray an ideology that manifests the exercise of power behind discourse. Metalinguistic commentaries about the language of Tejanos demonstrate how language ideology was constituted in preconceived notions of cultural and linguistic superiority. The language variety of Tejanos was explicitly evaluated in opposition to what observer's called "pure Castilian." Mary Joseph Patrick, an Irish nun of the Ursuline order commissioned to minister in San Antonio, observed that:

> The Mexican Spanish is not good; the children are here taught to improve their pronunciation. We are learning la lengua castellana and we hope soon to write to our Padre de Salamanca, Doctor Cooke. (McDowell 1977:178)

This statement underscores the social rather than linguistic basis of the negative evaluations of Tejano Spanish. The observer's authority to make distinctions between good and bad Spanish is in no way connected with her own communicative competence in the language, but rather is based on the view that she has a certain degree of expertise and training in language generally. Teresa Viele made a similar observation when describing communicative activity among San Antonio Tejanos in the 1850s:

> Very little conversation took place between them, and that little in a language called "Mex," a kind of Spanish patois, differing widely from pure Castilian! (1984:158)

Viele creates the same opposition between "pure Castilian" and Tejano Spanish, but she goes a step further in suggesting that this opposition is a barrier to communicative activity. In this way, she positions Tejano Spanish as a clearly inferior language variety. An anonymous observer in 1837 articulated this inferiority more explicitly:

The people speak the Spanish language but so adulterated and corrupted that it grates like harsh thunder upon the chaste ear of the polished Castilian. (Muir 1958:102)

The use of adjectives such as "adulterated" and "corrupted" signal the particular asymmetric configuration of the opposition between Castilian and Tejano Spanish. The asymmetric configuration, furthermore, appears to be grounded in perceptions of racial and ethnic difference. Another observer in 1840, for instance, made the following statement:

In point of character for intelligence, vigor or enterprise, the Mexicans are far inferior to Anglo-Americans or any class of Europeans . . . The language spoken by these people is a corrupt Spanish, altogether unlike the pure Castilian, from which it differs as far as does the rude dialect of a plantation Negro from the style of Addison. (Anonymous 1840:227-228)

The defective character of Tejano Spanish in this statement appears to be bound up with an essentialist view of racial inferiority. The inferior intelligence of the Mexican, according to this observer, prevents him from achieving mastery of his own native tongue.

The exercise of power behind discourse in nineteenth century South Texas thus cemented the language of Tejanos in a subordinate position. Anglo newcomers attributed to themselves a linguistic authority that justified and rationalized their observations of the Tejano tongue. They exercised this authority in the articulation of routine and emphatic devaluations of the language, thus stripping it of its linguistic integrity. Tejano Spanish was perceived as a degenerate and adulterated version of the Spanish language that was incapable of transmitting ideas and beliefs beyond any rudimentary level.

It is doubtful, however, that the reproduction of linguicism in South Texas, either in or behind discourse, was ever meant to induce language shift. The subordination and devaluation of the Tejano tongue was a centrifugal social force employed in the interest of maintaining the disparity of opportunity and privilege between the two groups. In this way, linguicism was more at the service of language maintenance than language shift. Euro-American newcomers offered a legitimate space for Spanish and other languages in Texas; however, they also acted as arbiters of the types of languages that should properly be inserted in those spaces. Racial ideologies set the parameters of these spaces and rationalized and justified the language ideologies that attempted to strip Tejano Spanish of communicative functionality and linguistic integrity. A clear indication of the coalescence of racial and language ideologies can be gleaned from the numerous accounts of newcomers' desires and attempts to learn Spanish. The Ursuline

Sisters, for instance, rationalized their desire to learn the language by stating: "Oh, how we long to be able to instruct the dear Mexicans! They are ignorant indeed, and dull, but many of them retain a strong love for the Faith" (McDowell 1977:197). Francis Latham, on the other hand, expressed far less noble designs in his attempts to learn Spanish:

> The Mexicans of Bexar are rather a diminutive, and a very ignorant, lazy, dastardly, treacherous, and yet, apparently a harmless people. Their inferior character, however, is not the least to be wondered at, and it would be a marvel were it otherwise, springing, as many of them have, from the prisons, abandoned soldiery, and worthless and vicious population of Mexico and Spain, and consisting, as no inconsiderable portion does, of the ragged relics of Santa Anna's miserable army, swept together from the streets, filthy lazarettos, and prisons of Mexico—conceived, nursed, educated in ignorance and villainy, and purposely restrained and chained down to their natural degradation, by an imbecile, oppressive, priest-ridden, pusillanimous and semi-barbarous government. The great wonder is that they are not worse people than they look to be and really are. They can hardly be considered a fair specimen of the Mexican population or character, though from the general tenor of accounts, they can be but little if any beneath the great mass of the Mexican people, in education or morals. They seem to be remarkably cleanly in apparel and well behaved, despising drunkenness; which virtues certainly form a happy offset to many of their shortcomings. In pedigree, they may be said to be the mongrel and illicit descendants of an Indian, Mexican and Spanish, penciled with a growing feint-line of the Anglo-Saxon ancestry. A trace of rich Castilian lineage is occasionally visible in the features of the females, some of whom are very fair, handsome and even beautiful. . . . . I remained in Bexar eight days, and amused myself daily in taking lessons in Spanish, from a most lovely girl. I thought it the sweetest and most musical language in the world; and certainly none can be more so, when its soft, liquid and varied accents trill and dance in the richest cadence, from the smiling lips of a Spanish girl "sweet sixteen," with her full, dark, tender eye beaming on yours, and sparkling with excited emotion. There is a modest earnestness and sincerity of expression in the eye of a Spanish girl, denoting great intenseness of feeling, sincerity and strength of attachment. And if a "gentleman of family" may be excused for talking about "love and girls" they really look as if they could love harder and more devotedly than any other women. However, it may be all in the eye after all. (Latham 1971:36-38)

Latham's inclinations to learn the language are clearly motivated by his reported sexual desire for his tutor. His evaluation of the language as the "sweetest and most musical language in the world," furthermore, is tainted by his impressions of the "smiling lips" from which the sounds emanated. In both cases, Latham's and the Ursuline Sisters', the learning and derived validation of the minority language is reduced to a scaffold of racial formation. In the case of the Ursuline Sisters, the rationale for learning Spanish was to save "ignorant" and "dull" Mexicans from the perils of their own fashioning. In the case of Latham, the rationale for learning Spanish was to take advantage of the perceived "natural degradation" and inferior morality of the young female tutor.

Resisting Linguicism in South Texas

Cultural conflict in nineteenth century South Texas was present on multiple levels and to varying degrees. Rosenbaum identifies "a conflict between cultures, and it occurred on two levels: often conflict grew out of misunderstanding, as neither group understood the other's socially established structures of meaning; at least as often, however, conflict was between meanings—each understood the other well enough and that was precisely the problem. They didn't want the same things" (1998:17). Conflicts of both sorts provoked a profound reaction among Anglos and Tejanos alike and led to bitter disputes fought out in both word and deed. As early as 1859, Juan N. Cortina prefaced a series of violent border skirmishes saying:

> Our object as you have seen, has been to chastise the villainy of our enemies, which heretofore has gone unpunished. These have connived with each other, and form, so to speak, a perfidious inquisitorial lodge to persecute and rob us, without any cause, and for no other crime on our part than that of being of Mexican origin; considering us, doubtless, destitute of those gifts which they themselves do not possess. To defend ourselves, and making use of the sacred right of self-preservation, we have assembled in a popular meeting with a view of discussing a means by which to put an end to our misfortunes. (Thompson 1994:14-15)

Cortina's *pronunciamiento* eloquently expresses the reactions of many Tejanos who felt the sting of ethnolinguistic subordination through the systematic processes of racial formation. His actions, furthermore, seem to have been nothing more than violent manifestations of a more discursively driven effort on the part of other Tejanos to defend "the sacred right of self-preservation." Throughout the nineteenth century, Tejanos resisted subordination through words and symbols. But in order to carry out this defense, they were forced not only to defend the underlying meaning of their own cultural existence, but also to defend and justify the very words that structured and conveyed this meaning. The resistance of linguicism in South Texas, therefore, permeated and solidified each and every mode of defense. One way of resisting linguicism was to simply keep talking—to continue using their language. Another way was to keep talking about talk—to elevate their language as a topic of rational discussion, and this is precisely what South Texas Tejanos did.

The first line of defense against linguicism was legal and political. Tejano and Anglo politicians alike sought to defend a space for the legitimate use of the Tejano tongue in matters pertaining to law and politics. Congressmen José Antonio Navarro and Juan N. Seguín argued before legislators that the laws of the land should be translated into Spanish (Matovina 1995:35). Such translations were eventually authorized by the Governor. Other legislators such as A. Supervielle proposed bills that would allow Tejanos to use their native language in official State-related matters. The July 28, 1856 issue of the San Antonio daily *El Ranchero* published a translation of congressman Supervielle's speech in which he laid out the legal and ethical bases of his proposal. The legislator's speech clearly recognizes language as a fundamental right in the establishment of equal access to and protection under the law.

> Pero no es simplemente un acto de justicia que yo pida del Senado y que mantenga con toda mi habilidad lo que yo también urgentemente demando para la parte de la población mejicana, a quien tengo el honor de representar sobre este suelo, es esa igualdad ante la ley que está escrita como una máxima de eterna justicia y de inmutable verdad en el acto fundamental que es la base de nuestras instituciones. Hasta este día, esa igualdad no ha existido para ellos pues en los precintos habitados exclusivamente por ciudadanos tejanos de origen americano, están privados de las ventajas que gozan otros ciudadanos con respecto a sus magistrados locales; en otras palabras estos precintos están excluidos de los privilegios de la justicia local no pudiendo los ciudadanos y jueces entender y mucho menos escribir el inglés satisfactoriamente y así sus procedimientos no se instituyen en este lenguaje y sus juicios que no se escriben en inglés son una nulidad y hacen que el magistrado les haga un objeto de ridículo para aquellos litigantes obstinados que jamás ceden sino cuando se les compete absolutamente. (*El Ranchero* July 28, 1856)

But even though the Senator recognized linguistic rights as fundamental to the civil rights of Spanish-speaking citizens, he also placed limits on the extension of these rights.

> No veo que merezca niguna objección, pues no se pide para aquellos que han emigrado a este país y que sabían antes de su venida que el inglés era el idioma legal del país, sino se quiere para favorecer a aquellos que tenían antiguamente posesión de él y sobre quienes hemos extendido nuestro idioma, instituciones y leyes; ni la población mejicana que reside en la parte occidental del Estado ha descuidado aprender nuestro idioma por alguna prevención contra el pueblo americano; por el contrario están

favorablemente dispuestos hacia nosotros y desde que han podido obtener maestros americanos; protegen las escuelas americanas con preferencia a las suyas propias, imbuyendo de este modo la mente de sus hijos con el amor de los principios liberales y de las instituciones republicanas. La nueva generación podrá antes de mucho tiempo comprender y hablar nuestro idioma; pero los muchachos no son magistrados y hasta que semejante generación tenga suficiente edad para manejar sus negocios, la ley que se pide es enteramente indispensable. (*El Ranchero* July 28, 1856)

The Senator, therefore, viewed linguistic rights as pertaining exclusively to those conquered peoples who had not yet had the time to master the "new" native language, and he confidently assured the legislative body that such rights would be relinquished in future generations. Supervielle's assurance was to be a self-fulfilling prophecy. By the end of the nineteenth century, the political tide had turned full circle. Congressmen, by that time, were not only arguing that Tejano's linguistic rights be relinquished but also that knowledge of the English language be a requirement for the enjoyment of other civil rights. The "Boehmar Bill" of 1913, for instance, proposed that the ability to read and write in English become a prerequisite for voting in Texas. Tejanos, however, continued to resist on the political front arguing that such legislation was meant to annul the voice of the Spanish-speaking majority. An editorial from San Antonio's *La Prensa* explains:

En el último periodo de sesiones de la Legislatura, Ryan fue a Austin a pedir que se pusiera en vigor la ley conocida con el nombre de "Boehmar Bill" que quita el derecho de votar a todas aquellas personas que no saben leer y escribir el idioma inglés. Para conseguir su objeto, se dirigió a los diputados que representan el Condado de Béxar pidiéndoles que apoyaran al proyecto, pero ellos, con toda entereza, rechazaron las proposiciones de Ryan. Este no desmayó ante el fracaso sufrido y sin pérdida de tiempo fue a ver al mismo Boehmer rogándole que presentara el proyecto como "ley de emergencia" para que inmediatamente fuera puesta en vigor en San Antonio y comprendiera las elecciones que están para verificarse. No era otro el objeto de Ryan al pretender que se aprobara el mencionado proyecto que nulifica a los votantes mexicanos ya que muchos no hablan ni escriben ni leen el inglés y otros a pesar de hablarlo no lo leen ni lo escriben. (*La Prensa* April 10, 1913)

The editors of *La Prensa* countered the attack on Tejano language rights by exposing the linguistic gerrymandering tactics of the San Antonio mayoral candidate. Tejano resistance on the political front was successful inasmuch as it protected linguistic rights in limited measures. However, the political and legislative gains were temporary at best and illusory at worst. Hernández-Chávez argues:

> It is clear that . . . laws concerning the use of Spanish were passed not in the interest of the people, but for the convenience of the State in administering the laws. Thus, the law of 1856 allowed the use of Spanish in the courts only in the counties with large Mexican populations. Even so, English was required where one of the parties did not speak Spanish . . . by 1905 a new law passed that specified that, except for foreign language instruction, all instruction had to be in English . . . The linguistic rights of Texas Mexicans became essentially non-existent. (1995:146)

Tejanos also resisted linguicism through what I call a unification ideology. In the face of devaluation from adverse language ideologies, Tejanos challenged the typological labels associated with their language by referring to it interchangeably as "español" and "castellano." The use of the term "castellano" created a historical connection between their language and that of the European homeland. This historical connection was not meant to separate different types of Spanish within the community but rather to symbolize a uniformity between Tejano Spanish and the Spanish of the old world, between Texas Mexicans and other heirs of Roman language and culture. The uniformity is clearly evinced in the following reactionary statement to *Know Nothing* nativism.

> Nosotros amamos a Tejas que es la tierra de nuestra adopción antes que todo y deseamos el bienestar y la paz de nuestros conciudadanos con preferencia al enriquecimento y conveniencia personal de individuos particulares. Los momentos son siglos en el cuadrante de la humanidad. Tratamos de reconstruir en Tejas el poder de una raza a quien nos ligan no sólo lazos de simpatías y amor, sino los que son aun todavía más fuertes para nosotros, los del origen y la nacionalidad. No hay tiempo que perder. Cada nuevo sol alumbra una agresión de parte de aquellos que nos quisieran estirpar . . . Haced que el pendón de la democracia cobije para siempre todo lo que de noble, caballerezco se conserva en nuestra raza, la pompa del rico idioma de Cervantes y Garcilaso y los nobles atributos del elemento latino que fluye en nuestras venas. (*El Ranchero* July 19, 1856)

In this statement, *Tejas* is conceived as a geo-political zone of contention, a zone in which a "noble race"—composed of foreign and native born alike– struggles against aggressive attempts to fragment and fracture it. The resistant posture is one of unity and solidarity in the face of aggression. The ties that bind, furthermore, are none other than language, *la pompa del rico idioma de Cervantes y Garcilaso*. A similar defensive posture is taken up in the July 4, 1856 issue of the same San Antonio newspaper. A call to the *Méjico-Tejanos* serves to warn against the separatist designs of "los Know Nothings que quieren engañaros, que han procurado siempre oprimiros . . ." 'the Know Nothings who want to fool you and who have always tried to oppress you' (*El Ranchero* July 4, 1856). Language once again serves as the strategic linchpin that unites Tejanos against the nativist, English dominant position of the Know Nothing Party.

> Por una parte el deseo de satisfacer las exigencias y súplicas de algunos mejicanos que no han podido permancer mudos e indiferentes en las graves y vitales cuestiones que han surgido en estos últimos tiempos y por otra parte las naturales simpatías que nos ligan a todos los pueblos de nuestra raza que hablan aquende los mares la lengua sonora de Castilla, nos han hecho prescindir de escrúpulos de poco momento . . . para que nos decidiéramos de un todo a mantener la lucha que en un día no lejano ha de dar por resultado el triunfo de las ideas progresistas y principios democráticos. (*El Ranchero* July 4, 1856)

The editors, thus, position themselves and their struggle within a larger context, *aquende los mares*, of Spanish speakers. While the discourse of *El Ranchero* is fueled by nativist tendencies attempting to restrict the civil rights of "foreigners," it emerges as an ideologically charged counter-hegemonic discourse relying on linguistic and cultural continuities. This unification ideology imbued the Tejano community with a sense of pride about their language and about the heritage that it embodied. It served, moreover, as an outright and incontrovertible challenge to the language ideologies that attempted to characterize the Tejano tongue as a deficient and corrupted version of the language of Castile.

At the same time that Tejanos defended their particular variety of Spanish molding it within a larger old world framework, they also spoke eloquently of their right to maintain and perpetuate the language among future generations. The ideology of preservation, however, was never a monolingual ideology. Tejanos vociferously claimed equal status for their language and equal protection for those who did not speak English, but they seem to have been just as vociferous in promoting the ideal of a bilingual citizenry. The editors of *El Bejareño*, for example, wrote:

> . . . nos empeñaremos siempre en promover la fundación y el formato de las Escuelas Públicas en las cuales, sin perder el idioma de Cervantes, los niños Méjico-Tejanos, adquirirán el idioma nacional, serán instruidos en los deberes de ciudadanos, su creencia religiosa será respetada, y se harán ciudadanos útiles y dignos de pertenecer a un país libre. (*El Bejareño* February 7, 1855)

The ideology of preservation in some respects echoes the sentiments of Congressman Supervielle. The difference, of course, is that while Supervielle's position extended linguistic rights only to those who had been directly affected by the 1848 cession, the preservation position takes linguistic rights to be a fundamental civil entitlement. In the January 8, 1910 issue of Laredo's *La Crónica*, Jovita Idar espoused a similar ideology.

> In our previous article we stated that "most regrettably, we have seen Mexican teachers teaching students of their race in English without taking into consideration, at all, their mother tongue." With that we did not intend to imply—not in the least—that the language of the land they inhabit should not be taught, as it is the medium available for direct contact with their neighbors, and that which will allow them to ensure that their rights are respected. What we wanted to suggest, simply, is that the national language should not be ignored, because it is the stamp that characterizes races and nations. Nations disappear and races sink when they forget their national language . . . We are not saying that English should not be taught to Mexican Texan children, but, whether appropriate or not, we are saying you should not forget to teach them Spanish. In the same way that arithmetic and grammar are useful to them, English is useful to those people who live among English speakers. (Kanellos 2002:142-142)

Idar's statement is characteristic of the ideology of preservation inasmuch as it attempts to strike a balance between the linguistic rights of Tejanos to use their native language and their linguistic responsibilities of learning and using the dominant language.

Throughout the nineteenth century Tejanos resisted linguicism in different ways. While much of the struggle was played out in courthouses and law-making sessions, another important part was manifested in day to day thought and discourse. Tejanos espoused a unification ideology which struck back at ideological attempts to devalue and degenerate the particular variety of Spanish spoken in the region. They also demonstrated a preservation ideology which denounced the ideological attempts to erase Spanish speakers from the political map. Tejanos were keenly aware, nonetheless, that the burden of bilingualism fell, justly or unjustly, on their shoulders. Thus, the preservation ideology spoke out in favor of a generalized bilingualism among Tejanos.

References

Almaguer, Tomás. 1994. *Racial Fault Lines: The Historical Origins of White Supremacy in California*. Berkeley: U of California P.

Anonymous. 1840. *Texas in 1840 or the Emigrants Guide to the New Republic*. New York: William and Allen.

Bourdieu, Pierre. 1991. *Language and Symbolic Power.* Cambridge, MA: Harvard UP.

Bracht, Viktor. 1931. *Texas in 1848.* Trans. Charles Frank Schmidt. San Antonio: Naylor Printing Co.

Canagarajah, A. Suresh. 1999. *Resisting Linguistic Imperialism in English Teaching.* Oxford: Oxford UP.

De León, Arnoldo. 1983. *They Called Them Greasers.* Austin: U of Texas P.

Dorian, Nancy. 1998. Western language ideologies and small-language prospects. In L. Grenoble & L. Whaley, (Eds.), *Endangered Languages* (pp. 3-21). Cambridge: Cambridge UP.

Durham, George. 1962. *Taming the Nueces Strip.* Austin: U of Texas P.

Fairclough, Norman. 1995. *Critical Discourse Analysis.* London: Longman.

Fairclough, Norman. 1989. *Language and Power.* London: Longman.

Fenley, Florence. 1939. *Oldtimers: Frontier Days in the Uvalde Section of Southwest Texas.* Uvalde, TX: The Hornby P.

Garza-Falcón, Leticia. 1998. *Gente Decente: A Borderlands Response to the Rhetoric of Dominance.* Austin: U of Texas P.

Hernández-Chávez, Eduardo. 1995. Language policy in the United States: a history of cultural genocide. In T. Skutnabb-Kangas, & R. Phillipson, (Eds.), *Linguistic Human Rights: Overcoming Linguistic Discrimination* (pp. 141-158). Berlin: Mouton de Gruyter.

Kanellos, Nicolás, Kenya Dworkin, José Fernández, & Erlinda Gonzales-Berry, (Eds.). 2002. *Herencia: The Anthology of Hispanic Literature of the United States.* Coordinator A. Balestra. Oxford: Oxford UP.

Latham, Francis. 1971. *Travels in the Republic of Texas, 1842.* Austin: The Encino P.

Lippi-Green, Rosina. 1997. *English with an Accent: Language, Ideology, and Discrimination in the United States.* New York: Routledge.

Limón, José. 1994. *Dancing with the Devil: Society and Cultural Poetics in Mexican-American South Texas.* Madison: U of Wisconsin P.

Matovina, Timothy M. 1995. *Tejano Religion and Ethnicity: San Antonio, 1821-1860.* Austin: U of Texas P.

McDowell, Catherine, Ed. 1977. *Letters from the Ursuline, 1852-1853.* San Antonio: Trinity UP.

Montejano, David. 1987. *Anglos and Mexicans in the Making of Texas, 1836-1986.* Austin: U of Texas P.

Muir, Andrew Forest, (Ed.) 1958. *Texas in 1837: An Anonymous, Contemporary Narrative.* Austin: U of Texas P.

Omi, Michael, & Howard Winant. 1994. *Racial Formation in the United States.* 2nd edition. New York: Routledge.

Phillipson, Robert. 1992. *Linguistic Imperialism.* Oxford: Oxford UP.

Rosenbaum, Robert. 1998. *Mexicano Resistance in the Southwest.* 2nd Edition. Dallas: Southern Methodist UP.

Sánchez, George I. 1970. Spanish in the Southwest. In H. Johnson & W. Hernandez, (Eds.). *Educating the Mexican American* (pp. 24-32). Valley Forge: Judson P.

Silverstein, Michael. 1979. Language Structure and Linguistic Ideology. In P. Clyne, W. Hanks, & C. Hofbauer, (Eds.), *The Elements: A Parasession on Linguistic Units and Levels* (pp. 193-247). Chicago: Chicago Linguistic Society.

Skutnabb-Kangas, Tove, & Robert Phillipson, (Eds.). 1995. *Linguistic Human Rights: Overcoming Linguistic Discrimination.* Berlin: Mouton de Gruyter.

Smithwick, Noah. 1935. *The Evolution of a State.* Austin: The Steck Co.

Sowell, Andrew Jackson. 1964. *Rangers and Pioneers of Texas.* New York: Argosy Antiquarian.

Thompson, Jerry, (Ed.). 1994. *Juan N. Cortina and the Texas-Mexico Frontier, 1859-1877.* El Paso: Texas Western P.

Viele, Teresa. 1984. *Following the Drum: A Glimpse of Frontier Life.* Lincoln: U of Nebraska P.

How the Californio Girls (and Boys) Lost Their Accents

María Irene Moyna and Wendy Beckman
Texas A&M University and San Diego State University

1. Introduction

The historical dimensions of California Spanish have until now been studied from a structural perspective (Blanco 1971, Perissinotto 1992, 1998, Acevedo 2000, Moyna and Decker 2005). Additionally, Balestra (2002) has analyzed the effects of social variation on specific linguistic variables of California Spanish. However, none of these studies has systematically considered the process of language shift as a result of contact with English (but cf. Trujillo 2000 and Martínez 2000:122-134, for studies of English borrowing into Spanish in post-Annexation New Mexico and Texas, respectively). The scarcity of studies on Spanish in the United States during the nineteenth century may be due in part because it has been obscured by the more dramatic contemporary examples. Also responsible for this neglect is the difficulty in accessing original documents and the unavailability of published or digital corpora.

The present study, then, comes to fill a gap in the history of Spanish in California by considering historical documents in light of general patterns of language shift as manifested today for immigrant communities in the United States.[1]

---

[1] In this regard, and without making any attempts at being exhaustive, one could mention general works on language shift in the United States (Fishman 1966, Veltman 1983). There is also a vast bibliography on language loss and maintenance specific to various U.S. Spanish-speaking communities, such as areas adjacent to the Mexican border in Texas (Amastae 1982, Bills et al. 1995), California (Aguirre 1982, Hidalgo 1993, Silva-Corvalán 2001:305-308), and New Mexico (Hudson-Edwards and Bills, 1982, Bills 1997). Other areas of the historical Spanish borderlands have also been studied, such as Colorado (Floyd 1992), and isleño (Coles 1991), as well as more recent immigration, such as Cubans in Miami (Pearson and McGee 1993), Puerto Ricans in New York (Pedraza 1985), and several immigrant groups in Chicago (Potowski 2004).

To do so, it focuses on personal correspondence written by the members of three families from southern California, whose lives spanned the second half of nineteenth century, after contact with English had begun.

Because the historical linguist only has recourse to written records, this paper also intersects with the study of contemporary written manifestations of code-switching in fictional and non-fictional prose, contributing to a field that has deserved fewer studies than its oral counterpart (but cf. Montes Alcalá 2001 for diaries, 2005 for notes and letters, Callahan 2001, 2002, 2004, and García Vizcaíno 2005, for code-switching in fictional prose, and Pfaff and Chávez 1986 for drama).

The aim of this study is, by examining the specific patterns of bilingual use in three families, to ascertain how the relationship between Spanish and English played out in everyday life. The letters provide information not just about the language choices authors made depending on their addressee, but also about the types of code mixing they employed in discourse and their awareness of their linguistic output.

2. Background

In what follows we provide general historical information about the social and demographic changes in California, in particular the San Diego area, as well as specific information about the three families.

2.1. California during the Nineteenth Century

By the time of the Mexican American War (1846-48), Alta California had been settled as a Spanish-Mexican territory for a little under a hundred years, during which time 21 missions had been founded along the Pacific shore. However, during the Spanish and Mexican periods it proved difficult to encourage migration to the rugged north, so that the Hispanic population was scanty and grew mostly through births (Mason 1998:40 *et passim*; Kessell 2002:337-8). However, with Mexican independence in 1821, the California missions fell under the rule of the new republic, which started to distribute the land to private citizens and to foster colonization in the early 1830s, so that the isolation of the previous period was somewhat broken (Mason 1998:113).

Additionally, American and European merchants and entrepreneurs had started arriving in California before Mexican independence, and their numbers grew steadily after that. For many merchants and sailors California offered the possibility of a sedentary life after years at sea, and the opportunity of continuing profitable trading ventures from dry land. As a result, by 1848 non-Hispanics accounted for 6,500 inhabitants, over a third of the total non-indigenous population (Francis 1976:153). These non-Hispanic settlers, mostly male, often converted to Catholicism and married Mexican women. In general they became wealthy and respectable by adoption into the *ranchero* elite, which accepted them as *hijos del país* "sons of the country." Their foreignness was never perceived as a threat, since they were willing to learn Spanish and adhere to the local customs (Gray 1998:52). For the Californio families, intermarriage and association with American and European entrepreneurs had its benefits, too. For one thing, it helped to "whiten" the local aristocracy and reaffirmed its claims to European extraction, widening the gap between them and the local *mestizo* class (cf. also Trujillo 2000:125). Additionally, it helped to integrate their rural economy into Western capitalism (Griswold del Castillo and De León 1996:21).

After American annexation in 1848 there were profound population changes in California. The territory was flooded by newcomers, attracted by the lure of gold and land, especially in the north. It is estimated that the non-indigenous population exploded to 200,000 by 1852 (Marschner 2000:7), a twelvefold increase in four years, making it impossible for the local Spanish-speaking population to retain its dominance. This in turn led to poor political representation in the new state's government, a disadvantage that would quickly result in social disenfranchisement and economic decline.

The Land Law of 1851 was particularly deleterious to the Californio interests. Although purportedly meant to uphold the Peace Treaty and guarantee the property rights of ranchers, it placed the burden of proving ownership on the landowners, who often lacked written documents to back their claims. They were thus left to fend for themselves before the courts against Anglo squatter farmers who said the lands were unoccupied and therefore available for settlement. Long and costly court battles led to the loss of all or part of the property, since lawyers often took what the squatters did not (Pitt 1966:86). Additionally, the American government took a different fiscal stance than its Mexican predecessor. *Rancheros* were now obligated to pay taxes on the property they owned regardless of its profitability, so that a couple of bad years could spell financial disaster. In the mining towns of the north, Spanish speakers also had their share of woes: although Sonorans, Peruvians, and Chileans were expert gold miners and taught the trade to many Anglos, their presence in the diggings was soon resented. In the lawless backwaters of northern California, this often led to summary arrests, lynchings, and other forms of intimidation and violence (Pitt 1966:50-1).

San Diego and its environs, the area where the three families lived, also witnessed demographic and social changes in the second half of the nineteenth century. Although the influx of immigrants was not as dramatic as in northern California and the growth of the town was slow, the population of the county did double between 1846 and 1850, and then tripled by 1870 (Table 1). Following general trends, San Diego Californio families tried to retain power by intermingling with newly arrived Anglos through marriage and business. However, an examination of the political rosters of the city and county shows the drastic shift in power and the Californios' loss of political clout and social status as the century progressed (San Diego Historical Society).

	1850	1860	1870
Town residents	233	293	319
Rural residents	499	438	1,981
Total	732	731	2,300

Table 1. Population of San Diego, 1850-1870 (modified from Griswold del Castillo 2006).

The internal make-up of the San Diego family also changed after annexation. Whereas in 1850 Mexican households in Old Town San Diego were more numerous than Anglo and mixed households combined, by 1870 they had become a minority. On the other hand, the number of Anglo-American households now constituted over 70% of the total, while the number of mixed households remained quite stable (Griswold del Castillo 2006) (Table 2).

Families with male head of household	1850	1860	1870
Anglo	13	103	8
Mexican	19	8	6
Mixed[2]	4	6	5
Families with male head of household			
Anglo	0	3	0
Mexican	5	7	3
Total number of families	41	34	52

Table 2. Family composition in Old Town San Diego 1850-1870 (modified from Griswold del Castillo 2006).

Both the increase in the numbers of English speakers and the presence of bilingual households changed the linguistic make-up of the area drastically. This was

---

[2] Mixed marriages were made up of an Anglo husband and his Californio wife.

coupled with a public school system not conducive to Spanish language maintenance, since education was conducted entirely in English except in the private sector (Griswold del Castillo 1979:169-70; Wilson 1942). The Catholic Church did not support the maintenance of Spanish either, since the American Catholic authorities instituted a policy of assimilation and focused their efforts on the adoption of English and the acculturation of immigrants (Pitt 1966:216; McKevitt 1979:39-40, 1990/91). All these factors are likely to have had an effect on the language patterns of the San Diego bilingual families. We now turn to the three households in our sample to illustrate the situation.

2.2. Californio families

The three mixed households in the study shared several features. For example, in each one of them, an English-speaking man had married a Spanish-speaking woman of Californio extraction. Two of the English speakers were from Britain, and one from Tennessee, in the eastern United States. In all certainty, both Spanish and English were spoken in all the homes. It is probable, however, that each family had its own dynamics, due to factors such as the political and social allegiances of the spouses, the dates of arrival of the men in California, and the ages of the spouses and children at the time of annexation. The aim of this section is to provide whatever pertinent information is available about the story of each family. In that respect, it must be borne in mind that not all families were equally well-known, so that some of this biographical information is sketchy and may change as new data becomes available.

2.2.1. The Forsters

The patriarch of this family was John Forster, known to the Californios as Don Juan Forster. He was ranked among California's most prominent *rancheros*, at one point owning several ranches consisting of over one hundred thousand acres of land. The information we can gather about his life comes mainly from his own extensive 1878 narration to Thomas Savage, one of the researchers who collected oral histories for William Bancroft's history of California (Tanner and Lothrop 1970) and also from Stant (1977) and Gray (1998).

Forster was born on September 16, 1814, in Liverpool, England. At the end of his primary education he traveled to Guaymas, Sonora, to assist his uncle James Johnson in his trading and smuggling business (Stant 1977:4). He arrived in Guaymas in April of 1831, and worked there and in Hermosillo for the following two and a half years. Eventually he moved to Los Angeles, where he started his own business. In 1837 he married Isidora Pico, sister of Don Pío Pico, a prominent Californio who was soon to become Governor of California

(1845). This marriage cemented Forster's position in Californio society. In 1840 he relocated to San Pedro, and three years later was appointed captain of Port.

In 1844 he took up residence in the San Juan Capistrano mission, 60 miles north of San Diego, which he purchased from the Mexican government (his brother-in-law Pico) for a nominal fee. The purchase of this land turned Forster into a wealthy *ranchero*; it would be followed by several other acquisitions totaling 105,460 acres of ideal land (Gray 1998:42 *et passim*). The Forsters lived in the San Juan Capistrano mission building for twenty years, in a lifestyle which has been described as "baronial." For example, in the 1860 U.S. Census, out of the twenty-one members of the household, only five were members of the nuclear family.[3] They were joined by three guests, probably from their extended family, one clerk, a cook, five *vaqueros*, and six servants (Gray 1998:44). However, Forster himself was not given to the excesses of other Californios and dutifully focused his energies on shoring up his economic empire with shrewdness and prudence (Gray 1998:65 *et passim*).

One of his prudent moves was his neutrality during the Mexican-American war, which translated into providing aid to both sides at different points. This was not a show of indecisiveness, but rather his way to guarantee the preservation of his family and his estate regardless of the outcome. Forster saw the American victory as a foregone conclusion but still wished to be on good terms with both sides (Gray 1998:49).

Unfortunately for Don Juan, after Annexation his family connection with the Picos, so beneficial earlier, became a liability: Pío Pico often needed Forster's financial backing to pay off mortgages on his own property as a result of bad business decisions (Gray 1998:213-4). Eventually, these divergent financial philosophies would cause the ties between Pico and Forster to break. In the year 1873, Pío Pico filed a lawsuit against Don Juan, accusing him of having swindled him out of the deed to his Rancho Santa Margarita y Las Flores. Years earlier, in 1864, Pico, who owed a large debt, had offered Forster half of the ranch if he would assume it. Forster had Pico sign a deed in English, which he knew Pico could not read; Pico signed all the same, trusting his brother-in-law blindly after years of familial bonds. The deed transferred the entire ranch to Forster, a fact discovered by Pico four years later. From Forster's perspective, the measure had been preventive: he could foresee that Pico's repeated financial blunders would eventually cause his bankruptcy and put the entire ranch they shared in jeopardy. The rationale behind his trickery had been to protect the title from creditors after Pico's inevitable economic collapse. In the meantime, he reasoned, he would support his brother-in-law by allowing him to remain on the

---

[3] The complete list of given names and birthdates of the Forster children is as follows: Marcos (1839); Francisco (1841); John (= Juanón) (1845); George (1847); Carolina (1848) (Stant 1977). In the 1860 U.S. Census, the Forster household claims only the three eldest children, however, suggesting that George and Carolina may have died at a young age.

land. Forster eventually won the lawsuit, since Pico was not able to prove the validity of the oral agreement between the parties and the written deed was deemed valid.

Forster's full integration into Californio society included the use of Spanish as the family language. Although Don Juan had learned Spanish in late adolescence, he adopted it fully as his own language, even when writing his private diaries (Gray 1998:190). Only Spanish was permitted in his *hacienda* (Stant 1977:44), so that the Forster children were raised in an exclusively Spanish-speaking household and preferred to speak and write to each other in that language (Gray 1998:202).[4]

2.2.2. The Stokes

Edward Stokes was an English sailor about whom little is known. In the 1830s he was first mate on a whaling vessel, whaling being an important industry which furnished oil for lamps and lubrication. He continued to work on various merchant ships in the south Pacific and the California coast into the 1840s, trading in hides and tallow. San Diego was probably one of his frequent ports of call, since it was active in commerce. In the early 1840s he married María del Refugio Ortega, daughter of José Joaquín Ortega, and thus became part of an influential local family by acquiring land in the area around modern-day Ramona, some 35 miles northeast of San Diego. For a time, he continued to trade along the California coast with the local *rancheros*. In those days ships functioned as floating trading posts, providing Californians with necessary industrial goods in exchange for furs, soap, liquor, tanned hides, saddles, boots, and figs. After receiving grants to the Santa María and Santa Isabel ranchos, he took up residence on dry land. He maintained neutrality during the Mexican-American war, but died suddenly after the battle of San Pasqual, of causes unknown (LeMenager 1989:37).

Edward Stokes and María del Refugio Ortega had had three sons, Adolfo, Eduardo, and Alfredo. After Edward's death, the children lived with their Spanish-speaking mother and had no English-speaking role model in the home. In 1852, María del Refugio remarried to Agustín Olvera, a widower and a judge for the Los Angeles county. The eldest son, Adolfo, worked mainly on his step-grandfather Joaquín Olvera's ranch, while the middle son, Eduardo, was sent away to boarding school at the Santa Ynez Mission on the central coast of California. The youngest son, Alfredo, does not seem to have left the family home, and was raised primarily by his mother and grandmother (Jane Cowgill, p.c.).

---

[4] The Forster correspondence in modern archives does not reflect the family's social prominence because of Don Juan's unfortunate habit of throwing away his letters (Gray 1998:111).

2.2.3. The Couts

Cave Johnson Couts is undoubtedly the best known, most public, and most colorful of the three patriarchs. Born in 1821 near Springfield, Tennessee, to a military family, he graduated from West Point in 1843. He served in the Indian frontier and in Mexico before being transferred to the San Diego area, where he escorted the first boundary team which established the U.S.-Mexico border between San Diego and the Colorado River. In 1851 he resigned his position with the army, but returned to public life as a captain in a volunteer company formed after the Garra Indian Revolt. Throughout his life, he took up several other public offices, such as sub-Indian agent, county judge, member of the Grand Jury and the County Board of Supervisors, and Justice of the Peace. He also took an interest in several business ventures, such as the establishment of a railroad to connect the San Diego area with the east coast (Annable 1965). In typical frontier fashion, however, Couts also had several run-ins with the law himself, most notably, two indictments for whipping Indians to death and a murder trial which ended in his acquittal (McKanna 1998; Gray 1998:111-12). His violent behavior was fueled in part by his propensity to drink, which would eventually bring about his own early death.

Couts' marriage to Isidora Bandini in 1851 had connected him to one of the most prominent Spanish Californio families and changed his future by turning him into a *ranchero*, since Isidora received Rancho Guajome as a wedding gift from her brother-in-law Abel Stearns, a Yankee married to her sister Arcadia. The ranch was a grant of 2,219.41 acres, some 40 miles north of San Diego in present-day Vista. On it Couts built a Spanish-style adobe house and embarked on the life of a landowner.

Although the second half of the nineteenth century spelled the demise of the large ranches in southern California through a combination of cattle price fluctuations, unfavorable weather conditions, and bad legislation, Couts succeeded in riding out the storm. He did so, on the one hand, by selling portions of his estate, and on the other, by diversifying his production and supplementing his cattle and horses with sheep as well as orange groves and vineyards.

Rancho Guajome was also the main residence of the Couts household, which grew with the birth of ten children.[5] To guarantee full literacy in English, the elder Couts hired English-speaking teachers to live and work with the family on the ranch while the children were young (McKanna 1998:260). Later on,

---

[5] The complete list of given names and birthdates of the Couts children is as follows: Abel Stearns (1852); María Antonia (= Toña) (1853); William Bandini (= Willy, Billy) (1854); Cave Johnson, Jr. (1856); Nancy Dolores (1857); Isidora Forster (1860); Helen (1862); Robert (1864); John Forster (1866); and María Carolina (1868) (Couts family Bible, Rancho Guajome). Abel Stearns died before his fourth birthday and Nancy Dolores, at age 11; all others reached adulthood. Notice that several of the children bear the names of family friends and *compadres* (Abel Stearns, Juan Bandini, John Forster).

the girls were sent to boarding school (thus, some of their letters are dated in Los Angeles, Oakland, and San Francisco and have references to nuns, possibly their teachers (Huntington Library, Couts Collection, CT 424). At least two of the boys went further afield, to Springfield, Tennessee, where they attended university under the tutelage of their paternal uncle (Huntington Library, Couts Collection CT 403, 404, 405, 406). Couts' local prominence and the size of his family contributed to the preservation of a wealth of documentary materials available for this study.

2.2.4. A Small World

In general, Californios were connected with one another in very dense social networks, and the families that we have just described were no exception. For example, although they had arrived in southern California at different times, John Forster and Cave Couts were close friends and neighbors, living seven miles apart (Gray 1998:109). They were so close, in fact, that Couts named two of his children after Forster, which suggests that the latter was their godfather. Moreover, after Pío Pico filed his lawsuit against Forster, Couts testified in Forster's favor, souring an already strained relationship with Pío's brother, Andrés (Gray 1998:174). Forster was also indirectly related to the third family in the sample, the Stokes, since his brother-in-law Pío Pico was the uncle of María Ortega, Edward Stokes' wife.

3. The Data

The documents used in the study are dated in southern California or written by authors from the area while corresponding with their families. They are all personal letters, although sometimes they refer to business topics, since family members were often involved in commercial ventures together. Of the 47 documents analyzed, 11 belong to the Stokes family, 8 to the Forster family, and 28 to the Couts. In all, 6 documents were written by speakers of the first generation, born before annexation, while 41 were written by people born around the time of annexation, which we have identified as the second generation (Table 3).

	Stokes	Forster	Couts	Totals
First generation authors	2	0	4	6
Second generation authors	9	8	24	41
Totals	11	8	28	47

Table 3. Totals of letters in the sample, classified by generation and family.

Of the 17 authors, 8 are men and 9 are women, although the former were normally more prolific, so that they are responsible for 33 out of the 47 letters. In general, they had some level of schooling, either in English or in Spanish, although some could not compose or read their correspondence and had to resort to scribes or readers.

The earliest letters are dated in 1865 and the last one is from 1900, so that they span almost the entirety of the second half of the nineteenth century. The bulk of the letters clusters around the twenty years between 1871 and 1890 (Table 4).

	Stokes	Forsters	Couts	Totals
1865-70	0	0	6	6
1871-80	4	7	13	24
1881-90	3	0	8	11
1891+	4	1	1	6
Totals	11	8	28	47

Table 4. Totals of letters in the sample by date.

Most of the letters were written in Spanish, but several of them exhibited portions written in English side by side with the Spanish, or English words interspersed in the Spanish text (Table 5, cf. Section 4.2.1).

	Stokes	Forster	Couts	Totals
English	0	0	9	9
Spanish	11	8	19	38
Totals	11	8	28	47

Table 5. Totals of letters in the sample, by language.

4. Findings

4.1. Patterns of language use

When all the families are considered together, distinct patterns of language use emerge among their members. Thus, in the case of the Forster family, all the available intra- and intergenerational correspondence, which is written by John Forster, Jr., is in Spanish, even after English became the majority language with the annexation of California to the United States. As noted before, Spanish had been adopted as the language of the family, and subsequent changes in political and social structures did not affect this choice. The clearest sign of maintenance is that this second generation writer preferred to communicate with his peers in Spanish in all the correspondence in the corpus (1).

> 1. Querido Hermano, I Recivi tu carta, y beo lo I que medise del trato que
>   piensas I aser, esta muy bueno [. . .] (F 3)
>   "Dear brother, I received you letter and I see what you said about the
>   agreement that you are thinking about, it is very good [. . .]"

The Stokes family also retained Spanish over the two generations, in spite of the English superstrate. As may be recalled, the patriarch of the family died while the children were still young, so that they were raised by their mother, grandmother, and Californio stepfather. This may have deprived them of the opportunity for acquiring English at home during childhood. Predictably, all their family correspondence is in Spanish for the remainder of the century. Again, like the Forsters, the Stokes preferred Spanish not just to address the older relatives but also their peers (2). It is possible that the children achieved some degree of proficiency in English, since, as may be recalled from Section 2.2, at least one of them attended a mission school after annexation. However, this was not enough to cause a shift to that language in intimate discourse.

> 2. Querido Hermano, I Pues asta ayier resibi tu apre I siable Carta (S 8)
>   "Dear brother, it was only yesterday that I finally received your
>   esteemed letter."

The Couts exhibit more complex patterns of language use and more willingness to adopt English. It is clear that the mother, Isidora Bandini de Couts, was a monolingual Spanish speaker and remained so all her life. All communication addressed to her was in Spanish if the author was proficient in the language. Thus, her two eldest sons, William and Cave, wrote to her in Spanish when they went away to study in Tennessee (Huntington Library, Couts Collection, CT 299, 328, 329, 330, 331, 332, 333, for Cave; CT 472, 473, 481, 482, for William). At least one of her daughters, Antonia, continued to write to her in Spanish into adulthood (Huntington Library, Couts Collection CT 2044, 2045, 2046), while another, Isidora Forster, admitted to limited proficiency in that language and opted to write in English with instructions to her brothers to do a sight translation for her mother's benefit (Huntington Library, Couts Collection, CT 715). It is clear that Isidora Bandini de Couts herself could not read or write in any language, since her letters are written in the hand of a number of different literate members of the family (cf. also the comment by her son Cave in 3).

3. [. . .] porsupuesto de U. no l espero contestacion directa pero de Billi sí, y U. podia l aser á Boby o Johny escrevir por U. (C 21)
"[. . .] of course, I don't expect a direct response from you, but I do from Billy and you could make Billy or Johny write for you."

On the other hand, the patriarch, Cave Johnson Couts, Sr., wrote both in Spanish and English. He conducted most of his ranching business by corresponding in Spanish with his *mayordomos* and farm hands. However, his letters relating to financial transactions and public affairs were generally in English, as were his exchanges with his brother-in-law and commercial partner, Abe l Stearns.[6] Within the family, Couts also used both Spanish and English. However, he reserved Spanish exclusively for communication with his wife, while he always wrote to his children in English and they in turn wrote back to him in the same language (cf., Couts Collection CT 472, 473, among many others). The shift to English is perhaps even more evident in the written communication among the second generation siblings, which is conducted in English generally, even if sometimes they show evidence of their knowledge of Spanish (cf. Section 4.2.2. for further discussion).

To sum up, although superficially the three families resembled each other in their ethnic make-up, the specific social circumstances of each were instrumental in determining the language(s) of communication. Thus, for instance, in the Stokes family, the death of the English-speaking patriarch led to the children being raised in a monolingual environment in their formative years and to their preference for Spanish as the language of the family throughout their adult life.

Yet, the languages spoken by the members of the household were not the only factor influencing language choice. Identification with one or the other linguistic community (Californio or Anglo) was also important. For example, English native speakers such as Forster, who had arrived before annexation, had accepted the position of Spanish as the prestige language, and chose not to teach English to their children. Therefore, the Forster boys, who could have learned English at home from their father during early childhood, did not. This was in spite of the fact that they were born around the time of annexation (the eldest, Marcos, was nine years old in 1848) and the practical usefulness of the language for conducting business was becoming increasingly evident. Yet, a combination of family

---

[6] Because these letters did not involve communication among the immediate family members, they were not included in the database under study here. They will, however, be the object of a larger scale investigation.

dynamics predating annexation and the relative isolation of the southern California ranches allowed the Forsters to continue to employ Spanish at home.

On the other hand, the Couts embraced the new American order, of which Cave Johnson, Sr. was a bulwark and an important local representative, his status as *ranchero* notwithstanding. Among other things, this led to very sustained efforts on his part to ensure that his children became proficient in English, in order for them to succeed financially and to guarantee their social prominence in American California. The Couts children thus transitioned to English in the course of their lifetime and tended to prefer it for communication within their cohort.

4.2. Features of language contact

If we consider the letters together, there are three major features that stand out as being a result of language contact. On the one hand, they show code mixing in the form of lexical borrowing and occasional code-switching of longer stretches. Additionally, there are a number of metalinguistic comments that show the authors' awareness and preoccupation with the effect of language contact on their proficiency. Finally, in some authors one finds evidence of attrition in the mother tongue, as well as strategies typical of non-native speakers in their second language. We shall discuss each one in turn.

4.2.1. Language mixing

In this category, we provide a rough measure of the frequency of code mixing in the documents, by quantifying its presence in the letters, not its density. The main type of code mixing found was the borrowing of individual lexemes, with or without some form of morphological or orthographic adaptation to the recipient language. We recognize the theoretical difference between borrowing and code-switching proper, i.e., the former can in principle be present in the speech of monolinguals whereas the latter is a feature exclusive to bilinguals (Pfaff 1979:295-6). However, in written documents from another historical period the lack of some crucial clues makes it virtually impossible to decide between borrowing and individual switches involving a single constituent. For example, one cannot base the distinction on phonetic clues, since orthography is a poor guide to pronunciation. It is also difficult to know whether a given term had already been incorporated into the lexical inventory of the other language as a borrowing, or was still an occasional switch. We therefore use code mixing as an umbrella term to include both of these features (Pfaff 1979:291).

Of the 47 letters, a total of 23 had examples of some form of code mixing (Table 6). Since only writers of the second generation ever mixed the two languages in our sample, only they were included in the table. It will be noted that not all families were equally likely to do so; for example, the Forsters did it a great deal less than the Stokes and the Couts.

	Stokes	%	Forster	%	Couts	%	Totals	%
Code mixing	6	66.7	1	12.5	15	62.5	23	56.1
No code mixing	3	33.3	7	87.5	9	37.5	19	43.9
Totals	9	100	8	100	24	100	42	100

Table 6. Totals and percentages of letters written by second generation writers with some form of Spanish-English code mixing.

Language mixing normally involved individual lexeme borrowing, mostly of nouns, sometimes adapted to the target language in orthography, phonology, and morphology. In their preference for individual switches, our authors were no different from bilingual writers of today, both of fiction and non-fiction (cf. Pfaff and Chávez 1986:232, Callahan 2004:90-91). Normally, these borrowings did not come to replace preexisting terms, but were associated with new cultural artifacts and institutions. They tended to cluster in certain semantic fields, such as personal titles and nicknames, and cultural notions more deeply entrenched in the lending language. The process worked both ways, with Californios adopting English for technological and legal innovations, and English speakers using Spanish terminology in ranching and for social terms and titles.

It was normally the case that people were referred to by their titles in their culture of origin (4). Nicknames were also revealing of people's linguistic allegiances (5), with younger family members often receiving Anglo appellations. Ironically, in a generation earlier their own Anglo fathers' names had been nativized to Spanish (e.g., John to Juan; Cave to Cuevas). It is interesting to note that even for speakers who opted to write in English, the Californio grandmother was referred to as *mamayita* or *vieja*, whereas the young generations of the family were referred to as *babies* even by authors who wrote in Spanish (6). Thus, it seems that the labeling associated the older generation with Spanish, while it assumed that the younger generation had been surrendered to the new order, and was therefore named in the language that represented it, even before they themselves had made a conscious choice in that regard.

4. a. [. . .] Mrs. Kittle dice que | ella y sus muchachas la sacaran | los dias de fiesta (C 20)
"Mrs. Kittle says that she and her girls will take her out on holidays."

b. Brother Chalmers y yo hemos estado | aquí desde aller (C 22)
"Brother Chalmers and I have been here since yesterday."

5. [. . .] lla savia | yo del casamiento de Bobby [. . .] (C 27)
"I already knew about Bobby's wedding."

6. Ya me muero por | ver a mis babies [. . .] (C 20)
"I am dying to see my babies."

As for the terminology borrowed from English to Spanish, it refers to innovations in communications (*el expres* "the express train," F 6, 1 16, *seguir en el Train* "continue on the train," C 20, l. 31.), the law (*mis taxes* "my taxes" S 11, l. 17, *esos escuates* "those squatters," C 10, l. 11), inventions and measurements (*el Thermometer*, C 13, l. 21; *acres* C 21, l. 28), and more mundane cultural innovations such as new holidays and foods associated with Anglo life (*el "Plum Pudding"* C 25, l. 57). Awareness of the foreignness of terms is evinced sometimes by overt flagging through special punctuation; other borrowings become integrated to the point that they are adapted to the Spanish phonology and morphology (cf. *escuates* < Engl. *squatters*).

On the other hand, Spanish sometimes appears in letters written in English, showing that Californio culture made inroads in the lives of English speakers in areas such as ranching and family relationships. A prime example is the Hispanic notion of *compadrazgo* (Griswold del Castillo 1984:42), which was extended beyond the family and often bestowed upon Anglos. Thus, for example, John Forster, Sr. and Cave Johnson Couts, Sr. addressed each other as *compadres* in their letters to each other, which are, of course, mostly in English.[7]

There are very few examples of code-mixing involving more than one lexeme at a time. However, a number of letters were addressed to two readers with different dominant languages (e.g., an English-dominant father and Spanish-dominant mother). In those cases the writers often opted to communicate with each one of them in their preferred language, with the result that the letter had portions in both English and Spanish, the length of each one also reflecting the writer's language dominance patterns. However, these are not strictly speaking examples of code-switching, which is normally considered to be the alternating use of two codes in the same speech act. Here the writer simply bundles up two speech acts into one letter (7).

7. Dear Father | We commenced to review our studies today [. . .] Your affect^e son | Willie |

---

[7] An example of this would be CT 732, which is not included in the database because it does not involve direct family members.

Querida Mama: I El padre de aqui tuvo I que hir a decir misa en otra parte
[. . .] I Su hijo I Billy (C 7)
"Dear Mother, the Father from here had to go perform mass somewhere
else."

In our entire database of 47 family documents, only one letter exhibits intrasentential code-switching. This is a letter of the later period, authored by a cousin of the Couts (cf. portions included in 8). Given the high level of monitoring possible in writing, this unusual example hints at the prevalence and acceptability of code-switching among the younger speakers, to an extent not unlike what one finds today in U.S. Spanish. If anything, (8) suggests the likelihood of much more frequent oral code-switching.

8. [. . .] no puedo ni I pasar por allí en el tren sin acer I UN STUPID OF MYSELF,
mucho menos I volver á vivir alli, pero estamos AT PRESENT viviendo en
un lugar muy bonito [. . .] (C 28)
"I can't even go by there on the train without making a fool of myself,
much less live there again; but right now we are living in a very pretty
place."

4.2.2. Metalinguistic references

Another element considered in the analysis of language shift and maintenance patterns is the speakers' own explicit assessment of their linguistic skills. From their comments, it is clear that the writers were aware of their proficiency or lack thereof in one or the other language (for a related phenomenon in fiction, cf. Callahan 2001). For example, the Forster children struggled to acquire English in southern California, which is ironic considering their father's imperfect acquisition of Spanish. At least one of them was sent to the north of the state, to San Francisco, apparently in the hopes that higher exposure to English would enable him to learn the language faster. Even while acknowledging its usefulness and commercial benefits, the young John Forster found the task difficult (cf. 9).

9. [. . .] mis de I seo son grandes de progresar cono siendo I el bien que me
vendrán, siendo una I idioma tan util sin ella nada se puede aser, siendo
la idioma comun del mu[n]do, yo siento el corto tiempo que tengo que
permanecer y no biendo vencido I las mayores dificultades del idioma.
[. . .] (F 4)
"[. . .] I have a strong desire to progress, knowing full well how good it
will be for me, since it is a useful language, without which one can't do
anything, and the common language of the world; I fear that I will not stay
here long enough to overcome the biggest difficulties of the language."

As for the Couts family, the eldest brothers remarked on their linguistic isolation when they moved away from southern California to Tennessee (10), which in all likelihood resulted in few opportunities to practice Spanish. The effects were soon evident. As their own comments show, speaking and writing Spanish became increasingly difficult and code switching more frequent, both in their written and oral discourse (11a,b).

10. No hay ninguno que sepa ablar en español aqui | masde nosotros tres (C 10)
    "There is no one who can speak in Spanish except for us three."

11. a. [. . .] me da mucho trabajo escribir en Español, tengo | mucho miedo que se me valla a olvidar, porque | cada vez que hablo Español se me entremete | el Ingles. (C 11)
    "It's really hard for me to write in Spanish, I am really afraid that I am going to forget it, every time I speak in Spanish, English mixes in."

    b. [. . .] la razon que no le he escrito hes | que apenas puedo escribir en español | he empesado varias cartas pero nunca | he podido acabar porque hago tantos | erores pero esta carta voy a mandar | de todos modos y voy a aser la prueba | para escribirle cada otra semana (C 13)
    "The reason why I haven't written is that I am barely able to write in Spanish, I have begun various letters but I haven't ever been able to finish them because I make so many mistakes, but this letter I am going to send anyway and I am going to try to write to you every other week."

Interestingly, neither the children nor their parents insisted on the usefulness of Spanish or the need to retain proficiency in that language to preserve this linguistic heritage. There were no references in the correspondence to any concerted effort to maintain the language, other than the very act of writing the letters.

This would not be so telling if the Couts brothers did not repeatedly express surprise at cultural and environmental differences such as weather, foods, and fashions (12), or make a point of commenting on their dutiful efforts to retain some other important features of their Hispanic upbringing, such as Catholic rites (13).

12. a. [. . .] ayer empeso el tiempo | frio otra vez, pero estamos con intenciones | que se cambian otra vez antes de la | Noche Buena, aunque no tengamos bu | ñuelos para esa noche (C 9)
    "Yesterday the weather turned cold again but we hope that it will change again before Christmas eve even though we don't have buñuelos for that night."

b. [. . .] tiza | es un articulo muy comun entre las | señoras de aquí y a Vd seguro no le | va a gustar eso, pero muy pronto se | acostumbrara, y lo usara tambien (C 9)

"[. . .] chalk is a very common article among the ladies here and I am sure that you won't like it, but soon you will grow accustomed to it and you will use it, too."

13. a. El Padre de aqui tuvo | que hir a decir misa en otra parte | y por fuerza tuvimos que estar sin | oir misa un Domingo. Es el segun | do Domingo que no hemos oido | misa desde que llegamos aqui. (C 7)

"The Father from here had to go perform mass somewhere else and we were forced to go another Sunday without mass. It is the second Sunday that we haven't gone since we got here."

b. Una muchacha Protestante se | va a-ser Catolica en cuatro ó cinco dias mas si encaso un | Padre viejo de Nashville viene en ese tiem[p]o, y yo voy | a ser el padrino de la hermosísima joven que por | cuatro meses ha sido ó fue una amiga muy grande (^de) su hijo | Billy (C 14)

"A Protestant girl is going to become Catholic in four or five more days if the old Father from Nashville comes at that time and I will be the god-father to the beautiful young girl that for four months has been or was a close friend of your son Billy."

The above comments give us a snapshot of a society in transition. Although Cal-ifornio identity seemed closely linked with language in the first generation, in the second generation linguistic allegiances started to weaken for some families, even if other cultural traits were maintained. Thus, although not all second gen-eration Californios became proficient in English to the same degree, all of them agreed on its importance for practical purposes. Loss of Spanish dominance was viewed by those who underwent it with some concern when it started to impede intrafamilial communication, but not with alarm since it did not jeopardize social or economic well-being.

4.2.3. Convergence, attrition, and second language acquisition

The final impact of language contact is constituted by the very structural features of Spanish and English in the letters. In the process of contact, speak-ers often start to adopt features from one language into the other. Traditionally, if this adoption results in the loss of features of one language, it has been called convergence, whereas if it involves the incorporation of new features from the other language, it is known as interference (Romaine 1995:75). However, as Myers-Scotton (2005:272) points out, the two processes often occur simultane-ously, as when a structure from one language is not just lost but replaced by one from the other. Here we will simply note deviations from the standard structures of Spanish and English which can be attributed to the simultaneous acquisition of both languages, without attempting to classify them as one or the other.

Because it is sometimes difficult to ascertain the mother tongue of a speaker, it is not always possible to distinguish cases of attrition, i.e., changes and impoverishment of the mother tongue through contact, from those of interlanguage, i.e., the features of intermediate stages in the acquisition of a second language. In what follows we will present the various structural features together.

The Spanish of the Californios included several examples of absence of obligatory morphological markers, such as verbal agreement (14a,b) and nominal concord (14c), as well as a blurring of the obligatory distinction between indicative and subjunctive mood (15a), and between *ser* and *estar* "to be" (15b). Some other distinctions were lost under the influence of English, such as the two-way split between *pero* and *sino*, both translatable as an adversative "but" in English, but the latter used exclusively in contraposition to a previous negative sentence (cf. 16, where standard Spanish requires *sino*).

14. a. tocante I del hombre que tu me dise (F 6)
"about the man that you tell-3p.s. me"

b. tan I pronto como buelba algunos Baqueros (F 8)
"as soon as some cowhands return-3.p.s."

c. siendo una ydioma tan util (F 4)
"it being such a-f.s. useful language-m.s."

15. a. Bese a todos mis hermanitos y usted I recibe lo mismo de su querido hijo (C 10)
"Kiss-2.s.imp.formal all my brothers and sisters from me and you receive-3.s.pr.ind. the same from your beloved son"

b. Yo le escrivi a tio Juanito diciéndole I que en mi opinión que U. habia mandado a Tio Baker I todos esos papeles i que el los habia entregado a Don I Alejandro Forbes, pero tal vez soy equivoco. (C 20)
"I wrote to Uncle Juanito telling him that I thought you had sent Uncle Baker all those papers and that he had given them to Don Alejandro Forbes, but perhaps I am wrong."

16. no solo ora que I estoy tan lejos pero despues (C 10)
"not only now that I am so far but also afterwards"

On the other hand, in English, the second generation Californios also exhibited occasional influence of Spanish, as in the lexical confusion of *leave* and *let* (with the same rendering, "dejar," in Spanish) (17), or features such as redundant past tense marking (18a) and lack of number concord (18b).

17. [. . .] my aunt says she will not I leave me go until my tooth I is well (C 1)

18. a. I wrote a letter to you I last month but I think you did I not received it (C 6)

    b. several of our good friend doubt their return (C 11)

On occasion, the syntax of Spanish was modeled on English word order or constructions. Thus, for example, (19a) is a calque on the English interrogative order, while (19b c) are lexically Spanish but structurally English (notice the use of *nunca* where the negative particle *no* would be standard in Spanish and the expression *cada otra semana*, calqued on "every other week" and whose equivalent in Spanish would have been *cada dos semanas*).

19. a. entiendo que la cadena, significa (S 5)
    "I understand what the chain means"

    b. yo nun[n]ca tenía una I idea que sería tanta caballada (F 6)
    "I never had any idea that there would be so many horses"

    c. voy a aser la prueva I para escribirle cada otra semana (C 13)
    "I am going to try to write you every other week"

In other cases the influence of English was less overt, but led to the preference of a less frequent over a more frequent construction in Spanish. Thus, in the formation of the passive, some writers prefer the *ser* + past participle instead of the less marked *se* construction (20). The overt use of the subject in cases where there is no special emphasis or contrast could also be attributable to English influence (21). On the other hand, complement pronouns that would be present in Spanish are sometimes eliminated as they would be in English (22).

20. Cuando Sali de San Francisco mi sueldo era $ 150.00/al I mes, luego que llegue fue subido a $ 175.oo (C 21).
    "When I left San Francisco my salary was $150.00 a month, but after I arrived here it was raised to $175.00."

21. Mr. Scott esta en I Sacramento fue a la oficina I del Agrimensor General para I atender negocios propios sobre I el Rancho de Buena Vista—El devia aberse ido antes (C 20)
    "Mr. Scott is in Sacramento; he went to the office of the Surveyor General to attend to his own business about Rancho de Buena Vista—he should have left earlier"

22. [. . .] y todo me tiempo ahora guardo para mis libros (C 14)
    "[. . .] and all my time now I devote to my books"

One would expect that the influence of English on Spanish would be greater in those writers who can be shown to be English dominant. However, signs of convergence are even evident in writers who by their own admission are not more proficient in English but rather the opposite. Thus, John Forster, who complained so bitterly about his hardships learning English (cf. 9), exhibited the most signs of convergence with English. On the other hand, Antonia Couts, who seems to have been quite a balanced bilingual, showed very few signs of convergence, and these tended to be quite subtle (cf. 21). This may have been related to the nature of the input they each received: at least part of what John heard was his father's non-native speaker Spanish, whereas Antonia heard native Spanish from her mother and native English from her father. However, one needs to be very cautious when assessing linguistic proficiency, since ascertaining it is complicated by the exclusive reliance on a written sample, which may show the effects of imperfect literacy, not just incomplete acquisition.

5. Conclusions

The analysis of our documents allows us to conclude that in the three families under study, the extent of loss of Spanish and the adoption of English were not uniform: while some families retained Spanish during the entire second half of the nineteenth century, others shifted to English in the second generation. In this regard, diverse social and political circumstances weighed more than any economic benefit to be derived from the mastery of English, showing that integrative factors exercised a stronger pull than merely instrumental motivation in language shift.

At the structural level, the evidence of language contact is constituted by a moderate incidence of code mixing in both English and Spanish. The documents show the usual preference for individual lexeme borrowing, a hallmark of language mixing in the written mode. With few exceptions, the English present in Spanish letters and the Spanish in English letters were limited to words or short phrases. Most writers were fully aware of these switches, sometimes flagging them overtly.

The effects of language contact in California can also be gleaned from metalinguistic comments, which present the writer's point of view about matters of language use and proficiency. These are further evidence of linguistic allegiances, sometimes at odds with economic and social convenience.

Finally, language contact is visible in features of structural convergence and individual attrition. In the first generation, the second language had been learned in adulthood, resulting in interlanguage strategies. In the second generation, patterns of language dominance are less clear. Whereas some writers exhibit native features in both languages, others show some degree of attrition in their stronger language, while at the same time exhibiting interlanguage features in L2. As stated earlier, though, determining the dominant language is complicated by the written mode, which eliminates several useful clues and makes others hard to interpret. A larger database may help to clarify matters.

This analysis of family correspondence could be profitably extended to the study of interactions between English and Spanish in public domains such as the law, banking, and various private business (ranching, etc.). The writing of Anglos may be as revealing in these domains as that of the Californios themselves and would complete the picture of language use in post-Annexation California.

Since this study covers only two generations, a natural extension would be to include third generation writers. A partial analysis suggests that, regardless of the usage of their parents, third generation Californios had completely embraced English, retaining Spanish only for sporadic emblematic words. If it had not been for the arrival of new immigrants in the wake of the Mexican revolution of 1910, Spanish in California might have been lost altogether.

Since it is only through documentary evidence like the one analyzed here that we can unearth the earliest layers of California Spanish, a natural corollary of this work is a call for more extensive recovery of documents from the period. If this task is to be undertaken with effectiveness, it seems imperative to create digital databases of whatever pertinent materials are available in Southwestern archives, since much evidence of interest remains untapped or inaccessible.

Document description

C 1. [1865] María Antonia Couts. Family letter. Written to her father, Cave Johnson Couts a. Los Angeles [E]. HL Box 34. CT 2036.

C 2. [1865] María Antonia Couts. Family letter. Written to her father, Cave Johnson Couts a. Los Angeles [E]. HL Box 34. CT 2040.

C 3. [c. 1865] Cave Johnson Couts a. Family letter. Written to his wife, Isidora Bandini de Couts. Rancho Santa Margarita, California [S]. HL Box 6. CT 299.

C 4. [1866] María Antonia Couts. Family letter. Written to her father, Cave Johnson Couts a. Los Angeles [E]. HL Box 34. CT 2036.

C 5. [1866]. María Antonia Couts de Scott. Family letter. Written to her mother, Isidora Bandini Couts [S]. Los Angeles. [In Spanish]. HL Box 34. CT 2044.

C 6. [1868]. Family letter. Written by Nancy Dolores Couts to her father, Cave Johnson Couts a. Los Angeles. [E]. HL. Box 8. CT 424.

C 7. [1871]. Family letter. Written by William Bandini Couts to his father, Cave Johnson Couts a and his mother, Isidora Bandini de Couts. Clarksville, Tenn. [E/S]. HL Box 9. CT 472.

C 8. [1871]. Family letter. Written by William Bandini Couts to his mother, Isidora Bandini de Couts. Clarksville, Tenn. [S] HL Box 9. CT 481.

C 9. [1871]. Family letter. Written by William Bandini Couts to his mother, Isidora Bandini de Couts. Clarksville, Tenn. [S] HL Box 9. CT 481.

C 10. [1872]. Family letter. Written by Cave Johnson Couts b to his mother Isidora Bandini de Couts. Clarksville, Tenn. [S] HL Box 6. CT 328.

C 11. [1872]. Family letter. Written by William Bandini Couts to his father, Cave Johnson Couts a and his mother, Isidora Bandini de Couts. Clarksville, Tenn. [E/S] HL Box 9. CT 473.

C 12. [1872]. Family letter. Written by Cave Johnson Couts to Isidora Bandini de Couts. Rancho San Luis. [S] HL Box 6. CT 300.

C 13. [1873]. Family letter. Written by Cave Johnson Couts b to his mother Isidora Bandini de Couts. Clarksville, Tenn. [S] HL Box 6. CT 329.

C 14. [1873]. Family letter. Written by William Bandini Couts to his mother, Isidora Bandini de Couts. Clarksville, Tenn. [S] HL Box 9. CT 482.

C 15. [1873]. Family letter. Written by Cave Johnson Couts a to his children William Bandini and Cave Johnson b. Rancho Guajome, California. [E] HL Box 6. CT 301

C 16. [1874]. Family letter. Written by Cave Johnson Couts a to his children William Bandini and Cave Johnson b. Rancho Guajome, California. [E] HL Box 6. CT 302.

C 17. [1875]. Family letter. Written by María Antonia Couts de Scott to her mother, Isidora Bandini Couts. San Francisco. [S] HL Box 34. CT 2045.

C 18. [1877]. Family letter. Written by Cave Johnson Couts b to his mother, Isidora Bandini de Couts. Los Angeles. [S] HL Box 6. CT 330.

C 19. [1877]. Family letter. Written by Cave Johnson Couts b to his mother, Isidora Bandini de Couts. Los Angeles. [S] HL Box 6. CT 330.

C 20. [1882]. Family letter. Written by María Antonia Couts de Scott to her mother, Isidora Bandini de Couts. San Francisco. [S] HL Box 34. CT 2046.

C 21. [1883]. Family letter. Written by Cave Johnson Couts a to his wife Isidora Bandini de Couts. San Francisco. [S] HL Box 6. CT 331.

C 22. [1883]. Family letter. Written by Cave Johnson Couts b to his mother Isidora Bandini de Couts. San José de Guatemala. [S] HL Box 6. CT 331.

C 23. [1883] Family letter. Written by Isidora Forster Couts Gray Fuller to her mother Isidora Bandini Couts. Oakland, California. [E] HL Box 12. CT 715.

C 24. [1884]. Family letter. Written by Cave Johnson Couts b to his mother, Isidora Bandini de Couts. Escuintla, Guatemala. [S] HL Box 6. CT 332.

C 25. [1884]. Family letter. Written by Cristina Estudillo Couts to her aunt, Isidora Bandini de Couts. Pasadena. [S] HL Box 7. CT 367.

C 26. [1885]. Family letter. Written by Cave Johnson Couts b to his mother Isidora Bandini de Couts. Temecula. [S] HL Box 6. CT 333..

C 27. [1886]. Letter forwarded by Cave Johnson Couts b to Isidora Bandini de Couts. Tucson. [S] HL Box 2. CT 70.

C 28. [1900]. Family letter. Written by Josefa Bandini Rhodes Thomas Dawsett to Isidora Forster Couts Gray Fuller London. [S/E] HL Box 10. CT 521.

F 1. [1871] Family letter. Written by John Forster b to his father, Don Juan Forster. San Francisco. [S]. HL.

F 2. [1871] Family letter. Written by John Forster b to his mother Isidora Pico de Forster. San Francisco. [S]. HL.

F 3. [1871] Family letter. Written by John Forster b to his mother, Isidora Pico de Forster. San Francisco. [S]. HL.

F 4. [1871] Family letter. Written by John Forster b to his father, Don Juan Forster. San Francisco. [S]. HL.

F 5. [1871] Family letter. Written by John Forster b to his mother, Isidora Pico de Forster. San Francisco. [S]. HL.

F 6. [1873] Family letter. Written by John Forster b to one of his brothers. San Diego. [S]. HL.

F 7. [1873] Family letter. Written by John Forster b to his mother, Isidora Pico de Forster. San Diego. [S]. HL.

F 8. [1875] Family letter. Written by John Forster b to his father, Don Juan Forster. Rancho Santa Margarita. [S]. HL.

S 1. [1873] Alfredo Stokes. Family letter. Written to his mother, Refugio Ortega de Olvera and his grandmother, María Pico de Ortega. San Francisco. [S] JC.

S 2. [1878] Alfredo Stokes. Family letter. Written to his mother, Refugio Ortega de Olvera. Nephi, Utah. [S] JC.

S 3. [1878] Balbina Cuevas. Family letter. Postscript written by Alfredo Stokes. Written to Alfredo's mother, Refugio Ortega de Olvera. San Francisco. [S] JC.

S 4. [1880] Unnamed author, widow of Ignacio del Valle. Family letter. Written to her niece, Dolores Olvera de Stokes. Camulos. [S] JC.

S 5. [1888] Alfredo S. Stokes. Family letter. Written to his grandmother, María Pico de Ortega. Los Angeles. [S] JC.

S 6. [1888] María Pico de Ortega. Family letter. Written to her daughter, Refugio Ortega de Olvera. Santa Barbara. [S] JC.

S 7. [1888] José Antonio María Ortega. Family letter. Written to his mother, María Pico de Ortega. Buckeye Rancho. [S] JC.

S 8. [1891] Eduardo R. Stokes. Family letter. Written to his brother, Alfredo Stokes. Las Vírgenes. [S] JC.

S 9. [1892] Josefa Olvera de Castillo. Family letter. Written to her stepbrother, Alfredo Stokes. Redondo Beach. [S] JC.

S 10. [1894] Adolfo Stokes. Family letter. Written to his mother, Refugio Ortega de Olvera. Nuevo. [S] JC.

S 11. [1894] Adolfo Stokes. Family letter. Written to his mother, Refugio Ortega de Olvera. Nuevo. [S] JC.

References

Acevedo, Rebeca. 2000. Perspectiva histórica del paradigma verbal en el español de California. In A. Roca (Ed.), *Research in Spanish in the U.S.*, (pp. 110-120). Somerville: Cascadilla.

Aguirre, Adalberto. 1982. Language use patterns of adolescent Chicanos in a California border town. In F. Barkin, E. A. Brandt, & J. Ornstein-Galicia (Eds.), *Bilingualism and Language Contact: Spanish, English and Native American Languages* (pp. 278-289). New York: Teacher's College P.

Amastae, Jon. 1982. Language shift and maintenance in the Lower Rio Grande Valley of Southern Texas. In F. Barkin, E. A. Brandt, & J. Ornstein-Galicia (Eds.), *Bilingualism and Language Contact: Spanish, English and Native American Languages* (pp. 261-277). New York: Teacher's College P.

Annable, Lyle C. 1965. *The Life and Times of Cave Johnson Couts, San Diego County Pioneer*. Unpublished master's thesis, San Diego State College.

Balestra, Mirta Alejandra. 2002. *Del futuro morfológico al perifrástico: Un cambio morfosintáctico en el español de California: 1800-1930*. Unpublished doctoral dissertation, University of Houston.

Bills, Garland D. 1997. New Mexican Spanish: Demise of the earliest European variety in the United States. *American Speech* 72, 154-171.

Bills, Garland D., Eduardo Hernández-Chávez, & Alan Hudson. 1995. The geography of language shift: distance from the Mexican border and Spanish language claiming in the Southwestern U.S. *International Journal of the Sociology of Language*, 114, 9-27.

Bills, Garland D., Alan Hudson, & Eduardo Hernández-Chávez. 2000. Spanish home language use and English proficiency as differential measures of language maintenance and shift. *Southwest Journal of Linguistics*, 19 (1), 11-27.

Blanco, Antonio. 1971. *La lengua española en la historia de California*. Madrid: Ediciones de Cultura Hispánica.

Callahan, Laura. 2001. Metalinguistic References in a Spanish/English Corpus. *Hispania*, 84(3), 417-427.

Callahan, Laura. 2002. The matrix language frame model and Spanish/English codeswitching in fiction. *Language and Communication*, 22, 1-16.

Callahan, Laura. 2004. *Spanish/English codeswitching in a written corpus*. Amsterdam / Philadelphia: John Benjamins.

188 ❖ ❖ ❖ ❖ ❖   *María Irene Montoya and Wendy Beckman*

Coles, Felice Anne. 1991. The *isleño* dialect of Spanish: Language maintenance strategies. In C. A. Klee, & L. A. Ramos-García (Eds.), *Sociolinguistics of the Spanish-Speaking World* (pp. 312-328). Tempe, AZ: Bilingual P / Editorial Bilingüe.

Decker, Wendy L. 2003. *A Time of Transition: A Linguistic Analysis of Californio Documents Written in Spanish in the 19th Century.* Unpublished master's thesis, San Diego State University.

Fishman, Joshua. 1966. *Language Loyalty in the United States.* The Hague: Mouton.

Floyd, Mary Beth. 1982. Spanish-language maintenance in Colorado. In F. Barkin, E. A. Brandt, & J. Ornstein-Galicia (Eds.), *Bilingualism and Language Contact: Spanish, English and Native American Languages* (pp. 290-303). New York: Teacher's College P.

Francis, Jessie Davis. 1976. *An Economic and Social History of Mexican California, 1822-1846: Volume I: Chiefly Economic.* New York: Arno P.

García Vizcaíno, María José. 2005. *The Pragmatics of Code-Switching in Chicano Narrative.* Unpublished ms.

Gray, Paul B. 1998. *Forster vs. Pico: The Struggle for the Rancho Santa Margarita.* Spokane, WA: Arthur H. Clark.

Griswold del Castillo, Richard. 1979. *The Los Angeles Barrio: 1850-1890. A social history.* Berkeley, CA: U of California P.

Griswold del Castillo, Richard. 1984. *La familia: Chicano Families in the Urban Southwest, 1848 to the Present.* Notre Dame, IN: U of Notre Dame P.

Griswold del Castillo, Richard, (Ed.) 2006. *Mexicans without Borders: Chicana/o Cultural Space and the Struggle for Justice in San Diego.* Tucson, AZ: U of Arizona P.

Griswold del Castillo, Richard, & Arnaldo De León. 1996. *North to Aztlán. A History of Mexican Americans in the United States.* New York: Twayne.

Hidalgo, Margarita. 1993. The dialectics of Spanish language loyalty and maintenance on the U.S.-Mexico border: A two-generation study. In A. Roca, & J. M. Lipski (Eds.), *Spanish in the United States. Linguistic Contact and Diversity* (pp. 47-73). Berlin: Mouton de Gruyter.

Hudson-Edwards, Alan, & Garland D. Bills. 1982. Intergenerational language shift in an Albuquerque barrio. In J. Amastae, & L. Elías-Olivares (Eds.), *Spanish in the United States. Sociolinguistic aspects* (pp. 135-153). Cambridge: Cambridge UP.

Huntington Library. Special Collections. Couts and Forster Collections.

Kessell, John L. 2002. *Spain in the Southwest.* Norman: U of Oklahoma P.

LeMenager, Charles R. 1989. *Ramona and Round About. A History of San Diego County's Little Back Country.* Ramona, CA: Eagle Peak.

Marschner, Janice. 2000. *California 1850: A Snapshot in Time.* Sacramento: Coleman Ranch P.

Mason, William M. 1998. *The Census of 1790. A Demographic History of Colonial California.* Menlo Park, CA: Ballena P.

Martínez, Glenn. 2000. *Topics in the Historical Sociolinguistics of Tejano Spanish, 1791-1910: Morphosyntactic and Lexical Aspects.* Unpublished doctoral dissertation, University of Massachusetts, Amherst.

McKanna, Clare V., Jr. 1998. "An old town gunfight": The homicide trial of Cave Johnson Couts, 1866. *Journal of San Diego History*, 44(4), 258-273.

McKevitt, Gerald. 1979. *The University of Santa Clara: a History, 1851-1977.* Stanford, CA: Stanford UP.

McKevitt, Gerald. 1990/1991. Hispanic Californians and Catholic higher education. The diary of Jesús María Estudillo, 1857-1864. *California History*, 69(4), 320-331.

Montes Alcalá, Cecilia. 2001. Written codeswitching: Powerful bilingual images. In R. Jacobson (Ed.), *Codeswitching Worldwide* (pp. 193-219). Berlin/New York: Mouton de Gruyter.

Montes Alcalá, Cecilia. 2005. "Dear amigo": Exploring code-switching in personal letters. In L. Sayahi, & M. Westmoreland (Eds.), *Selected Proceedings of the Second Workshop on Spanish Sociolinguistics* (pp. 102-108). Somerville, MA: Cascadilla.

Moyna, María Irene, & Wendy Decker. 2005. A historical perspective on Spanish in the California Borderlands. *Southwest Journal of Linguistics*, 24(1), 23.

Myers-Scotton, Carol. 2005. *Multiple Voices. An Introduction to Bilingualism.* Malden, MA: Blackwell.

Pearson, Barbara Zurer, & Arlene McGee. 1993. Language choice in hispanic-background junior high school students in Miami: A 1988 update. In A. Roca, & J. M. Lipski (Eds.), *Spanish in the United States. Linguistic Contact and Diversity* (pp. 91-102). Berlin: Mouton de Gruyter.

Pedraza, Pedro. 1985. Language maintenance among New York Puerto Ricans. In L. Elías-Olivares, E. A. Leone, R. Cisneros, & J. R. Gutiérrez, (Eds.), *Spanish Language Use and Public Life in the United States* (pp. 59-71). Berlin / New York / Amsterdam: Mouton.

Perissinotto, Giorgio. 1992. El español de los Presidios y Misiones de California en 1782. *Estudios de Lingüística Aplicada*, 10 (15-16), 35-47.

Perissinotto, Giorgio, (Ed.) 1998. *Documenting Everyday Life in Early Spanish California.* Santa Barbara: Santa Barbara Trust for Historic Preservation.

Pfaff, Carol W. 1979. Constraints on language mixing: Intrasentential code-switching and borrowing in Spanish-English. *Language.* 55(2), 291-318.

Pfaff, Carol W., & Laura Chávez. 1986. Spanish/English code-switching: Literary reflections of natural discourse. In R. von Bardeleben, D. Briesemeister, & J. Bruce-Novoa (Eds.), *Missions in Conflict: Essays on U.S.-Mexican Relations and Chicano Culture* (pp. 229-254). Tübingen: Gunter Narr.

Pitt, Leonard. 1966. *The Decline of the Californios: A Social History of the Spanish-Speaking Californians, 1846-1890.* Berkeley: U of California P.

Potowski, Kim. 2004. Spanish language shift in Chicago. *Southwest Journal of Linguistics*, 23(1), 87-116.

Romaine, Suzanne. 1995. *Bilingualism* (2nd ed.). Oxford / Cambridge, MA: Blackwell.

San Diego Historical Society. Website: http://www.sandiegohistory.org. Accessed July 7, 2006.

Silva-Corvalán, Carmen. 2001. *Sociolingüística y pragmática del español.* Washington D.C.: Georgetown UP.

Stant, James E. Jr. 1977. *Don Juan Forster, Southern California Pioneer and Rancher.* Unpublished master's thesis, University of San Diego.

Tanner, John D. Jr., & Gloria R. Lothrop. 1970. Don Juan Forster, Southern California Ranchero. *Southern California Quarterly*, 52(3), 195-230.

Trujillo, Juan Antonio. 2000. Socioeconomic identity and linguistic borrowing in pre-statehood New Mexico legal texts. *Southwest Journal of Linguistics*, 19(2), 115-128

Veltman, Calvin. 1983. *Language Shift in the United States.* Berlin / New York / Amsterdam: Mouton.

Wilson, Harlan L. 1942. *A History of the San Diego City Schools from 1542 to 1942 with Emphasis upon the Curriculum.* Unpublished master's thesis, Los Angeles: University of Southern California.

Dialect Death:
The Case of Adaeseño Spanish
in Northwest Louisiana

Comfort Pratt
Texas Tech University

1. Establisment of the Adaeseño Community

The Spanish became the first Europeans to set foot in the territory now known as the United States when Juan Ponce de León and his men landed in Florida in 1513. Numerous Spanish expeditions into the territory followed, and by the end of the sixteenth century, the Spaniards had explored the entire southern part of North America, including the territories now occupied by Texas, Tennessee, Florida, Georgia, the Carolinas, Alabama, Louisiana, Mississippi, Arkansas, and New Mexico. However, they abandoned the region in 1693 and moved further south because they did not find the treasures they were looking for. In the second decade of the eighteenth century, the activities of the French, who had successfully established trade with the native Indians, lured the Spanish back, and they occupied Texas once again and started their defensive activities in the region. Many groups of missionaries traveled to the banks of the Mississippi and the Gulf Coast by way of Mexico and established missions in East Texas.

On 29 September 1717, two of the missionaries, Fathers Antonio Margil de Jesús and Francisco Hidalgo, founded a mission to the east of the Sabine River in Northeast Texas among the Adaes Indians, and named it San Miguel de Linares. The mission was located near the border of Spanish Texas and French Louisiana, fifteen miles from Natchitoches, where the French had already built a fort, St. Jean Baptiste. The mission, which was the easternmost Spanish settlement in the Province of Texas, was established with the aim of converting the Indians to the Catholic faith and winning their loyalty to Spain. There were only three residents in the mission at that time—two priests and a soldier—, yet seventeen Indians were baptized to the Catholic faith that year. In 1718, partly due to Spanish fears of the growing influence of France in Louisiana after the establishment of New Orleans that year, Spanish presence in the area was strengthened with an expedition comprised of seventy-two people under the command of Captain Martín de Alarcón, Governor of Coahuila and Texas. The group renamed the mission San Miguel de Cuéllar. In 1719, due to the war of the Quadruple Alliance in Europe that had pitted Spain against England, Holland, Austria, Sicily, and France, the residents of the French post in Natchitoches attacked the Spanish mission and drove out the occupants, causing the Spanish to abandon the area and return to San Antonio, Texas. Two years later, the Spanish returned to the mission, and the Viceroy of Mexico sent another group led by Marqués de San Miguel de Aguayo, the new Governor of Coahuila and Texas, to fortify Spanish presence, fight the French, and build more missions in the region. Aguayo arrived at the mission on August 29, 1721 with a military force comprised of 3,900 horses, 600 mules laden with food, clothes and six cannons, 200,000 piastres, and 584 men, with the intention of building presidios to protect the East Texas border. Forty-four of the one hundred eighteen conscripts that came with him were Spanish. Also among them were twenty-one *coyotes*, thirty-one mulattos, one *lobo*, one free black, and one Indian (Fuster 2001:148, Lipski 1987a:114).[1]

Aguayo and his men drove away the French and recovered the Texas territory for Spain. Suspicious of the intentions of the French, they also built a presidio, Nuestra Señora del Pilar de Los Adaes, that year after coming to an agreement with the Adaes Indians who inhabited the territory.[2] The presidio was located about a mile and a half east of the mission. It was built with a stockade of painted logs, two and three-quarters yards high all around it. It was hexagonal in shape with three bulwarks placed on alternate corners, each protecting two sides (Castañeda 2:144-45). On 12 October 1721, the Feast Day of Nuestra Señora del Pilar de Zaragoza, the presidio and the mission were dedicated, and the following year, Los Adaes became the residence of the Governors of Texas.[3] Los Adaes protected the missionaries and the converted Indians and was guarded by a garrison of one hundred men. The mission prospered significantly due

---

[1] The piastre was a unit of currency originally equal to one silver dollar or peso. A *coyote* is the offspring of an Indian and a non-Spanish. A *lobo* is the offspring of a black person and an Indian.

[2] The presidio is generally referred to simply as Los Adaes.

[3] Our Lady of Pilar is the Patron Saint of Spain. Her statue, placed on a marble pillar in the Basilica of Zaragoza, is worshipped in remembrance of the apparition of the Virgin Mary to Saint James.

to the good relations between the Spanish and the Indians. The Spaniards founded many missions in Texas and on the coast of California and used them to Christianize and promote the Spanish language and culture. With the passing of time, Spain became more and more disinterested in the settlement. The military strength waned, and the settlement underwent many hardships. Los Adaes and other Spanish settlements in East Texas were very far from the supply center in New Spain (Mexico). The *Camino Real* (the Royal Highway), which was the main route between Los Adaes and New Spain, was a path where traveling was made difficult by the rivers and the Indians. Due to the lack of adequate supplies, the soldiers were forced to raise animals and cultivate their own food, especially corn, but they could not produce adequate food to feed themselves, because the land was not good. Eventually they started to depend on the French post in Natchitoches for supplies, and ended up getting involved in an illegal trade in alcoholic beverages, tobacco, and ammunitions with the French. In 1725, the stockade used to build the presidio started to rot, and it was all replaced with timber the following year. More problems erupted when the military force was reduced from one hundred to sixty in accordance with the *Reglamento* of 1729.[4] An inspection carried out by Brigadier Pedro de Rivera in 1727 on the orders of the Viceroy of Mexico, Marqués de Casafuerte, had ended with a recommendation that since the French were no longer a threat and had only twenty-five soldiers at St. Jean Baptiste, Los Adaes had no need for many soldiers. Furthermore, the annual salary of the soldiers was reduced. Many presidios which were considered no longer useful were closed at that time. In spite of the hardships it was facing, Los Adaes was named capital of the Province of Texas in 1729, and the Spanish continued their Christianization and trading activities with the Indians and the French for many decades.

2. Closure of Los Adaes

In 1762, France ceded the Louisiana territory to Spain by the Treaty of Fontainebleau. Louis XV of France gave the land to the west of the Mississippi to his Spanish cousin, Carlos III, as a gift for helping him in the Seven Years War against England. It is speculated that perhaps the only reason why Spain accepted the territory was in order that it would not fall into the hands of the English (Din 1972). As a result of this transfer, the French ceased to be a threat. The absence of confrontations with the French led Spain to determine that it was no longer necessary to keep Los Adaes open and decided to close it down and transfer the capital to Béxar (San Antonio). Besides, an inspection carried out in September 1767 by Marqués de Rubí, who had been commissioned by the

---

[4] A *Reglamento* is a by-law.

Spanish Crown to inspect all the Spanish missions in Texas, had revealed that only sixty-five soldiers and twenty-five horses were fit and many soldiers did not have adequate clothes. It also revealed that there were not adequate supplies for the maintenance of the presidio, and that the then Governor, Martos y Navarrete, had violated several regulations (Castañeda 4:238-39). The order was given in the *Reglamento* of 1772. In spite of the protests of the residents, who were unwilling to leave their homes and occupations, the Adaeseños,[5] approximately five hundred in all, abandoned the presidio on 24 June 1773, led by the veteran José González. They left behind almost all of their belongings. By the time the Adaeseños left, the latest records indicated that there had been 103 Indian baptisms, 256 baptisms of people living close to the presidio, 64 marriages, and 116 deaths at the mission (Avery 1996:63).

About a quarter of the Adaeseños died during the three-month journey to San Antonio. On their arrival, some of the soldiers joined the troops in San Antonio and others retired, but bad living conditions forced most of them to return. They left in 1779, led by Antonio Gil Ybarbo (Ybarburu), who founded Nacogdoches on their way back. They settled along the Sabine River and in small communities such as Laguna Española (now Spanish Lake) near Robeline, Vallecillo (later called Bayou Cie and now known as Zwolle), and Bayou Piedras (now Rocks Creek) in Louisiana. Many of the Adaeseños never went to San Antonio, including the mother, the brother and the sister-in-law of Ybarbo (Lipski 1987a:117; Bolton 1921:114-15). The Adaeseños participated in a very fruitful trade with the rest of Texas and Mexico. Many of them dedicated themselves to cattle rearing, blacksmithing, wood-cutting and farming, and it is known that some of them, even Ybarbo himself, were involved in the sale of contraband goods.

3. Present Situation

Today, the Adaeseños no longer have communities. They can be found scattered on both sides of the Sabine River, along the *Camino Real* in Texas and Louisiana. They know very little about their origins. Some of them say they are Spanish, some say they are Spanish and Indian, and others do not know what they are. Many of them live under poor conditions and do menial work, and the young ones have moved to the big cities. Some of them live in Nacogdoches, Moral, and Cherry Grove in Northeast Texas and the rest are scattered about in Spanish Lake, Zwolle, Ebarb, and Noble in Northwest Louisiana.[6]

---

[5] The name "Adaeseño" is a term created from Los Adaes by authors to refer to the residents of Los Adaes and their descendants. Other versions are "Adaesaño" and "Adaesano."

[6] For this study, the author concentrated on the Adaeseños in Louisiana alone.

A lot of their names are a clear indication of their origin. Some of the common ones are: Bargas (Vargas), Bascus and Basco (Vázquez), Cardaway (Córdoba), Corrales, Cortínez, Ebarb (Ybarbo), Flores, Garza, Garci, Garcie and Garsee (García), Leone (León), Manshack (Menchaca), Martines (Martínez), Moore (Mora), Paddie (Padilla), Parré and Parrie (Parrilla), Procella and Procell (Procela), Ramides, Remedes, Remedios and Remedies (Ramírez), Rivers (del Río), Santos, Sepulva and Sepulvado (Sepúlveda) and Solice (Solís).[7] Some of these names appear in the old documents about the residents of Los Adaes, the military payrolls, the list of the parishioners, and the diary of Father José de Solís, who visited Los Adaes in 1767 (Nardini 1961:20).

4. Methodology

4.1. Informants

Due to restrictions imposed by the fact that very few Adaeseños who have any knowledge of the dialect could be found, the study was carried out with seventeen informants. There were nine from Spanish Lake and eight from the Zwolle-Ebarb-Noble area, and they represented three generations—90 years and above, 70 to 89 years, and 50 to 69 years. Their ages ranged from 55 to 91 years. In accordance with a pre-investigation agreement, all the informants were given fictitious names in order not to reveal their real identity. Their names from oldest to youngest were Marielena, Juan, Luis, Berta, Diana, Prudencia, Gloria, Alberto, Miguel, Virginia, Simón, Juanita, Flora, Jaime, Francisco, Rosa, and Roberto. The original plan was to include an equal number from each generation, but only one person in the 90 years and above group was found. Furthermore, given that only eight informants could be found for the 70 to 89 generation, only eight from the 50 to 69 group participated in order to have an equal number representing both groups. The three generational groups were determined only with the intention of finding out if there was any correlation between the ages and the proficiency levels. It became obvious early in the investigation that the older the participants were, the more proficient they were in Spanish. The groups were not intended to be used for any further purpose.

All the informants had received either very little formal education in English or none at all. They never received any formal education in Spanish. All the Spanish they knew was learned orally. The 91-year-old—Marielena—was a Spanish-English bilingual speaker. She was equally fluent in both languages and code-switched on occasion. Eight of the 70 to 89 group—Berta, Gloria, Juan, Alberto, Diana, Prudencia, Luis, and Miguel—were bilingual Spanish-English

---

[7] The orginal names are in parentheses.

speakers too but were more fluent in English than in Spanish due to the fact that they had not spoken Spanish for at least four decades. They code-switched frequently. As the interviews progressed, they remembered more Spanish. The rest of the group were fluent in English but not in Spanish, although they understood most of the Spanish that was spoken to them. The 50 to 69 group were only rememberers, that is, they only remembered frequently used isolated Spanish words and phrases they had overheard, but they had never used Spanish as a means of communication. They were monolingual English speakers.

4.2. Procedure

The study was carried out by means of interviews, which took place between April and December, 1999. The interviews were guided by a questionnaire prepared by the investigator based on the *Atlas Lingüístico de Hispanoamérica* (1984) by Manuel Alvar and Antonio Quilis and the *Atlas Lingüístico de México* (1990b) by Juan Lope Blanch as well as preliminary interviews carried out by the investigator. The questionnaire was divided into five parts (Interviews 1 to 5)—general conversation, lexicon, morphology, syntax, and narration respectively, and each one lasted approximately thirty minutes. For the general conversation, the investigator solicited information covering a wide range of topics including family, language, occupations, food, celebrations, traditions, religion, education, and culture. It was used to determine the informants' proficiency levels as well as to gather sociolinguistic information. For the second interview, which centered on lexicon, the participants were given pictures and asked to identify the objects in them. In cases where there were no pictures, the information was solicited through descriptions. The objective was to determine their level of lexical competence as well as which areas they were still knowledgeable about. In the third and fourth interviews, the informants were asked specific questions pertaining to the fields of morphology and syntax respectively. This was done in different ways. Some of the information was solicited through descriptions. The informants were also given a series of expressions and asked which ones they would use. They were asked questions which made them demonstrate their use of aspects of the language such as gender, number, tense, and mood, and they were also asked to translate some expressions from English into Spanish. The fifth interview, which consisted of a narration of interesting events which occurred in the past, focused on discourse competence. The informants were asked to talk about any past event they found interesting. The interviews were conducted by the investigator in the homes of the informants. All the interviews were recorded. The Spanish-English bilingual speakers were interviewed in Spanish and they participated in all the five interviews. The monolingual English speakers were interviewed in English and only participated in Interviews 1 and 2.

4.3. Analysis

The first and fifth interviews of the bilingual speakers were transcribed phonetically and used for the phonological analysis of the dialect. The features were divided into consonants and vowels and grouped according to their places of articulation. The number of allophones pertaining to the different phonemes as well as the number of occurrences of each allophone and its environment were determined. Where there was an alternation of allophones in the same environment, a quantitative study was carried out to determine the number, percentages, and ratios of occurrence. The data obtained from the remaining interviews was used for their corresponding analyses and narratives. Only the data gathered from the nine bilingual speakers was used for the linguistic analysis.[8]

5. Characteristics of the Adaeseño Dialect[9]

Due to lack of documentation, it is not known what characterized the original Adaeseño dialect. However, this study was able to document its current features. Because of the origins of the residents of the Los Adaes settlement, the dialect is similar to Castilian and rural Mexican Spanish of the seventeenth and eighteenth centuries. It also has Nahuatl elements, because that was the language of the Indians who inhabited Mexico at the time of the Spanish occupation and the Spanish spoken by the recruits who were brought to Los Adaes from Mexico had many Nahuatlisms. There are also archaic features as a result of the isolation of the Adaeseños from other Spanish speakers and from the modernizations in the language. A few French and English influences are also present due to the coexistence of the communities. The Adaeseño dialect exhibits characteristics typical of vestigial and rural varieties of Spanish. However, the unique combination of features distinguishes it from the other dialects.

5.1. Phonological Features

Characterized by a wide range of allophones and phonemic changes, the phonological elements are the most distinctive features of Adaeseño. There is a massive weakening and elision of consonants and a reduction of the vocalic system, accompanied by transpositions and nasalizations.

---

[8] More information about the interviews can be obtained from Pratt 2004.

[9] For a more detailed description and tables, see Pratt 2004.

Due to the weakening of consonants, the plosives /b/ and /d/ do not exist in Adaeseño. Both are exhibited in the form of the fricatives [β] and [δ], which alternate with a wide range of allophones. There is frequent retention of the voiced labiodental fricative [v] in place of the voiced bilabial fricative [β] in words that retain the etymological *v*, as in *vasu* ['va.su] "glass" (Standard Spanish *vaso* ['βa.so]).

Although the alternation [b]/[v] has disappeared almost completely in the Peninsula since the sixteenth century, it has remained in some dialects, such as in Arizona, Los Angeles, Paraguay, Puerto Rico, Mexico, among the Isleños and the Brules of Louisiana, and in Valencia, Spain (Boyd-Bowman 1960:64, Post 1975, Alarcos Llorach 1983:133, Lipski 1990a:15, 1994:309, Holloway 1997a:106, Pratt 2004:53). By the time the alternation disappeared in the Peninsula, it had already been transferred to the Americas, as is evidenced in Nebrija's grammar of 1492 and Valdés' *Diálogo de la lengua* of 1535.[10] The alternation has been maintained in isolated dialects and is therefore common among vestigial dialects. In Isleño and Brule, the bilabial is substituted with the labiodental even in words which do not have the etymological *v*. The maintenance of the [β]/[v] contrast in Adaeseño can be attributed principally to the isolation of the dialect from other Spanish-speaking communities. The overall retention rate recorded in this study was 61%.

The voiced bilabial fricative is elided in syllable-final position, as in *oselvá* [o.sɛl.'va] "to observe" (Standard Spanish *observar*) and *otuvo* [o.'tu.vo] "obtained" (Standard Spanish *obtuvo*). This phenomenon forms part of a systematic reduction of consonants in syllable-final position which occurs in dialects that are generally only acquired orally, and it can be found in almost all vestigial and rural Spanish dialects. The elision of the bilabial in any position is even more frequent when it is preceded or followed by a similar phone, such as in *tamién* [ta.'miɛn] "also" (Standard Spanish *también*).

There is sporadic substitution of the bilabial fricative with the velar fricative [ɤ] when it precedes the back vowel *u*, as in *güelito* [ɤwɛ.'li.to] "grandpa" (Standard Spanish *abuelito*). Together with the substitution of the bilabial with the velar when it precedes the back vowel *o*, this is a common phenomenon in rural speech in the south of Spain and rural regions of Latin America, such as among the Gauchos of Argentina, the Isleños, and the Brules. MacCurdy (1950:52) discovered [te.ɤu.'ron] "shark" (*tiburón*) among the Isleños while Holloway (1997a:106) found *gomitar* in place of *vomitar* "to throw up" among the Brules (Lipski 1985a:975, 1994:180, Pratt 2004:55).

The voiced dental fricative [δ] is elided in many positions, such as in *guaran* ['gwa.ran] "they keep" (Standard Spanish *guardan*), *usté* [us.'tɛ] "you"

---

[10] Although it was written in 1535, it was not published until 1737.

(Standard Spanish *usted*), and *icir* [i.'sir] "to say" (Standard Spanish *decir*). In some cases, the entire syllable is deleted, as in *pue* ['pwε] "she/he can" (Standard Spanish *puede*), leading to relexification in some cases, such as in *lantal* [lan'tal] "apron" (Standard Spanish *delantal*). The weakening and subsequent elision of the dental is found in many dialects of Spanish, such as in the Caribbean, Mexico, and Texas (Espinosa 1930:1, 229-30, Cárdenas 1975:2, Pratt-Panford 1997:27-28). The dental alternates with the alveolar tap [r] in intervocalic position, as in *elgarito* [εl.ga.'ri.to] "slim" (Standard Spanish *delgadito*) and *marera* [ma.'rε.ra] "wood" (Standard Spanish *madera*). The fricative/tap/elision alternation ratio in intervocalic position recorded in the study was 7:28:65. The [d]/[r] alternation is a common phenomenon in Spanish dialects, such as in the Caribbean region, the Pacific coast of Colombia, the northwestern coast of Ecuador, and in Nicaragua, and has been attributed to both internal and external factors. Internally, it is caused by a lack of closure in the articulation of the dental, especially in rapid speech. It has also been attributed to a possible influence from English, given the fact that the English /r/ alternates with its equivalents /t/ and /d/ in intervocalic position in words such as *latter* and *ladder* (Lipski 1990b:4). Lipski also observed the alternation among the youngest semi-speakers of Isleño. Sometimes the alternation results in the creation of new words, such as *gurón* [gu.'ron] "cotton" (Standard Spanish *algodón*). Another type of lexicalization occurs with the group *dr* when the /d/ is sporadically vocalized to [i] as in *maire* ['mai.re] "mother" (Standard Spanish *madre*). In certain dialects, such as Isleño, there is further sporadic elision of the [i], producing words such as *mare* "mother" and *pare* "father" (Standard Spanish *padre*). When the cluster *nd* precedes *e*, there is sporadic assimilation of /d/ to [n], such as in *onne* ['on.ne] "where?" (Standard Spanish *¿dónde?*), a frequent phenomenon in vestigial dialects (MacCurdy 1950:34, Holloway 1997a:109).

The voiceless labiodental fricative /f/ is aspirated to the glottal fricative [h] when it precedes the diphthongs *ui* and *ue*, as in *jueron* ['hwε.rõ] "they were" or "they went" (Standard Spanish *fueron*). This velarization originates from medieval Spanish and existed in Peninsular Spanish until the sixteenth century. Although it still exists in some rural areas in Andalusia, it has disappeared in almost all varieties of Spanish except some rural Spanish American dialects and some vestigial dialects of southwestern United States, Ecuador, and Peru (Lipski 1994:271, Pratt 2004:56). The aspiration rate recorded in this study was 81 percent.

Aspiration and deletion of the voiceless alveolar fricative /s/ is a common phenomenon in many dialects of Spanish. However, in Adaeseño, the alveolar is very resistant. In preconsonantal position, the ratio retention/aspiration/deletion was 52:3:45; in intervocalic position, the ratio was 62:11:20, with the rest being changes to the voiced alveolar [z]. When the alveolar precedes -*otro*-, it is aspirated, such as in *nojotro* [no.'ho.tro] "we" (Standard Spanish *nosotros*). Sometimes there is loss of internal syllables such as in *lotros* ['lo.tros] "the others" (Standard Spanish *los otros*). This feature occurs in rural and archaic dialects, such as in central Colombia and among the Isleños (Lipski 1994:209, MacCurdy 1950:35, Pratt 2004:62).

In keeping with the general weakening of the consonant system, there is also sporadic elision of the alveolar nasal /n/ in intervocalic position, such as in *bueo* ['βwɛo] "good" (Standard Spanish *bueno*). In word final postvocalic position preceded by the vowels *a*, *e* or *i*, there is elision of the alveolar accompanied by the nasalization of the preceding vowel, such as in *jadí* [ha.'dɾ] "garden" (Standard Spanish *jardín*). Nasalization of vowels is a common feature in vestigial dialects. MacCurdy (1959:554) and Holloway (1997a:102) also discovered it among the Isleños and the Brules.

Unlike many dialects of Spanish such as in the Caribbean region and the Canary Islands, Adaeseño exhibits very little liquid migration, which is the alternation of the alveolar lateral /l/ and the alveolar tap /r/. This phenomenon occurred only in final prevocalic position in the study at a rate of 13%, and all the cases were lambdacisms, that is, /r/>[l]. There were no rotacisms. Lambdacism occurs in the majority of the Hispanic world, such as in Andalusia (Alonso 1961:219), the Caribbean region (Pratt-Panford 1997:29-30), Argentina, Chile, Ecuador, and Mexico (Canfield 1981:7, Lipski 1994). Due to its assimilation to the following consonant, there is also sporadic elision of the lateral in final preconsonantal position, such as in ['ɛ no 'pwɛ a.'βla] "He cannot speak" (Standard Spanish *Él no puede hablar*). The elision rate recorded in the study was 28%. There is also elision of the alveolar tap in final position, such as in [no 'pwɛo tɛ.'nɛ 'na] "I cannot have anything" (Standard Spanish *No puedo tener nada*), a feature which occurred in the study at a rate of 87%.

Due to the weakening of the palatal nasal /ñ/, there is sporadic neutralization of the opposition /ñ/ / /y/, such as in *spayol* [spa.'yol] "Spanish" (Standard Spanish *español*). The rate of occurrence of the palatal fricative in the study was 19%. This feature can also be attributed to English influence since the nasal does not exist in English. The probability is further supported by the fact that this phenomenon seems to be a new development in Adaeseño, given that it never occurred in the speech of the oldest speaker, who clearly pronounced the word as [spa.'ñol].

Very common in Adaeseño is the elision of phones, phonic groups, and entire syllables, which in some cases results in the creation of new words, such as in *mikano* [mi.'ka.no] "Mexican" (Standard Spanish *mexicano*). This phenomenon forms part of the irregularities that have developed in many dialects as a result of simplification. There are also frequent transpositions of phones, such as in *puelbo* "village" (Standard Spanish *pueblo*) and *comites* "you ate" (Standard Spanish *comiste*), and metatheses, such as in *miraglo* "miracle" (Standard Spanish *milagro*). These features are common in rural dialects of Spanish (Azevedo 1992:80, Pratt 2004:75).

There is a tendency to reduce the vocalic system of five vowels to three (/i/, /a/, /u/), thus fusing the front spread /e/ / /i/ and back rounded /o/ / /u/ oppositions. There is therefore frequent substitution of /e/ with /i/ and /o/ with /u/, such as in *mijó* [mi.'ho] "better" (Standard Spanish m*ejor*), and *hermanu* [ɛr.'ma.nu] "brother" (Standard Spanish *hermano*). The rate of substitution of /o/ for /u/ in the study was 68%. This phenomenon also occurs among bilingual Quechua and Aimara speakers of Peru and Bolivia respectively (Lipski 1994). The vowels are also nasalized when they occur between nasals, such as in *telminá* [tɛl.mr.'na] "to finish" (Standard Spanish *terminar*). This feature is common to rural and vestigial dialects and is also found in the Canary Islands, the Caribbean, and New Mexico (MacCurdy 1950:28, Holloway 1997a:100, Espinosa 1930:1, 94-95, Foster 1976:24).

There is sporadic apocope of non-tonic preconsonantal syllable-final /e/, as in *tien que llamale* ['tiɛn ke ya.'ma.le] "she/he has to call him" (Standard Spanish *tiene que llamarle*), and it is always elided in prevocalic position, such as in *eran sieten toa la familia* ['ɛ.ran 'siɛ.tɛn 'toa la fa.'mi.lia] "They were seven in the whole family" (Standard Spanish *Eran siete en toda la familia*). All the other vowels are also always elided in prevocalic position. When /e/ forms part of the group *uer* in initial-syllable position, it centralizes to /a/, as in *puata* ['pwa.ta] "door" (Standard Spanish *puerta*). The /a/ in the group *uar* also raises to [ae] or [ɛ], such as in *cuetu* ['kwɛ.tu] "room" (Standard Spanish *cuarto*). There is also the tendency to elide the /e/ or the /o/ in word-initial position in the sequence #esCV and #osCV, where C is a voiceless plosive, such as in *scuela* ['skwɛ.la] "school" (Standard Spanish *escuela*), a common phenomenon in southwestern United States and in vestigial dialects (Lastra de Suárez 1972:63, MacCurdy 1950:28, Holloway 1997a:104-5). This feature occurred in 85% of the cases studied. On occasion, there is aphaeresis of the entire initial syllable, producing words such as *ta* ['ta] "she/he is" (Standard Spanish *está*) and *cuela* ['kwɛ.la] "school" (Standard Spanish *escuela*). Adaeseño also exhibits aphaeresis and sporadic syncope of non-tonic /a/, as in *ora* ['o.ra] "now" (Standard Spanish *ahora*). In word-final position, the /a/ tends to centralize more, raising to [ə] as in ['va.kə] "cow" (Standard Spanish *vaca*), a feature which is typical of Mexico. The ratio [a]/[ə]/[ø] in word-final position was 6:26:68.

Finally, by means of diphthongization and reduction, the hiatus *eí* becomes *i, eo* becomes *o* or *io, ee* becomes *e,* and *aí* becomes *ai,* as in *fri* ['fri] "to fry"

(Standard Spanish *freír*), *antojos* [an.'to.hos] "eyeglasses" (Standard Spanish *anteojos*), *cre* ['krɛ] "to believe" (Standard Spanish *creer*), and *mais* ['mais] "corn" (Standard Spanish *maíz*). There are also non-etymological diphthongizations which change verbal paradigms, such as in *dijieron* [di.'hiɛ.rõ] "they said" (Standard Spanish *dijeron*) and *cociniá* [ko.si.'nia] "to cook" (Standard Spanish *cocinar*). Lope Blanch observed this phenomenon in Texas, New Mexico, Arizona, and California (1990a:17), and Lipski (1990a:36) and Holloway (1997a:127) found it among the Isleños and the Brules. A very notable characteristic of Adaeseño is the prolongation of tonic vowels, such as in *tomatitos* [to.ma.'ti:.tos] "tomatoes" and *tres hijos* ['trɛ.si:.hos] "three children." As the vowel is prolonged, the tone is lowered, resulting in a peculiar tone. This feature is also found in Yucatán, Mexico.

5.2. Morphosyntactic Features[11]

The morphosyntactic system is characterized by the simplification and modification of structures, and archaisms, which are common to vestigial and rural dialects of Spanish. There is a tendency to use rustic genders in the nominal system. Among these are *la mar* "sea" (*el mar*), *la calor* "heat" (*el calor*), *la hacha* "axe" (*el hacha*), *el sartén* "frying pan" (*la sartén*), and *la puente* "bridge" (*el puente*). There are frequent neutralizations of gender, such as in *Hay uno viva* "There is one alive" (*Hay uno vivo*), and *Si hacían un baile, invitaban todo la familia* "If they had a dance, they invited the whole family" (*Si hacían un baile, invitaban a toda la familia*). These fluctuations, caused by disuse, are common in vestigial dialects, such as Isleño and Brule (Lipski 1990a:36-37, Holloway 1997a:128). The formation of the plural in Adaeseño presents both standard and non-standard forms, the latter being the use of the allomorph /-ses/, such as in *pieses* "feet" (*pies*). This form occurs in rural dialects in words that end in a stressed vowel. It is common in Santo Domingo and Puerto Rico (Navarro Tomás 1966:116) and also in Isleño (MacCurdy 1950:43).

The pronominal system also exhibits some notable features, which can be attributed to the exclusively domestic and oral usage of the dialect as well as its vestigial state. There is non-standard usage of grammatical categories and functions, such as the substitution of prepositional pronouns with subject pronouns, as in *Yo me dijieron que la trujeron patrás* "They told me they brought her back" (*A mí me dijeron que la volvieron a traer*). In imperatives, there is pluralization of the clitics *se* and *lo* instead of the verb, such as in *siéntesen* "sit down" (*siéntense*) and *démelos* "give it to me" (*dénmelo*), a phenomenon which can lead to

---

[11] The words in parentheses in this section are the standard Spanish versions.

loss of information by converting singular object pronouns into plurals. *Naide, naiden, nadien,* and *naigen* are used in place of the indefinite pronoun *nadie* "nobody," and *los dos* is used in place of *ambos* "both." Such colloquial and rustic forms, which result from processes such as metatheses, paragogues, and velarizations, are still used in rural areas in the Hispanic world and are common in vestigial dialects (Lipski 1990a:38).

Of particular significance is the use of the second person plural informal subject pronoun, *vosotros* "you," which is almost non-existent in the dialects of the New World where the formal pronoun *usted* is used all the time. The use of *vosotros* goes back to the presence of Spaniards among the original residents of Los Adaes, and its maintenance in the dialect over the centuries can be attributed to the lack of contact between Adaeseño and other dialects in the region. Another notable feature is the redundancy of subject pronouns, such as in *Mi güelita ea hablaba spayol* "My grandma spoke Spanish" (*Mi abuelita hablaba español*) and *No lo sé yo* "I do not know" (*No lo sé*). This feature is commonly found in the Caribbean, South America, and the Canary Islands, in addition to vestigial dialects. It is attributed to the loss of final verbal morphemes and the influence of English, in which case the use of the pronoun is indispensable. Closely related to the redundancy of subject pronouns is the use of the genitive construction *noun phrase + de + subject pronoun,* or *possessive adjective + noun + de + subject pronoun* to express possession, such as in *la casa de ella* (*su casa*) and *su abuelo de ella* (*su abuelo*), which is also common among vestigial dialects. Another feature is the inverted word order in interrogative sentences, that is, the pronoun precedes the verb, such as *¿Qué tú quieres?* "What do you want?" (*¿{Tú}qué quieres?*). This construction is common in the Caribbean and rural dialects of Panama, Venezuela, Colombia, and Ecuador (Lipski 1990a:40, Holloway 1997a:140).

The verbal system exhibits archaisms, such as *vide* in place of *vi* "I saw," *vido* in place of *vio* "she/he saw," *truje* in place of *traje* "I brought," and *trujo* in place of *trajo* "she/he brought." There is a notable absence of the subjunctive, which is replaced by either the infinitive or the indicative, such as in *Quieren que nosotros tené una famila* "They want us to have a family" (*Quieren que tengamos una familia*) and *Toy contenta que vinites* "I am glad you came" (*Me alegro de que hayas venido*). This modal neutralization usually occurs in varieties of Spanish which are in contact with English. They tend to lose the subjunctive as a result of the lack of an equivalent in the English language, a phenomenon referred to as "negative transfer" by Gutiérrez and Silva-Corvalán (1993). In the United States, it is very common among the bilingual speakers of Los Ángeles (Ocampo 1990) and can also be found among vestigial varieties such as Isleño and Brule. It has also been documented in the Philippines and

Trinidad (Lipski 1985a:974). Neutralization of the *ser/estar* opposition is also common among the Adaeseños, such as *Cuando staba nueva, vivía con mis padres* "When I was young, I lived with my parents" (*Cuando era joven, vivía con mis padres*) and *Y la casa era hecho de puros palos* "And the house was made of only wood" (*Y la casa estaba hecha de sólo palos*).

Certain tenses have disappeared from the dialect. The synthetic future is replaced with the periphrastic future, such as in *vamos a salir* for "we will go out" and *vamos a comprar* for "we will buy" in place of *saldremos* and *compraremos* respectively. This phenomenon forms part of the simplification process where synthetic structures are replaced with more analytical forms, and it is common in the United States and among vestigial speakers. The conditional is not used in Adaeseño, and the imperfect tense is often replaced with the present tense, as in *Mi madre prepara dumplings* "My mother used to prepare dumplings" (*Mi madre preparaba bolas de masa hervida*). There is neutralization of the distinction between regular and irregular imperatives in favor of the regular, such as in *hácela* in place of *hazla* "do it" and *pónelo* in place of *ponlo* "turn it on." Adaeseño also exhibits the agreement of impersonal verbs with apparent subjects, such as *Hacen dos años que viven aquí* "They have been living here for two years" (*Hace dos años que viven aquí*) and *Habían muchos estudiantes en la clase* "There were many students in the class" (*Había muchos estudiantes en la clase*), a common feature of rural dialects.

There is a tendency to eliminate articles and prepositions, such as in *Prendí tocá música* "I learned to play music" (*Aprendí a tocar música*) and *Yo no me acuedo to eso* "I do not remember all that" (*Yo no me acuerdo de todo eso*). Prepositions are normally composed of very few words and their absence often does not hinder comprehension. They therefore tend to disappear more frequently than other elements in vestigial and rustic dialects. This feature occurs frequently in the Caribbean region, the Philippines and Trinidad, and has also been found in Isleño and Brule.

There is some syntactic calquing from English. *Para atrás* is used to translate "back," as in *Tuvo que irse patrás al hospital* "She had to return to the hospital" (*Tuvo que volver al hospital*), and *no más*, which literally means "no more," is used for "only" (*solamente*). This is a common phenomenon among bilingual English-Spanish speakers, and has been documented in Gibraltar, Berlice, and Trinidad, and among people of Puerto Rican, Cuban, and Mexican descent in the United States, the Isleños (Lipski 1990a:117) and the Brules (Holloway 1997a:145).

Finally, with regard to complex structures, Adaeseño exhibits a simplification of all the three categories of subordination, namely nominal, such as in *Es importante pa hacer* "It is important that they do it" (*Es importante que lo hagan*) and *No pienso que lo hizo* "It is doubtful that he has done it" (*Es dudoso que lo haya hecho*); adjectival or relative, such as in *La muchacha, le dieron una pojoleá, lloró* "The girl, who had been beaten, wept" (*La muchacha, quien había sido pegada, lloró*) and *Los tragos que no le gustó vendieron* "The drinks which they didn't like were sold" (*Las bebidas que no les gustaban fueron vendidas*); and circumstantial or adverbial, as in *Habló mucho y perdió la voice* "She talked so much that she lost her voice" (*Habló tanto que perdió la voz*) and *Sta muy contenta cuanno viene* "She becomes very happy when he arrives" (*Se pone muy contenta cuando él llega*). Nevertheless, despite the loss of some structure, the message is almost always very clear.

5.3. Lexical Features

The Adaeseños still use sufficient lexicon covering many semantic fields, especially parts of the body, animals, food, and utensils. The fact that there is a common lexicon among the speakers is proof of the existence of a functional system. The foreign elements present in the dialect are almost exclusively limited to the lexicon. Most of the foreign elements are Nahuatlisms. According to Armistead (1991:287), the Nahuatlisms undoubtedly connect the dialect with Mexico and the southwest of the United States. Some of the Nahuatl words in Adaeseño include *amole* "cassava" (*yuca*),[12] *chapulín* "little child" (*niño*), *guajolote* "turkey" (*pavo*), *huerco* "little child" (*niño*), *jicote* "wasp" (*avispa*), *metate* "square stone used for grinding corn," *molcajete* "stone or clay mortar," *tamal* "tamale," and *tuza* "mole" (*topo*).

The Los Adaes settlement was isolated from other ethnolinguistic communities. As a result, the Adaeseños maintained their dialect in its archaic state, which explains why it has a lot of archaic elements. They include: *crevá* "to break" (*quebrar*), *duse* "sweet" (*dulce*), *encino* "oak" (*roble*), *fierro* "iron" (*hierro*), *lumbre* "fire" (*fuego*), *mamavieja* "grandma" (*abuelita*), *noria* "well for water" (*pozo*), *peje* "fish" (*pez*), *palo* "tree" (árbol), *prieto* "black" (*negro*) and *túnico* "dress" (vestido) (Lapesa 1981:394-95, Lerner 1974, Boggs et al. 1946, Baldonado 1975).

There was very little French influence on the Adaeseño dialect. The Gallicisms include: *camino de hierro* "railroad" (*chemin de fer*),[13] *casquete* "axe" (*casse-tête*), *cauén* "large sea turtle" (*caouane*), *charón* "little pail" (*chaudron*), *cude* "patio" (*cour*), *grega* "tea pot" (*grègue*), *pasaportú* "saw for cutting" (*passé-partout*), *romana* "dress" (*romaine*), and *sedrón* "frying pan" (chaudron) (Armistead and Gregory 1986).

---

[12] The words in parentheses in this section and the next are the standard Spanish versions.
[13] The words in parentheses in this section are the French words from which the Gallicisms arise.

The few Anglicisms in Adaeseño include *casa del corte* "city hall" (*ayuntamiento*),[14] *goober* "peanuts" (*cacahuetes*), *lonche* "lunch" (*almuerzo*), *mashina* "machine" (*máquina*), *maestro* "boss" (*jefe*), and *papel* "newspaper" (*periódico*).

Other words used in Adaeseño include: *bolillo* "white person" (*blanco*), *bujero* "hole" (*agujero*), *chipilote* "eagle" (*águila*), *chuchonta* "mockingbird" (*sinsonte*), *cusca* "buzzard" (águila ratonera), *chuparrosa* "hummingbird" (*colibrí*), *encantado* "mixture of Indian and white" (*mezcla de indio y blanco*), *finisia* "spasms which accompany high fever" (*espasmos*), *lacrante* "scorpion" (*alacrán*), *negrito* "black tree" (*árbol negro*), *niblanito* "light in weight" (*livianito*), *sancud* "mosquito" (*zancudo*), and *tapanco* "roof" (*techo*).

6. The Death of Adaeseño

According to Swadesh (1948:226) and Cook (1989:235), language death is one of the most common consequences of acculturation, when the contact involves languages of unequal status. It is a gradual process of loss of fluency. There are different stages and forms of language death. It can be a language that 1) is written but not spoken, or vice versa; 2) is no longer used in public or for commercial activities but is still used in the home; 3) has lost speakers in a social class although there are still speakers in other social classes; or 4) whose use has been reduced and only a few small groups still use it, sometimes for a long period of time. The loss of Adaeseño has advanced beyond all these stages. Despite the fact that it has not been used on a daily basis for more than four decades, it still has quite a solid system with clear tendencies, most of which are in accordance with the norm. However, the linguistic system is not the only thing that is at stake. The whole community is at risk of extinction. According to the theory of language loss, the factors that determine the disintegration and extinction of languages are: the status of the dominant language; the prestige the subordinate language has in the community and the official support available to it; what the language is used for; the social relationship between the subordinate and the dominant communities; and the level of the individual acculturation of the members of the subordinate community in the new community (Coles 1993:122, Dorian 1987, Fishman 1985). These have been precisely the determining factors in the case of Adaeseño.

The coexistence of the Adaeseños with the Adaes Indians was of no consequence with regard to influence, because the Indians did not have a stable community. Unlike what happened in other Spanish-speaking communities in Louisiana, their contact with the French did not have any consequences either.

---

[14] The words in parentheses in this section and the next are the standard Spanish versions.

In the case of the Isleños, most of the French influence occurred in the churches, and in the case of the Brules, the French priests changed their Spanish names into French names (Hawley 1976:21). However, the case was different with regard to the contact between the Adaeseños and the English. When the Adaeseños returned from San Antonio, a series of events occurred which reduced Spanish presence in the region considerably and led to a systematic reduction in the use of their language.

In 1802, in a surprising turn of events, Spain returned the Louisiana territory to France by the Treaty of San Ildefonso. However, just a year later on April 30, 1803, Napoleon sold it to the United States because he needed funds for an imminent war with England, and the Louisiana Purchase was signed on May 2, 1803. Before the Louisiana Purchase, there was not much contact between the Adaeseños and the English-speaking community, because unlike the French and the Indians who had ties with the Adaeseños with regard to religion and trade, there was nothing that linked the English to them, which explains the scarcity of Anglicisms in Adaeseño (Armistead and Gregory 1986). As a result of the purchase, the English-speaking population increased significantly in the region, because there was a rapid infiltration of English-speakers into the territory due to a constitutional convention which gave them more rights than any other linguistic groups. The English-speaking population was soon the majority, and they took over all the good lands, forcing the Spanish to move further out to the poor lands. There was also an economic boom, which resulted in road constructions and improvements in communication that brought an end to the isolation of the Adaeseños and exposed them to the English language and culture.

Spain was unhappy with the sale of the Louisiana territory to the United States and sent troops to Louisiana under the command of General Herrera to try to reclaim the territory which belonged to them before the Treaty of Fontainebleau. After a long conflict between the Spanish and the Americans, the territory between Arroyo Hondo and the Sabine River, where Los Adaes and other Adaeseño communities were situated, was declared No Man's Land or Neutral Strip by an agreement signed on February 6, 1806. The agreement prohibited both Spain and the United States from having control over the territory. As a result of the lack of control and supervision, it became the refuge of criminals who, due to the lack of laws, carried out unlawful activities in Spanish Town and other towns in the area. The conflict was resolved when Spain relinquished its claim to the land. On 22 February 1821, the Adams-Onís Treaty, which extended the western border of the United States to the Sabine River and transferred ownership of the Neutral Strip to the United States, was signed in Washington, D.C. between the United States and Mexico. This decision was strongly opposed by the Spanish, French, and Indian residents.

In 1812, a group of buccaneers initiated a fight for the independence of Texas from Mexico. In 1821, Mexico became independent. In 1835, the Caddo Indians sold their lands to the United States. In 1843, the United States purchased New Mexico, Utah, Nevada, and Wyoming, and in 1845, Texas joined the Union. But perhaps the most serious blow Adaeseño suffered was the law that made English the sole medium of communication in public and in the schools. This had a very crippling effect on the Adaeseño community and its language, and the consequent situation of inferiority in which they found themselves caused them to even renounce their own language. They spoke Spanish only at home and in their small groups for a period of time, but eventually it was not used anywhere anymore, a situation which Lipski (1987a:120) describes as a "linguistic transmutation without exception." In 1900, the arrival of Mexican workers in Zwolle to help build the Kansas City Southern Railroad helped maintain the Hispanic culture alive (Gregory 1978), but the deterioration of the Spanish communities continued.

7. The Future of Adaeseño

All these factors contributed in some way to the eventual vestigial state in which Adaeseño is at present. There are very few speakers left, and its future is very bleak. The maintenance of a threatened language depends primarily on its social status with respect to the political and social powers. It is directly related to its pragmatic value and the extent of the opposition it faces. According to Coles (1993:123), the number of speakers and the restoration efforts of the members of the community are also of great importance. Fishman (1985:47) also affirms that even small groups can maintain their language if they live together and are separated physically, economically, and culturally from other linguistic groups. The attitude of the government toward the language is also very crucial, and contact with other communities who speak the same language is necessary. The Adaeseños have been in a disadvantageous situation most of the time. Even though the settlement was established under the protection of the Spanish Crown, it had to fend for itself most of the time because it was too far from the supply centers, and later, the Adaeseños were abandoned because Spain lost its control over the territory. Also, Adaeseño is beyond the point of being salvaged, because there are no communities to work with and there are very few speakers left, who live far from each other. The new generation of Adaeseños have recently founded the Adaesaño Foundation to help protect their heritage and document as much of their history as possible. The foundation organizes annual symposia and publishes newsletters with the aim of recovering the Adaeseño heritage and keeping it alive, but their task is very difficult because there are no communities to work with. The Isleños, on the other hand, have been able to revitalize their language by means of the creation of a cultural society, *Los Isleños Heritage and Cultural Society*, because they still have communities. Adaeseño faces an imminent death which cannot be avoided, because there will soon be no speakers left. According to Fishman's scale of classification of intergenerational interruption (1991:182), which ranges the state of threat to languages from 1 to 8 with higher numbers implying higher threat, Adaeseño is already at 8. In spite of this, it is still quite homogeneous with clear tendencies and very few deviations from the norm.

8. Conclusion

Adaeseño Spanish came about as a result of the founding of a Spanish-speaking community among the Adaes Indians in 1717. The settlement was in the form of a mission and a presidio, and was the capital of Spanish Texas for forty-four years. The inhabitants were a mixture of Spaniards, Mexicans, Indians, and people of mixed descent. Although the settlement was abandoned in 1773 when the capital was moved to San Antonio, and adverse political, social and economic conditions have led to the deterioration of the communities and the dialect, some of the Adaeseños can still be found in Northwest Louisiana today. The Adaeseño dialect shares many characteristics with other vestigial and rural dialects of Spanish, but its unique combination of features distinguishes it from the others. Notwithstanding the fact that it has not been used as a means of daily communication for at least forty years, it is still very functional. However, its death is imminent, because there are very few speakers left and there will soon be nobody to speak it. Through the efforts of the Adaesaño Foundation, the new generation hopes to keep the Adaeseño heritage alive in spite of the death of the language.

Bibliography

Alarcos Llorach, Emilio. 1983. *Fonología española*. Madrid: Gredos.
Alonso, Amado. 1961. *Estudios lingüísticos: Temas hispanoamericanos*. Madrid: Gredos.
Alvar, Manuel. 1955. Las hablas meridionales de España y su interés para la lingüística comparada. *Revista de Filología Española,* 39, 284-313.
Alvar, Manuel. 1996. *Manual de dialectología hispánica.* Barcelona: Ariel.
Alvar, Manuel, & Antonio Quilis. 1984. *Atlas lingüístico de Hispanoamérica.* Madrid: Instituto de Cooperación Iberoamericana.
Armistead, Samuel. 1978. Romances tradicionales entre los hispanohablantes del estado de Luisiana. *Nueva Revista de Filología Hispánica* 27:39-56.

Armistead, Samuel. 1981. Spanish language and folklore in Louisiana. *La Crónica*, 9.2, 187-89.

Armistead, Samuel. 1983a. Más romances de Luisiana. *Nueva Revista de Filología Hispánica* 32:41-54.

Armistead, Samuel. 1983b. Spanish Riddles from St. Bernard Parish. *Louisiana Folklore Miscellany*, 5,3, 1-8.

Armistead, Samuel. 1985. Adivinanzas españolas de Luisiana. In Dámaso Alonso et al. (Eds.), *Homenaje a Álvaro Galmés de Fuentes* (pp 251-62). Madrid: Gredos.

Armistead, Samuel. 1991. Tres dialectos españoles de Luisiana. *Lingüística Española Actual*, 13, 279-301.

Armistead, Samuel, 1992. *The Spanish tradition in Louisiana: I. Isleño folklore.* Newark, DE: Juan de la Cuesta.

Armistead, Samuel & Hiram Gregory. 1986. French loan words in the Spanish dialect of Sabine and Natchitoches Parishes. *Louisiana Folklife*, 10, 21-30.

Avery, George. 1996. *Annual Report for the Los Adaes Station Archaeology Program.* Natchitoches, LA: Northwestern State U.

Azevedo, Milton. 1992. *Introducción a la lingüística española.* Englewood Cliffs, NJ: Prentice Hall.

Baldonado, Joan Martín. 1975. Problems in New World lexical "Survivals." *Romance Philology*, 29,2, 229-40.

Bergen, John (Ed.) 1990. *Sociolinguistic Issues.* Washington, D.C.: Georgetown UP.

Boggs, Ralph et al. 1946. *Tentative Dictionary of Medieval Spanish.* Chapel Hill, NC.

Bolton, Herbert. 1905. The Spanish abandonment and re-occupation of East Texas, 1773-1779. *Quarterly of the Texas State Historical Association*, 9,2, 67-137.

Bolton, Herbert. 1921. *The Spanish Borderlands.* New Haven, CT: Yale UP.

Boyd-Bowman, Peter. 1952. La pérdida de vocales átonas en la planicie mexicana. *Nueva Revista de Filología Hispánica*, 6, 138-40.

Boyd-Bowman, Peter. 1960. *El habla de Guanajuato.* Mexico City: UNAM.

Campbell, Lyle, & Martha Muntzel. 1989. The structural consequences of language death. In N. Dorian (Ed.), *Investigating Obsolescence: Studies in Language Contraction and Death* (pp. 181-96) Cambridge: Cambridge UP.

Canfield, Delos. 1981. *Spanish Pronunciation in the Americas.* Chicago: U of Chicago P.

Cárdenas, Daniel. 1975. Mexican Spanish. In E. Hernández-Chávez, A. Cohen, & A. Beltramo (Eds.), *El lenguaje de los chicanos* (pp. 1-6). Arlington, VA: Center for Applied Linguistics.

Castañeda, Carlos. 1936-1958. *Our Catholic Heritage in Texas, 1519-1936.* Seven Volumes. Austin, TX: Von Boechmann-Jones.

Coles, Felice. 1991. *Social and linguistic correlates to language death: Research from the Isleño dialect of Spanish.* Unpublished doctoral dissertation, University of Texas, Austin.

Coles, Felice. 1993. Language maintenance institutions of the Isleño dialect of Spanish. In A. Roca & J. Lipski (Eds.), *Spanish in the United States: Linguistic Contact and Diversity* (pp. 121-33). Berlin: Mouton de Gruyter.

Cook, Eung-Do. 1989. Is phonology going haywire in dying languages? Phonological variations in Chipewyan and Sarcee. *Language in Society,* 18, 235-55.

Din, Gilbert. 1972. Early Spanish colonization efforts in Louisiana. *Louisiana Studies,* 11, 31-49.

Dorian, Nancy. 1978. The fate of morphological complexity in language death: Evidence from East Sutherland Gaelic. *Language,* 54, 590-609.

Dorian, Nancy. 1982. Language loss and maintenance in language contact situations. In R. Lambert & B. Freed (Eds.), *The Loss of Language Skills.* (pp. 44-59) Rowley, MA: Newbury House.

Dorian, Nancy. 1983. Natural and second language acquisition from the perspective of the study of language death. In R. Andersen (Ed.), *Pidginization and Creolization as Language Acquisition* (pp. 158-67). Rowley, MA: Newbury House.

Dorian, Nancy. 1986. Making do with loss: Some surprises along the language death proficiency continuum. *Applied Psycholinguistics* 7, 257-76.

Dorian, Nancy. 1987. The value of language maintenance efforts which are unlikely to succeed. *International Journal of Sociology,* 68, 51-67.

Espinosa, Aurelio. 1930. *Estudios sobre el español de Nuevo Méjico.* Buenos Aires: Biblioteca de Dialectología Hispanoamericana.

Fishman, Joshua. 1985. *The Rise and Fall of the Ethnic Revival: Perspectives on Language and Ethnicity.* Berlin: Mouton de Gruyter.

Fishman, Joshua. 1991. *Recovering Language Shift.* Clevedon: Multilingual Matters Ltd.

Foster, David. 1976. The phonology of Southwest Spanish. In J. D. Bowen, & J. Ornstein (Eds.), *Studies in Southwest Spanish* (pp. 17-28). Rowley, MA: Newbury House.

Fuster, Miguel. 2001. El adaeseño: Génesis y regresión de una variedad de español de América. In *Contacto interlingüístico e intercultural con el mundo hispano,* 1 (pp. 145-68). Valencia, Universitat de València.

Gregory, Hiram. 1978. *Personal Communication.* Natchitoches: Northwestern State U.

Gregory, Hiram. 1983. Los Adaes: The archaeology of an ethnic enclave. *Geoscience and Man* (Baton Rouge), 23, 53-57.

Gregory, Hiram, & James McCorkle. 1980-81. *Los Adaes Historical and Archaeological background.* Natchitoches, LA: Northwestern State U.

Guerra, Pancho. 1977. *Obras completas III: léxico de Gran Canaria.* Las Palmas: Excma. Mancomunidad de Cabildos.

Gutiérrez, Manuel. 1990. Sobre el mantenimiento de las cláusulas subordinadas en el español de Los Ángeles. In J. Bergen (Ed.), *Spanish in the United States: Sociolinguistic issues* (pp. 31-38). Washington, D.C.: Georgetown UP.

Gutiérrez, Manue, & Carmen Silva-Corvalán. 1993. Spanish clitics in a contact situation. In A. Roca, & J. Lipski (Eds.), *Spanish in the United States: Linguistic Contact and Diversity* (pp. 75-89). Washington, D.C.: Georgetown UP.

Hawley, Francis. 1976. *Spanish Folk Healing in Ascension Parish, Louisiana.* Unpublished master's thesis, Louisiana State University, Baton Rouge.

Henríquez-Ureña, Pedro. 1931. Observaciones sobre el español en América. *Revista de Filología Española,* 18, 120-48.

Holloway, Charles. 1997a. *Dialect death. The Case of Brule Spanish.* Amsterdam: John Benjamins.

Holloway, Charles. 1997b. Divergent Twins: Isleño and Brule Spanish in Louisiana. *Southwest Journal of Linguistics,* 17, 55-72.

Lapesa, Rafael. 1981. *Historia de la lengua española.* Madrid: Gredos.

Lastra de Suárez, Yolanda. 1972. El habla y la educación de los niños de origen mexicano en Los Ángeles. In E. Hernández-Chávez, A. Cohen & A. Beltramo (Eds.), *El Lenguaje de los chicanos* (pp. 61-69). Arlington, VA: Center for Applied Linguistics.

Lerner, Isaías. 1974. *Arcaísmos léxicos del español de América.* Madrid: Ínsula.

Lipski, John. 1985a. Creole Spanish and vestigial Spanish: Evolutionary parallels. *Linguistics,* 23, 963-84.

Lipski, John. 1985b. /s/ in Central American Spanish. *Hispania,* 68, 143-49.

Lipski, John. 1987a. El dialecto español de Río Sabinas: Vestigios del español mexicano en Luisiana y Texas. *Nueva Revista de Filología Hispánica,* 35, 111-28.

Lipski, John. 1987b. Language contact phenomena in Louisiana Isleño Spanish. *American Speech,* 62,4, 320-31.

Lipski, John. 1990a. *The Language of the Isleños.* Baton Rouge: Louisiana State UP.

Lipski, John. 1990b. Sabine River Spanish: A neglected chapter in Mexican-American dialectology. In J. Bergen (Ed.), *Spanish in the United States: Sociolinguistic Issues* (pp. 1-13). Washington D.C.: Georgetown UP.

Lipski, John. 1994. *Latin American Spanish.* London: Longman.

Lope Blanch, Juan. 1990a. *El español hablado en el suroeste de los Estados Unidos.* Mexico City: UNAM.

Lope Blanch, Juan. 1990b. *Atlas Lingüístico de México, Vol 1.* Mexico City: Colegio de México/Fondo de Cultura Económica.

MacCurdy, Raymond. 1950. *The Spanish Dialect in St. Bernard Parish, Louisiana.* Albuquerque: U of New Mexico P.

MacCurdy, Raymond. 1959. A Spanish word-list of the "Brulis" dwellers of Louisiana. *Hispania,* 42, 547-54.

Morales, Amparo. 1986. *Gramáticas en contacto. Análisis sintáctico sobre el español de Puerto Rico.* Madrid: Playor.

Morales, Amparo. 1990. *El habla culta de San Juan.* Río Piedras: Universidad de Puerto Rico.

Nardini, Louis. 1961. *No man's land: A history of El Camino Real.* New Orleans: Pelican.

Navarro Tomás, Tomás. 1948. *El español de Puerto Rico: contribución a la geografía lingüística hispanoamericana.* Río Piedras: Universidad de Puerto Rico.

Navarro Tomás, Tomás. 1966. *El español de Puerto Rico.* Río Piedras: Universitaria.

Nebrija, Antonio de. 1492. *Gramática de la lengua castellana.* Salamanca.

Ocampo, Francisco. 1990. El subjuntivo en tres generaciones de hablantes bilingües. In J. Bergen (Ed.), *Spanish in the United States: Sociolinguistic Issues* (pp. 33-48). Washington, D.C.: Georgetown UP.

Post, Anita. 1975. Some Aspects of Arizona Spanish. In E. Hernández-Chávez, A. Cohen and A. Beltramo (Eds.), *El lenguaje de los chicanos* (pp. 30-36). Arlington, VA: Center for Applied Linguistics.

Pratt, Comfort. 2002. El español del noroeste de Luisiana: Orígenes y pervivencia. *Interlingüística,* 13,3, 283-303.

Pratt, Comfort. 2004. *El español del noroeste de Luisiana: Pervivencia de un dialecto amenazado.* Madrid: Editorial Verbum.

Pratt-Panford, Comfort. 1997. *La variedad lingüística de la mujer del área metropolitana de San Juan, Puerto Rico.* Unpublished master's thesis, Texas A&M University, College Station.

Romaine, Suzanne. 1989. Pidgins, Creoles, Immigrant and Dying Languages. In N. Dorian (Ed.), *Investigating Obsolescence: Studies in Language Contraction and Death* (pp. 369-83). Cambridge: Cambridge UP.

Ross, John. 1980. La supresión de /y/ en el español chicano. *Hispania,* 63, 442-54.

Schmidt, Annette. 1985. *Young People's Dyirbal: An Example of Language Death from Australia.* Cambridge: Cambridge UP.

Shoemaker, Janet. 1988. *The "broken" Spanish of Ebarb: A study in language death.* Unpublished master's thesis, Louisiana State University, Baton Rouge.

Stark, Louisa. 1980. Notes on a dialect of Spanish spoken in Northern Louisiana. *Anthropological Linguistics,* 22,4, 163-76.

Swadesh, Morris. 1948. Sociologic notes on obsolescent Languages. *International Journal of American Linguistics,* 14, 226-35.

Tsitsipis, Lukas. 1984. Functional restriction and grammatical reduction in Albanian language in Greece. *Zeitschrift für Balkanologie,* 20, 122-31.

Valdés, Juan de. 1737. *Diálogo de la lengua.* Madrid: Editorial Porrúa.

Contributors

Alejandra Balestra is currently an independent scholar in Albuquerque, New Mexico. She received her Ph.D. from the University of Houston, where she also served as a visiting assistant professor and the coordinator of the Recovering the U.S. Hispanic Literary Heritage Project. Most recently she served as an assistant professor at the University of New Mexico. The author of numerous published articles, she coordinated the anthologies *Herencia: The Anthology of Hispanic Literature in the United States* (Oxford University Press, 2002) and *En otra voz: antología de literatura hispana de los Estados Unidos* (Arte Público Press, 2002).

Wendy Beckman graduated from the Masters' program in Spanish Linguistics at San Diego State University.

Magdalena Coll is Profesora Adjunta of the Instituto de Lingüística of the Facultad de Humanidades y Ciencias de la Educación (Universidad de la República, Uruguay). She teaches Historical Linguistics and her principal areas of research are related to the history of Spanish and Portuguese in America and particularly in Uruguay.

Debbie S. Cunningham is a Ph.D. candidate in the Hispanic Studies program at Texas A&M University. Her research includes textual analysis of Spanish colonial manuscripts for historical research and interpretation relevant to the history of the Southwest.

Patricia Gubitosi holds a Ph.D. from the University of Houston, where she worked as a Research Assistant at the prestigious Recovering the U.S. Hispanic Literary Heritage Project under the direction of Dr. Nicolás Kanellos. Cur-

215

rently, she is Assistant Professor at the University of Massachusetts, Amherst, where she teaches undergraduate and graduate courses, such as Linguistic Variety and Pluralism, Bilingualism and Language Contact, and Discourse Analysis among others.

Glenn Martínez is Associate Professor of Spanish and chair of the Department of Modern Languages and Literature at the University of Texas Pan American. He is the author of *Mexican Americans and Language: Del dicho al hecho* (University of Arizona Press) and numerous articles on the sociolinguistics of Spanish in the United States Southwest.

María Irene Moyna is an assistant professor at Texas A&M, where she teaches a variety of linguistics and advanced language courses. She was the associate editor for the 5th edition of the *University of Chicago Spanish Dictionary* (University of Chicago Press, 2002), and her scholarly work has appeared in journals such as the *Southwest Journal of Linguistics*, *Spanish in Context*, *Studies in Hispanic and Lusophone Linguistics*, and in several edited collections.

Comfort Pratt is Assistant Professor of Curriculum and Instruction in the College of Education at Texas Tech University. She holds degrees in Spanish, French, Linguistics, and Translation from the University of Ghana, Universidad Complutense de Madrid, Spain, Texas A&M University and Louisiana State University. Her areas of specialization and research include sociolinguistics, dialectology, foreign language pedagogy and curriculum development. Dr. Pratt is the author of *El español del noroeste de Luisiana: Pervivencia de un dialecto amenazado* (Spanish in Northwest Louisiana: Survival of a Threatened Dialect), published in 2004 by Editorial Verbum of Madrid, Spain, and *In-Class Communicative Projects*, published in 2008 by Prentice Hall.